IMAGES
of America

TEWKSBURY

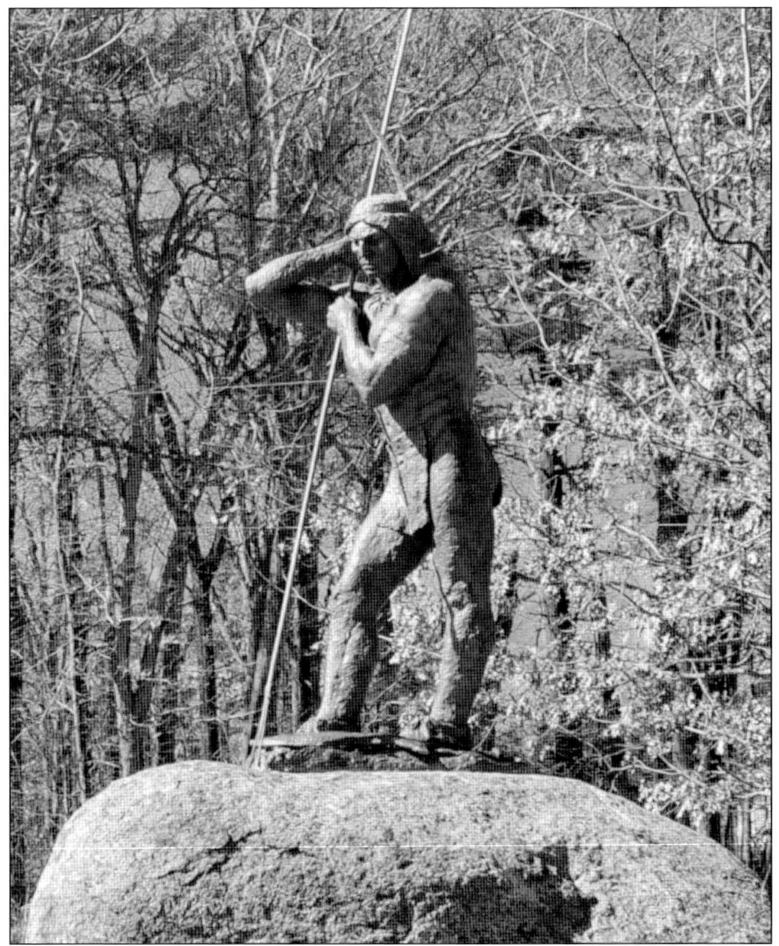

Tewksbury sculptor Mico Kaufman's Wamesit Indian Statue stands proudly on Main Street in the Wamesit section of town. The commemorative plaque reads as follows below. (Courtesy of the Tewksbury Historical Society.)

The Wamesit Indian Park
Dedicated in memory of a proud, peace loving people, who inhabited these lands under the rule of Passaconaway, the Great Sachem and Bashaba, as recorded by the Reverend John Eliot in the year of 1648.
Donated through
The Committee of Interested Citizens Inc.
Tewksbury, Massachusetts
June 17, 1989.

On the Cover: Students marching in the 200th Anniversary Parade in 1934 are smiling from ear to ear, waving their American flags, all dressed in their best outfits. Walking the parade route in front of Sycamore Hall, the community spirit and love of country can be seen in the flags and patriotic buntings outfitting the viewing stands on the Town Common. (Courtesy of the Tewksbury Historical Society.)

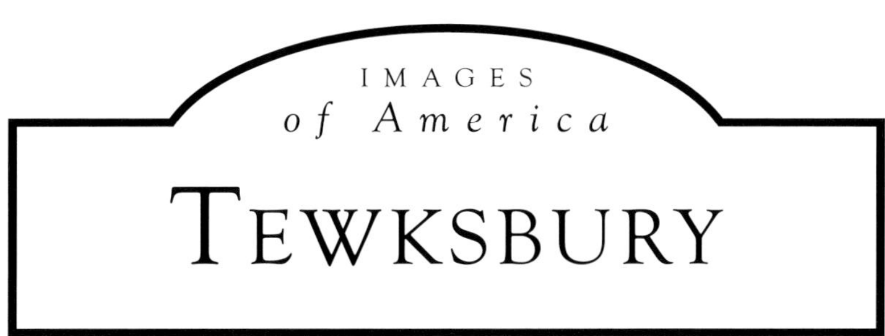

Rev. Douglas W. Sears, JD, and Nancy Reed

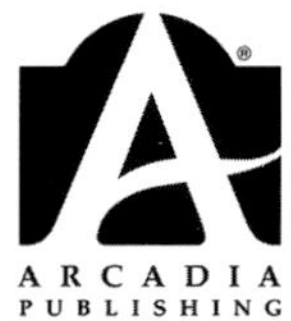

ISBN 978-1-4671-6248-7

Published by Arcadia Publishing
Charleston, South Carolina

Printed in the United States of America

Library of Congress Control Number: 2024951603

For all general information, please contact Arcadia Publishing:
Telephone 843-853-2070
Fax 843-853-0044
E-mail sales@arcadiapublishing.com

Visit us on the Internet at www.arcadiapublishing.com

Contents

Acknowledgments

To the noble men and women,
Our ancestors, brave and true,
Who by their sacrifices, courage and loyalty,
In both times of peace and war,
Our good old
"Town of Tewksbury"
Was established and preserved . . .
We render all honor and gratitude.

This is the foreword to Harold Patten's 1965 book *Ask Now of the Days That Are Past, A History of Tewksbury, Massachusetts, 1734–1964*. It is also the foreword to *Ye Towne Book*, published by the 200th Anniversary Committee in 1934. Harold Patten was a member of the 1934 Anniversary Committee, and there is no doubt he made significant contributions to that booklet. We think it is fitting that we use the same foreword again here, as it would be difficult to do a better job with it than Harold has done.

Unless otherwise noted, all images are from the Tewksbury Historical Society.

Introduction

Today's Tewksbury is primarily a commuter suburb of 30,000-plus, located 23 miles north of Boston in Middlesex County, intersected by major highways that whisk motorists in all directions of the compass. Its beginnings and its development tell a story of struggle and perseverance common to our neighbors but with a particular pride of place that makes Tewksbury unique.

Much of the history of early New England towns begins across the pond. Historians have yet to find any link with "Tewkesbury" in Gloucestershire, England, where, in 1471, the most decisive battle in the War of the Roses took place. However, we remain "sister cities," sharing our history and culture, officially and unofficially, as occasions arise.

What we do know is that the Puritan Rev. Peter Bulkeley (1583–1659) was removed from his pulpit in Bedfordshire for not reading to his congregation an edict from King Charles I (1625-1649). The *Book of Sports* proscribed athletic and other events on Sundays. Bulkeley's congregation sold all their possessions and sailed on the "Susan and Ellen" to Boston, Massachusetts, in 1635.

Among the passengers was Bulkeley's younger friend William Hunt (1604–1667), who brought along his wife and children, including his two-year-old son Samuel (1633–1706). Bulkeley, in 1636, became the first minister of Musketaquid, later Concord. He served as minister from 1637 to 1659. History accords Rev. Peter Bulkeley as the founder of Concord.

Samuel Hunt I left Concord for Ipswich, where he became a carpenter. His son, Samuel Hunt II (1657–1742), was born in Ipswich. He appeared in Billerica in 1689, living near the Merrimack River. In 1691–1692, Hunt bought one-fifth part of the Winthrop Farm of 3,000 acres. In 1640, the legislature granted this land to Governor Winthrop's widow. She only allowed Wamesit Indians to live there—no settlers.

Waitstill Winthrop, grandson of the founding governor of the Massachusetts Bay Colony, conditioned the land's sale on his maintaining a garrison (block) house on a bluff overlooking a basalt dike used by Wamesits as a fording point on the river. Hunt's Falls perpetuates his name. Hunt's job was to guard against Indians (Mohawks), unfriendly to both Wamesit and English settlers from crossing.

The Wamesits were assembled from tribes decimated by Mohawk raids and epidemics that had wiped out villages. Their territory of about 1,000 acres east of the falls ran south along the Concord River. Wamesit translates as "a place for meeting." Mico Kaufman's statue of a Wamesit brave holding a salmon fishing spear memorializes the dignity and culture of these Indigenous residents.

Another Puritan minister, Rev. John Eliot (1604–1690), was known as "the apostle to the Indians." He was determined to carry out the 1644 legislative mandate to bring the gospel to the Indians. In 1663, Eliot translated the Bible into the Massachusetts language. An important part of Eliot's ministry was to convert the Indians he met to Christianity. Eliot thought he was doing the right thing.

At one time, there were 14 praying Indian communities. Wamesit, at the confluence of the Concord and Merrimack Rivers, was Eliot's fifth. Under Eliot's leadership and Chief Passaconaway's wise counsel, the Wamesits did not get caught up in King Philip's War (1675–1678), in which Metacomet almost succeeded in driving the English colonists into the sea. However, many Wamesit fled north.

The Wamesits were peace-loving but not pacifists. They were battle-scarred by wars with the Mohawks. They wanted to live in peace with other tribes and with the English settlers. However, those who remained suffered indignities brought on them by the behavior of tribes elsewhere. They became indentured servants and farmers. Their land holdings were liquidated. Little of Reverend Eliot's efforts survived.

The Puritans, such as Samuel Hunt I, did not come to these shores for freedom of religion. They came to practice their religious beliefs in their own way. The mandate to convert the Indians was a major objective for the colonists. Church and state were intimately bound together. The minister was the religious and secular power in these early communities. The Wamesits as a tribe eventually faded away.

In 1653, the "Shawshin Wilderness" was settled. The First Parish Church in Billerica was founded in 1658 to serve the settlers who arrived from England. Attendance was not optional. Samuel Hunt II and families who settled in the northeasternmost part of Billerica declared that traveling to that church building was too hot in summer and too cold in the winter. They wanted a meetinghouse of their own.

In 1725, Hunt petitioned to create Wamesit as a town separate from Billerica. The petitioners obtained approval but failed to call a minister or build a meetinghouse. In 1734, Hunt and several families asked Billerica "to erect a meetinghouse in the centre, or so as to accommodate the northerly part of the town, upon the Town's cost, or set them off, so that they may maintain preaching amongst themselves."

At first reluctant, Billerica finally voted to grant their petition and set them off with "two thirds of the land between the Billerica meetinghouse and the Andover line, by a parallel line extending from the Concord River to the Wilmington line, if the inhabitant on the southeasterly side of "Shawshin River be willing to join with them." Tewksbury was incorporated as a town on December 23, 1734.

For these and other efforts, history accords Samuel Hunt II as the founder of Tewksbury.

Tewksbury called Rev. Sampson Spaulding (1711–1796) of Chelmsford to minister to the First Congregational Church (built 1736–1737). The congregation built him a home (in 1737–1738) that still stands. Reverend Spaulding was struck with paralysis during a church service in 1791. When he died in 1796, Reverend Spaulding was the first to be buried at what is known as the Old Cemetery on East Street, near his home.

Massachusetts was the last state to disestablish. In 1833, the 11th Amendment to the Massachusetts Constitution declared that towns no longer would support the minister through tax receipts. Church membership and funding were entirely voluntary. Religious societies had the right to hire their own clergy, to build their own churches, and to manage their own membership rolls.

In 1842, the First Baptist Church, founded in Town Center, moved to North Tewksbury. In 1883, the Missionary Oblates of Mary Immaculate arrived in Tewksbury to serve the spiritual needs of the poor, infirm, and indigent at the State Almshouse (Tewksbury Hospital). St. William of York Church and the Oblates serve the Roman Catholic community to this day. The United Methodist Church was founded in 1911.

On April 19, 1775, a rider alerted Capt. John Trull (Samuel Hunt's grandson) of the British Regulars on the march toward Lexington. As previously agreed, Trull fired three shots across the Merrimack River to rouse General Varnum in Dracut. Trull rode his horse to the Town Center, where Minutemen under his command were armed and ready to march along Billerica Road to Concord.

Tewksbury and Billerica Minutemen engaged the retreating Regulars at Meriam's Corner. Tewksbury men were also represented at Charlestown, Boston, Cambridge, Roxbury, Rhode Island, New York, and Ticonderoga. One hundred years after Metacomet almost drove the English settlers into the sea, the newly minted Americans sent the Hessian hired guns of King George III back across the sea.

The textile industry was one of the first to become mechanized. In 1812, Francis Cabot Lowell, a Boston merchant who, disguised as a country farmer, visited British power looms in textile mills and memorized their design. In 1813, Lowell and his partners founded the Boston Manufacturing Company in Waltham, Massachusetts, on the Charles River.

The Merrimack River showed greater potential for hydropower looms. When Lowell died in 1817, his partners founded the Merrimack Manufacturing Company in E. Chelmsford. The area was incorporated as the Town of Lowell in 1826 and as the City of Lowell in 1836. Business was booming as the Industrial Revolution took hold.

The success of the mills in Lowell had a major effect on Tewksbury. Lowell was where the jobs were. Young men and women flocked from all over New England to work in the mills. As Lowell needed space to expand, Tewksbury land became part of it. Lowell annexed 384 acres of Belvedere Hill in 1834, doubling its size; 210 acres in 1874; 220 acres in 1888; and 1,087 acres in 1906.

Tewksbury's poor farm took care of those unable to care for themselves. It was located on the Kittredge Estate, where Wang Laboratories was headquartered on North Street. In 1854, the Massachusetts Legislature built the Tewksbury State Almshouse (now Tewksbury Hospital) for those with mental and physical challenges. Today, it is the largest Public Health Hospital in the commonwealth.

The hospital's most significantly remembered resident is Anne Sullivan (1866–1936). Her parents emigrated from Ireland to Feeding Hills, Massachusetts. They could not keep taking care of their children, Anne, 10 years old, and James, 7 years old (in 1876). There was nearly 100 percent mortality for children of James's age. He died of meningitis and was buried somewhere on the property without a marker. Anne vowed she would never love another.

Anne went on to graduate from the Perkins School for the Blind in South Boston. She met a deaf/blind woman named Laura Bridgman, who taught her how to fingerspell. By the side of the Town Hall, internationally acclaimed artist Mico Kaufman sculpted a bronze statue of two seated women. The older woman is Anne, spelling "water" into the palm of young Helen Keller (1880–1968).

In 1861, the school committee voted that the Constitution of the United States be read once a term in the Tewksbury Public Schools. War drums were beginning to beat across the land as the Civil War began to unfold. Tewksbury was not spared. Tewksbury men mustered into Company K of the 6th Regiment Volunteer Infantry for nine-month tours of duty in Louisiana and Texas. Others served elsewhere.

In 1906, retired Union general Adelbert Ames (1835–1933) purchased 700 acres on Prospect Hill. The castle he built was torn down in 2012. Ames, a Mainer, was a ship captain's son who aspired to be a clipper ship captain. Ames graduated from West Point in 1861. He was severely injured at the Battle of Bull Run. Ames received the Congressional Medal of Honor for his bravery on that battlefield.

After the war, he succeeded Confederate president Jefferson Davis as senator from Mississippi. In 1876, he was the last Republican governor of Mississippi. Democrat politicians who disliked his kindness to former slaves pushed him out of office. Ames retired to his home on Tewksbury's highest hill and lived a long life. Ames was the last full-rank Civil War general to die.

The narrative rests here.

The photographs that follow largely center on the years after the Civil War until about 1950. As we look ahead to the town's 300th anniversary, we hope this pictorial essay captures the extraordinary lives of Tewksbury's citizens over those years. May this book illustrate for posterity the pride and perseverance of those who came before us in this unique New England town.

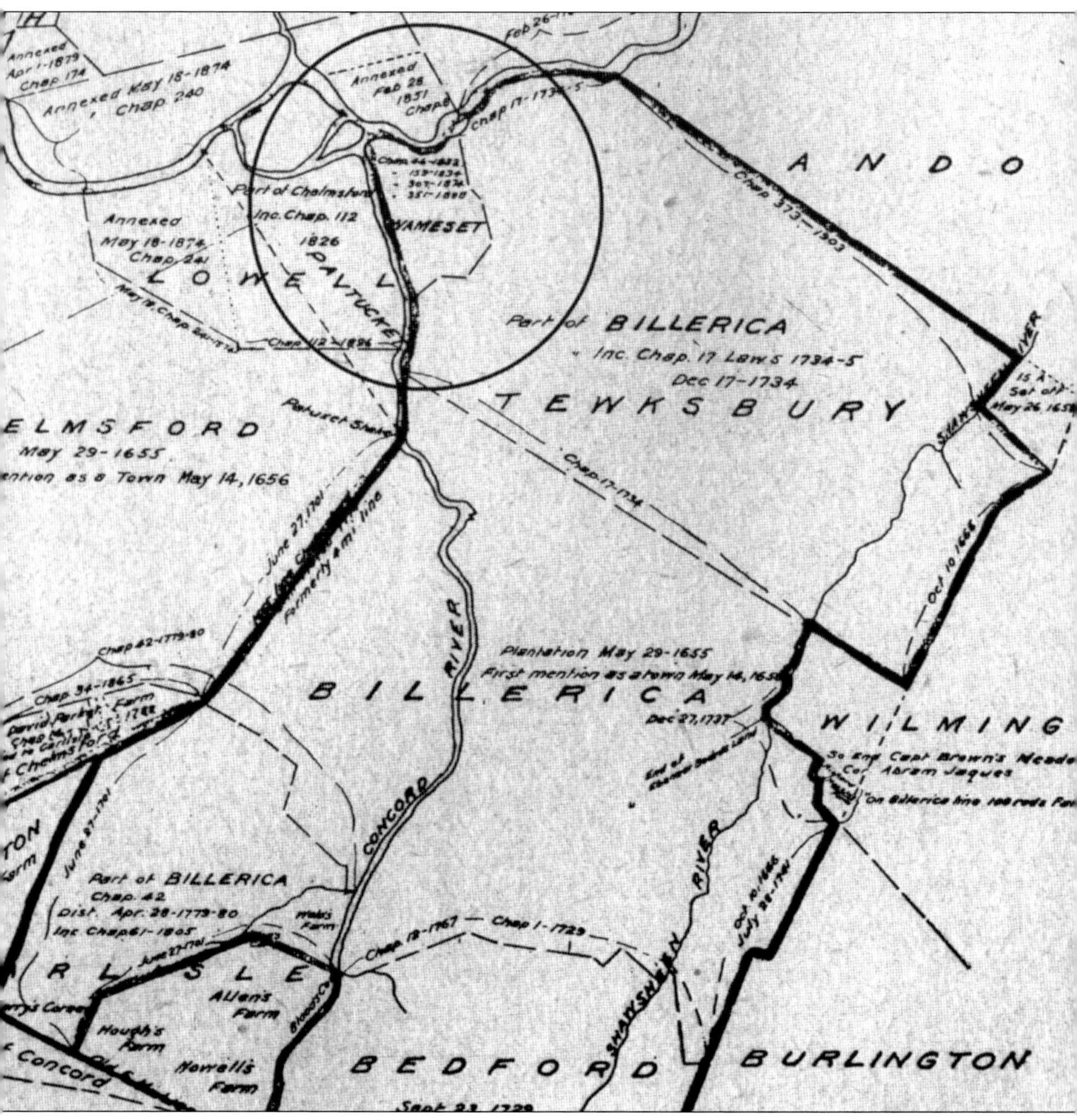

This map by Henry B. Wood, from the *History of Chelmsford* by Wilson Waters, published in 1917, illustrates the early changes in town lines in the 16th and 17th centuries. Note that the encircled area is labeled "Wameset" and its relationship to adjoining towns and rivers.

One

200th Anniversary Celebration

In 1934, the Town of Tewksbury, Massachusetts, celebrated its 200th anniversary of incorporation with a three-day event, on August 25, 26, and 27. There was a magnificent parade, which started on the State Infirmary grounds and traveled down East Street, to Chandler Street, and onto Main Street, ending at the Town Common. Historical exhibits, including Native American relics found in town, were displayed on the first floor of the Foster School. Pageants were performed on Town Common and depicted the traditions and history of the town as written by Rev. Edward Pride in 1888. There were 12 Episodes ranging in topics from the settling and incorporation of the town to World War I. Each church in the town held special services on that Sunday morning in honor of Tewksbury Anniversary Sunday. The 200th Anniversary Committee produced a 76-page booklet entitled *Ye Towne Book*, including a brief history of the town, with pictures of the town's historic homes, churches, and schools. The book also included pictures of their committee members, along with programs for all the events and advertisements from businesses and supportive citizens. The Tewksbury Historical Society's photograph collection includes pictures of decorated buildings, parade floats, and marching groups, which are not included in the *Ye Towne Book*. It was a grand patriotic event that honored Tewksbury's founding and early culture.

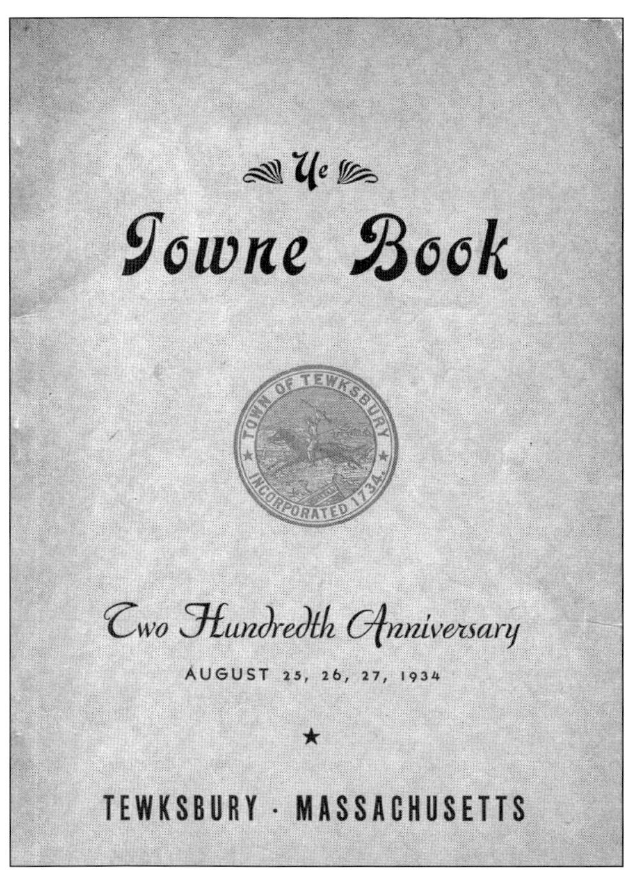

The cover of the *Ye Towne Book* in 1934 by the 200th Anniversary Committee is the starting point for the plan of events for the commemoration of the town's incorporation and its history. Proudly welcoming all to the town's three-day celebration, this book has become an important historical resource for insight into life in the 1930s in the town and country.

Leading the August 25, 1934, parade on Main Street in the Town Center, representing Tewksbury's part in the 1776 American Revolution, is a drum and fife portrayal. The image is noted with the names John Patton, Alger Johnson, and Herbert Larrabee, with the fife. In the background is the Town Common viewing stand with town dignitaries of the time, including Harold Patten, Herbert Trull, and Mark Roper of the 200th Anniversary Committee.

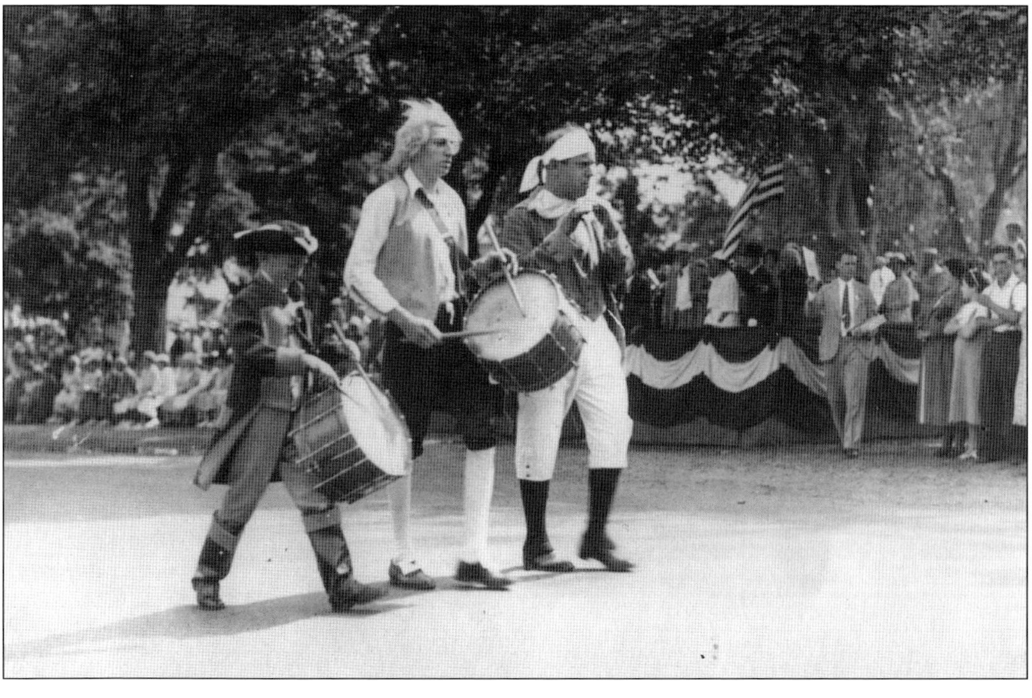

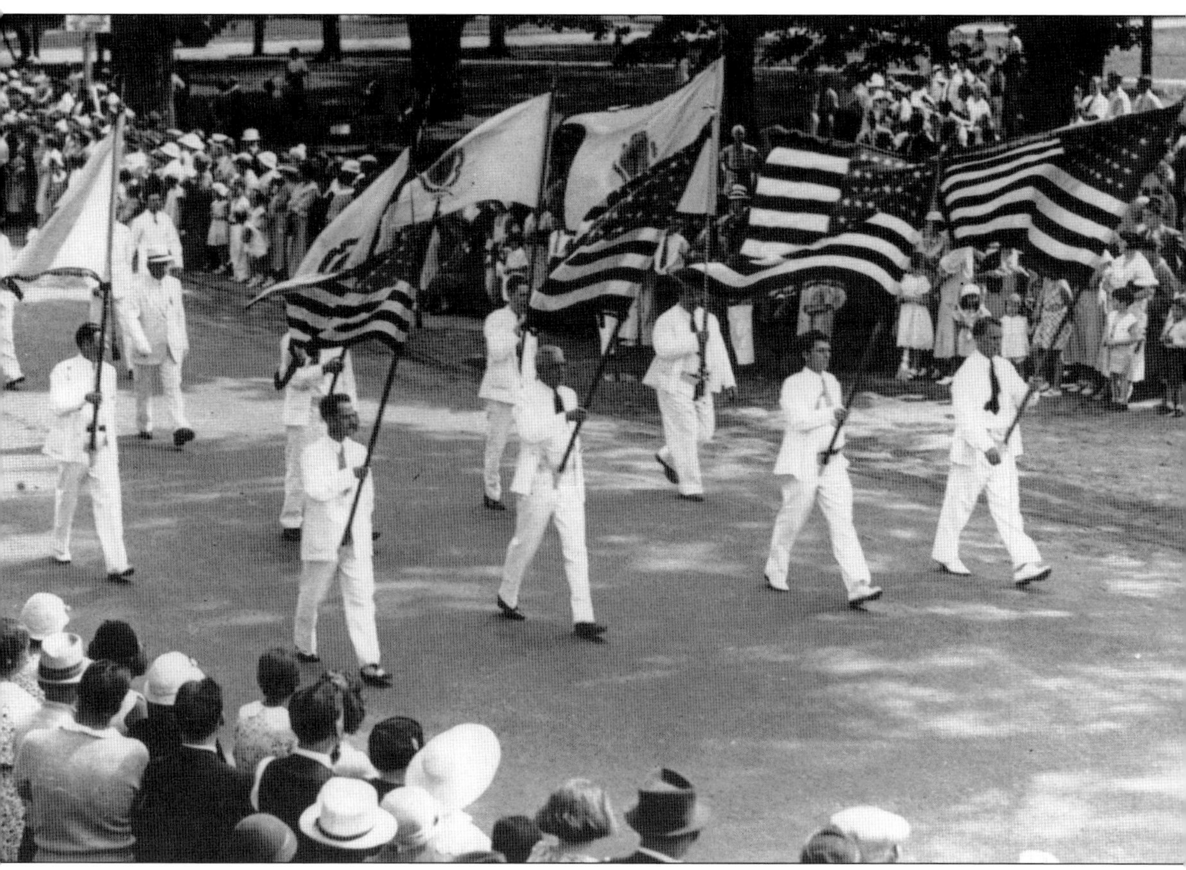

Established in 1854 as a state almshouse, Tewksbury State Hospital was an important cultural partner to the citizens of the town. Here, the hospital's color guard marches to lead off the hospital's several floats and participants.

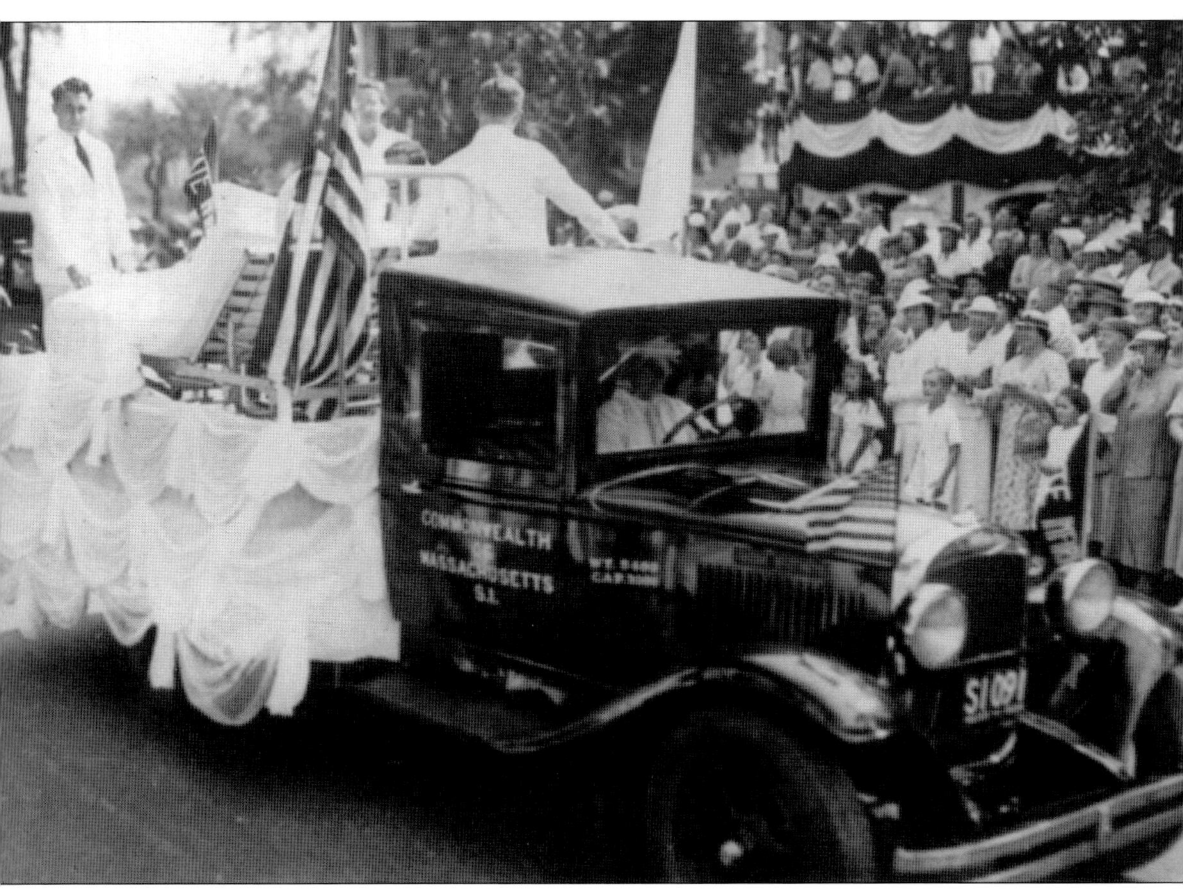

This Commonwealth of Massachusetts truck with an exhibit on the back representing doctors, nurses, and a patient in bed adds insight into what happens at the State Hospital. The Town Common bandstand is in the background, in its original elevated form, decorated with patriotic buntings.

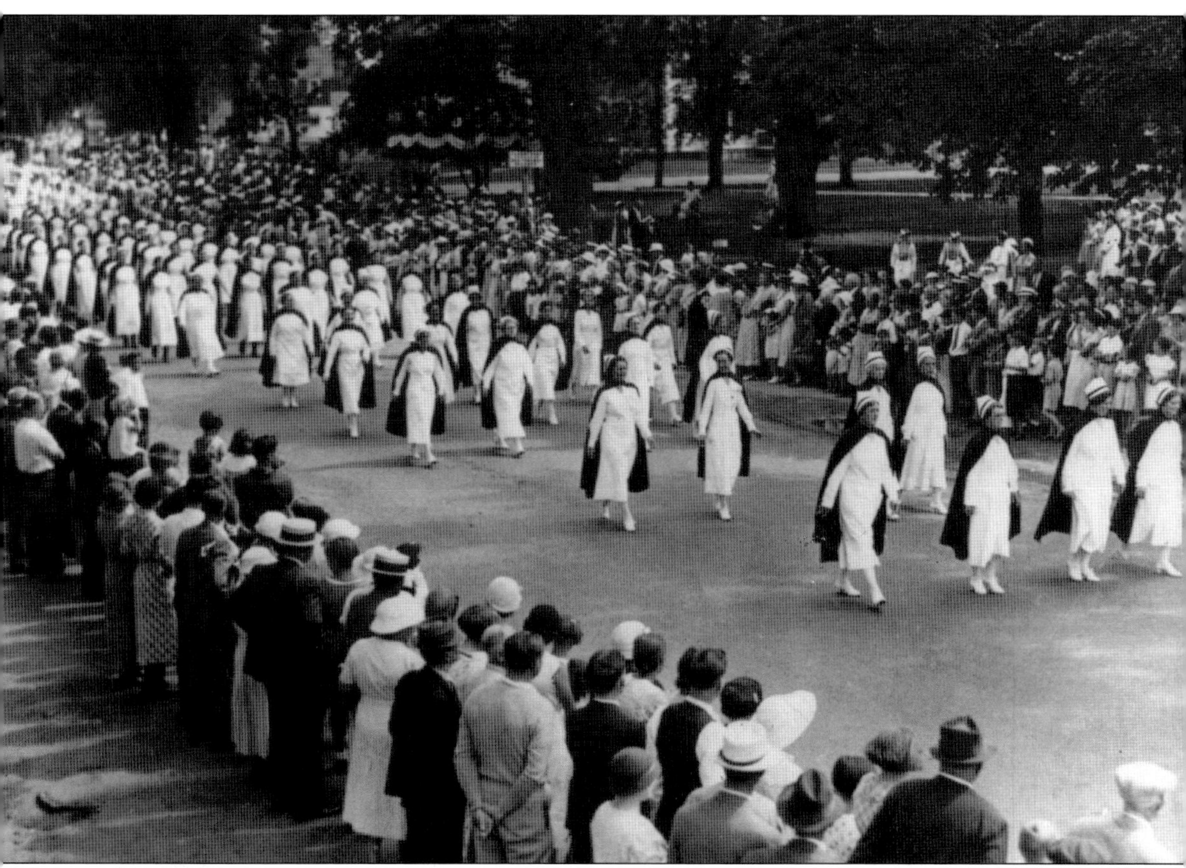

Tewksbury State Hospital nurses march in their starched white uniforms and wool capes, which became their trademark. Many of the hospital's staff nurses earned their degrees at the on-site nurse's training school, which opened in 1894. This training empowered them to be employed in their field, serve the hospital, and gain a sense of identity and independence. Note the spectators, with their equally appropriate outfits in respect of the day's festivities.

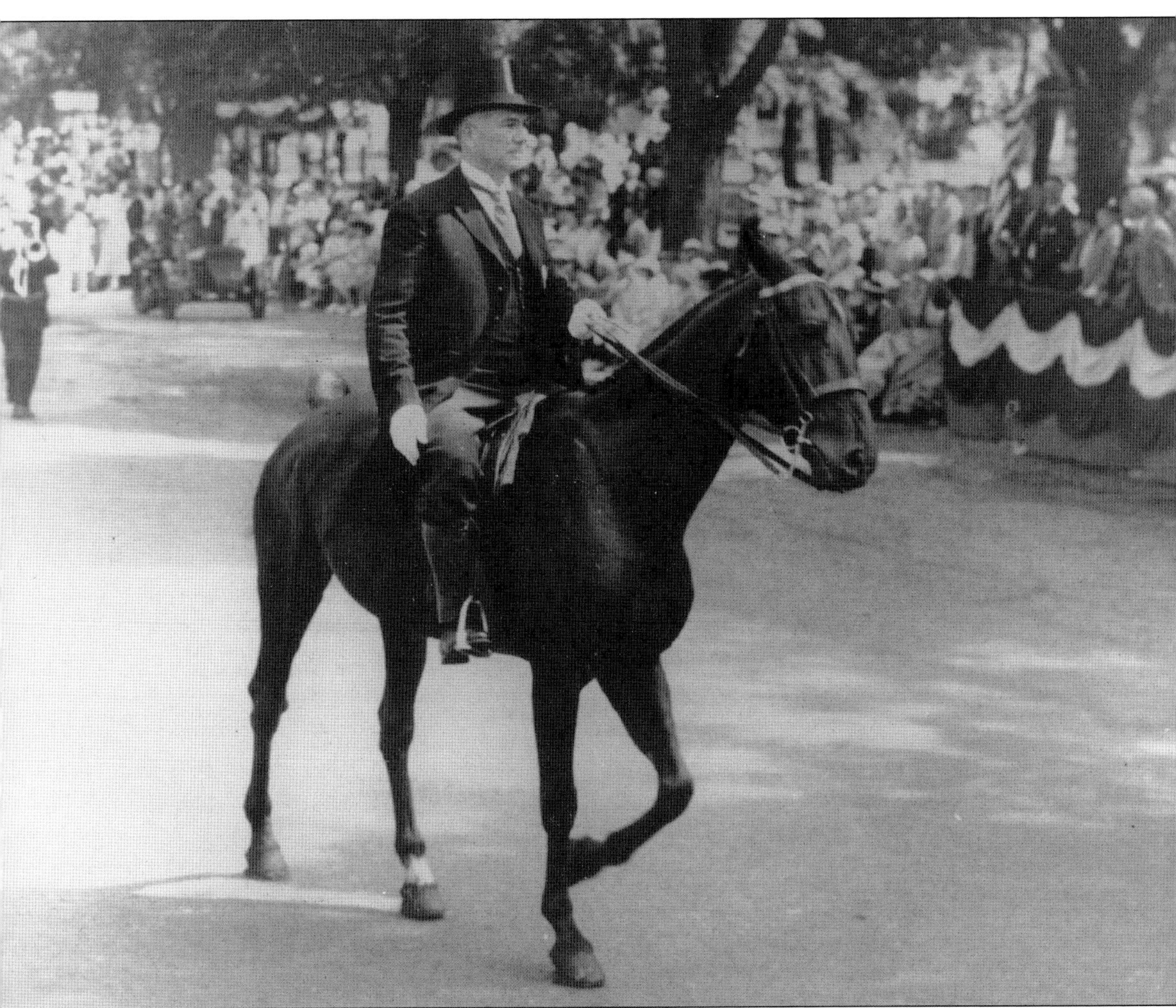

Melvin G. Rogers, Tewksbury's town meeting moderator for 40 years, is on horseback in the parade. He served as the chairman of the speaker committee for the 200th-anniversary events. Melvin was also a lawyer and the last of five generations of the Rogers family to bear the name in the town. He attended the West Tewksbury school. His family's name is found on Rogers Street, where the family homestead was at the corner of Whipple and Rogers Streets, and at Rogers Park, where his family had donated land to the Town of Tewksbury.

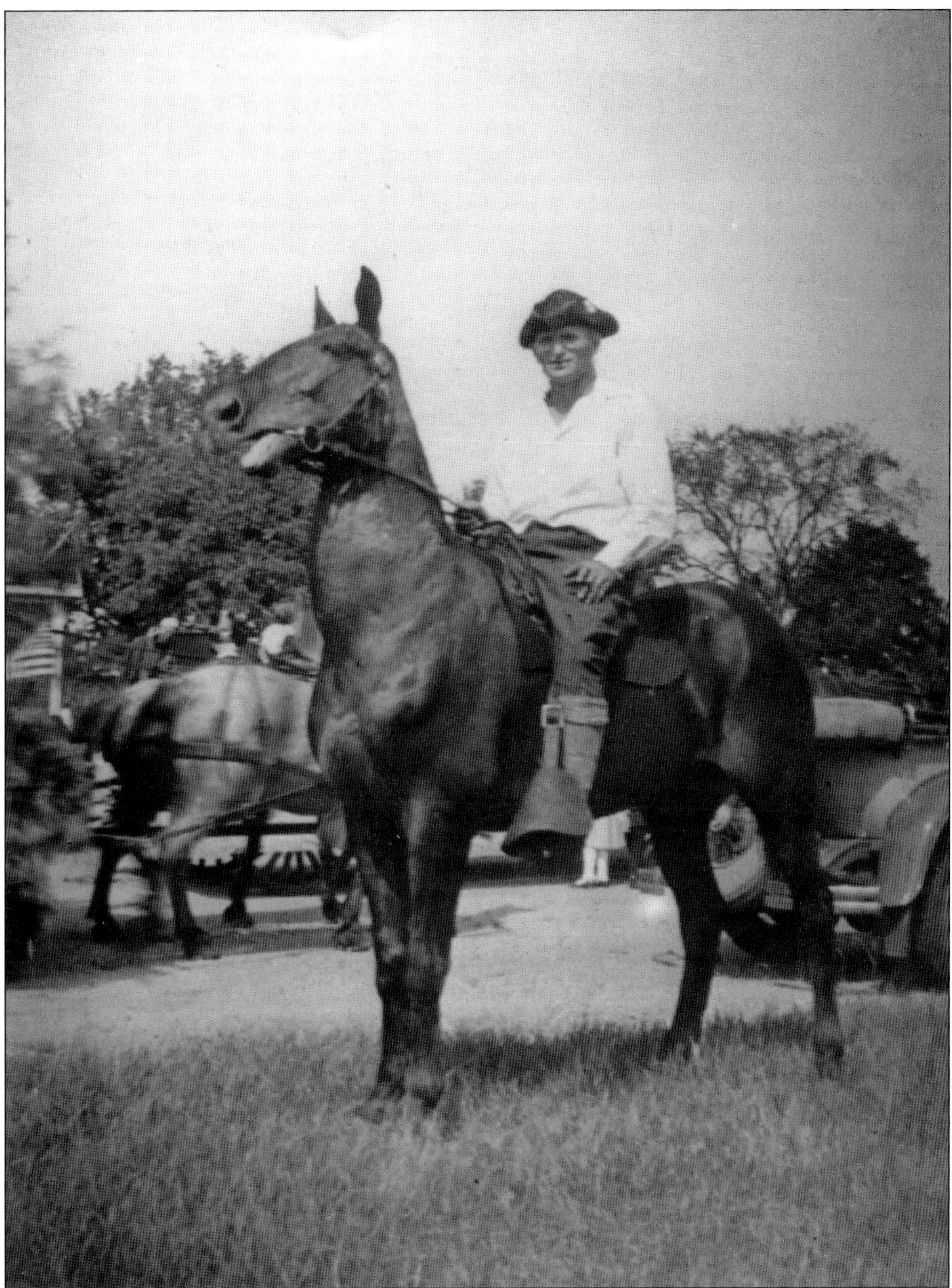

Phaida Joseph "Joe" Roux, a Town Center resident in a Paul Revere costume on horseback, is ready to march in the parade. Born in Quebec, Canada, in 1889, he came to Tewksbury in 1901. He became a naturalized citizen in 1919 and served as a farrier in World War I. The sign above his shop, pictured in about 1910, on Pleasant Street, reads, "P.J. Roux, Professional Horseshoer, Repairer of all Kinds." Roux was known to be always ready to help anyone in need.

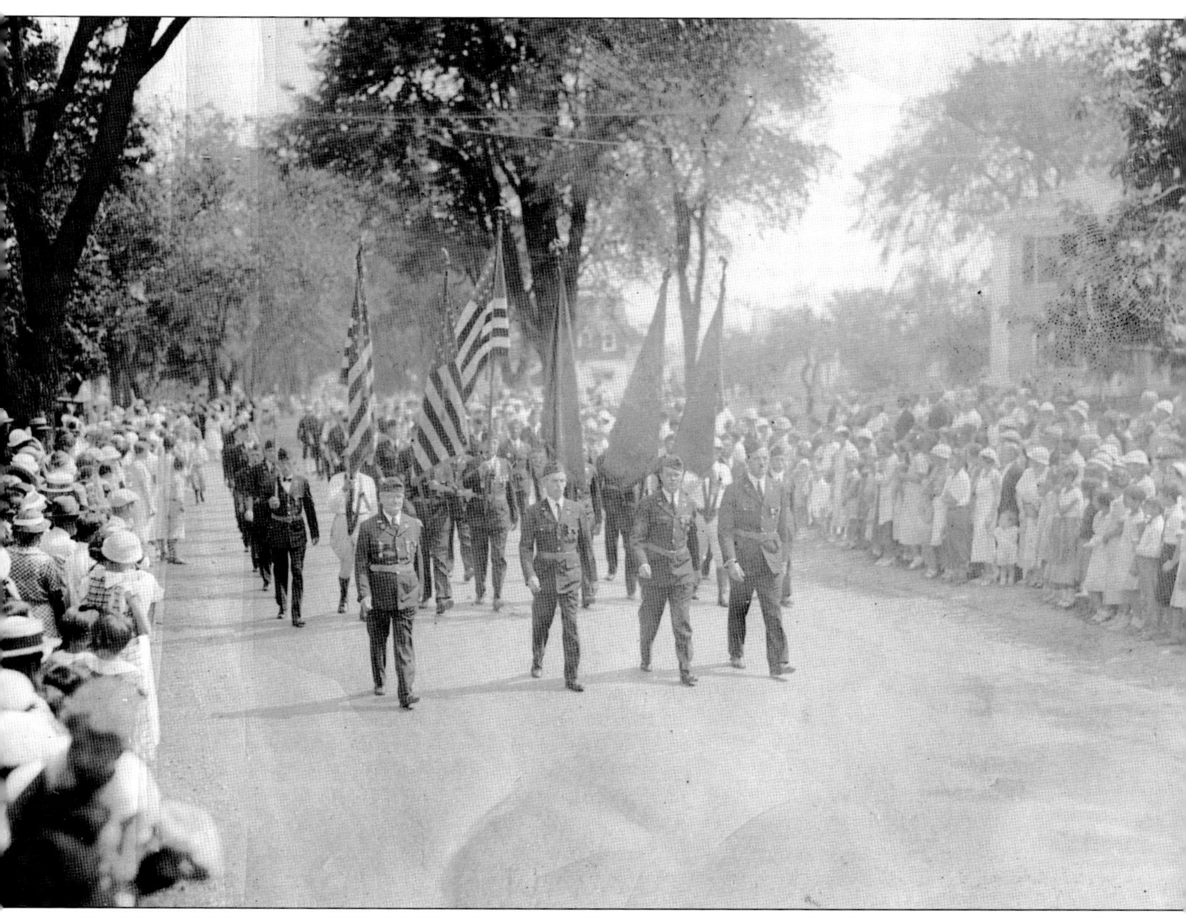

Tewksbury's Veterans of World War I are proudly marching in the 1934 parade. War memorial tablets of the town's World War I veterans were placed in the lobby of the new Town Hall in 1920. The 1806 Sycamore Hall, once the parsonage of Rev. Jacob Coggin of the First Congregational Church, can be seen on the right.

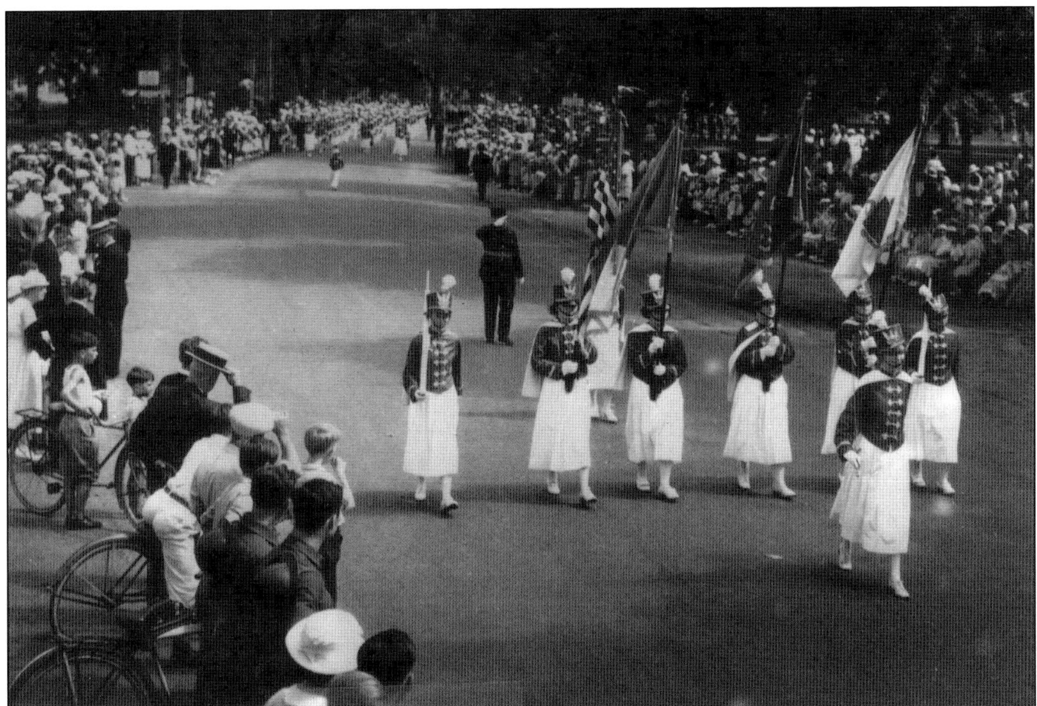

A women's color guard marches while residents watch from the streetside. Notice the gentleman on the left tipping his hat and the other adults and children on their bicycles.

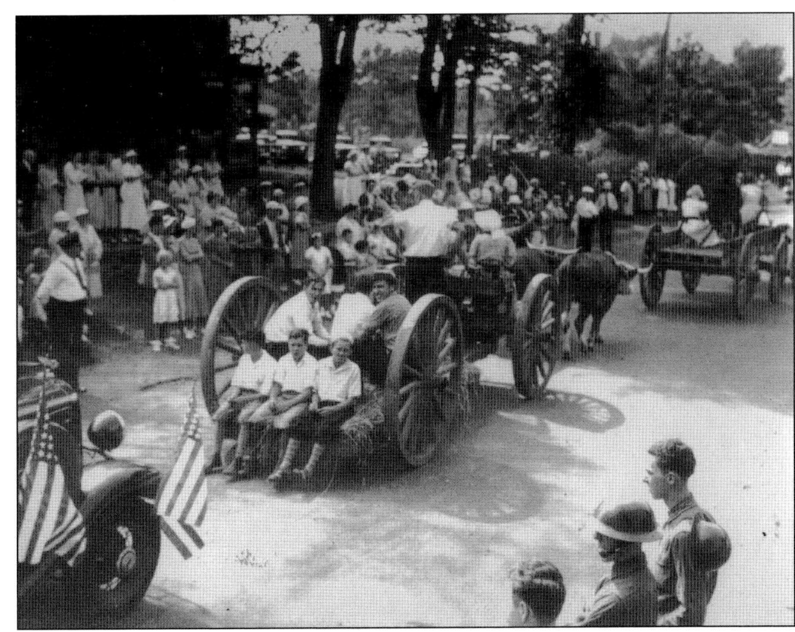

Oxen pull a wagon with a family dressed in colonial-period attire. They represented Tewksbury's early days as a farming community. This image is noted as being the Battles and Jaques family members, both farming families in the town going back over 100 years.

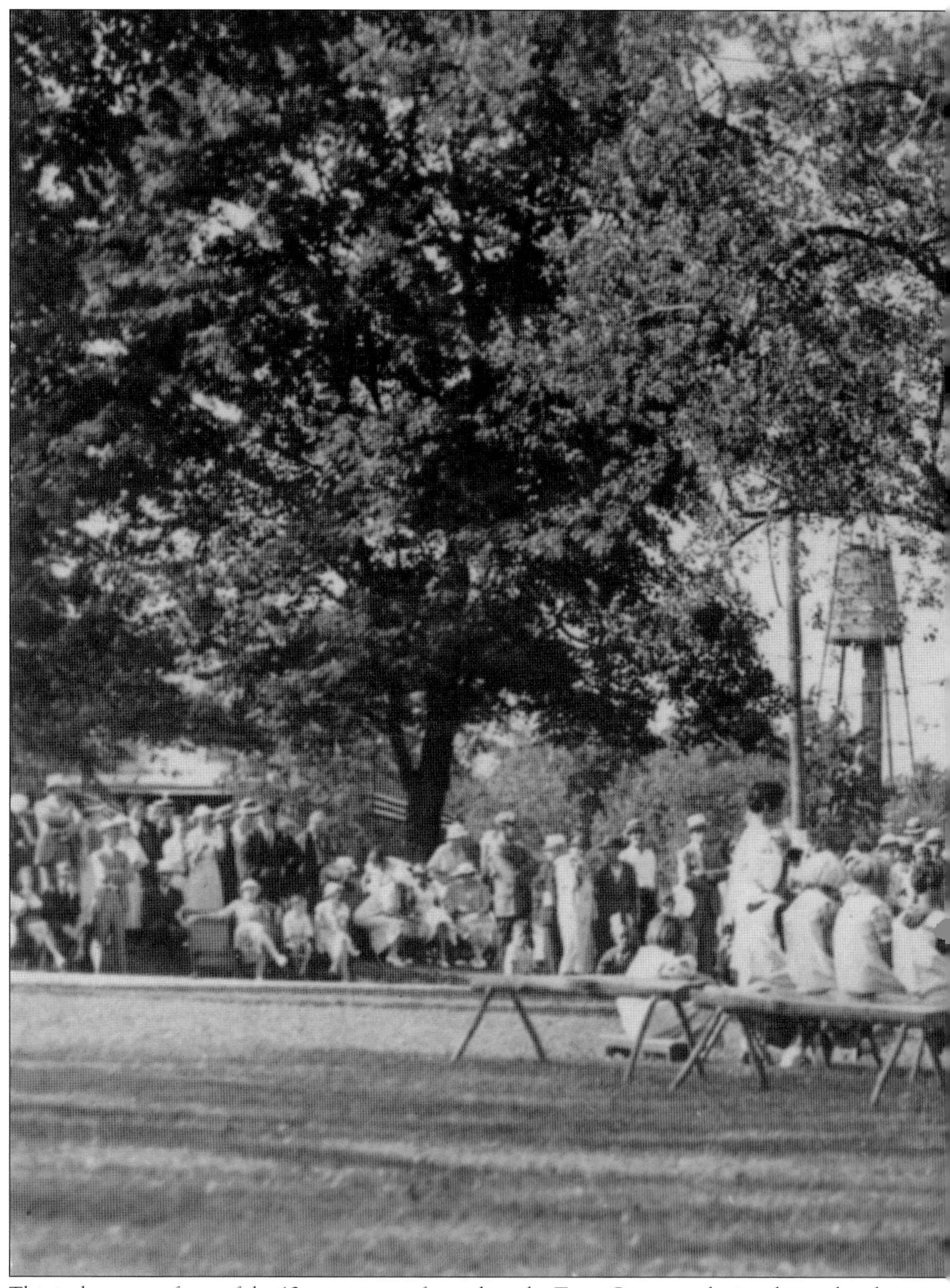

This is the scene of one of the 12 pageants performed on the Town Common during the weekend of festivities for the 200th anniversary. This was episode four, representing the founding of the town's schools, with children and teachers in clothing from those early days. In the background

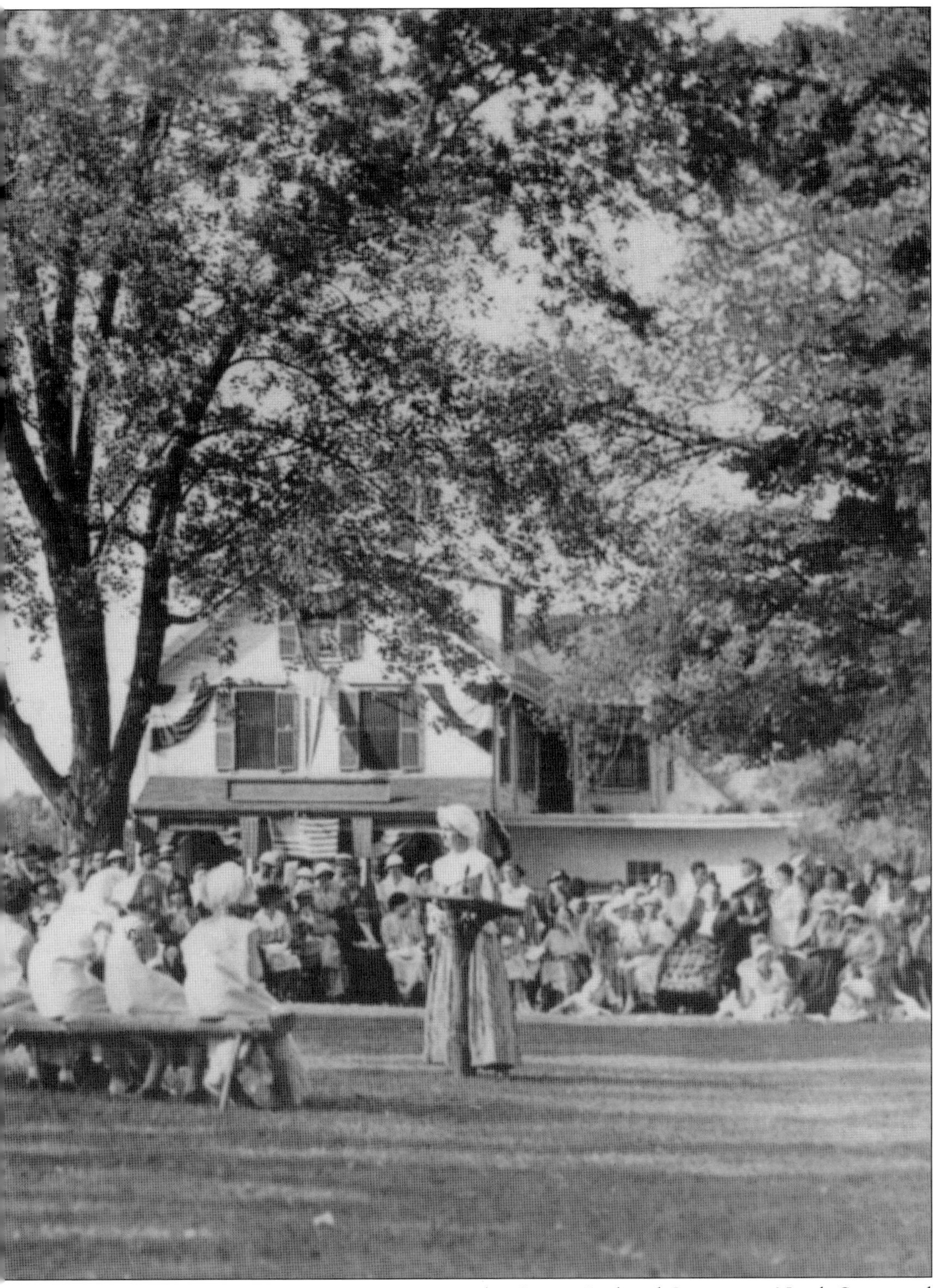

of Town Common are a water tower serving the Center Railroad Station on North Street and Fairgreive's Store.

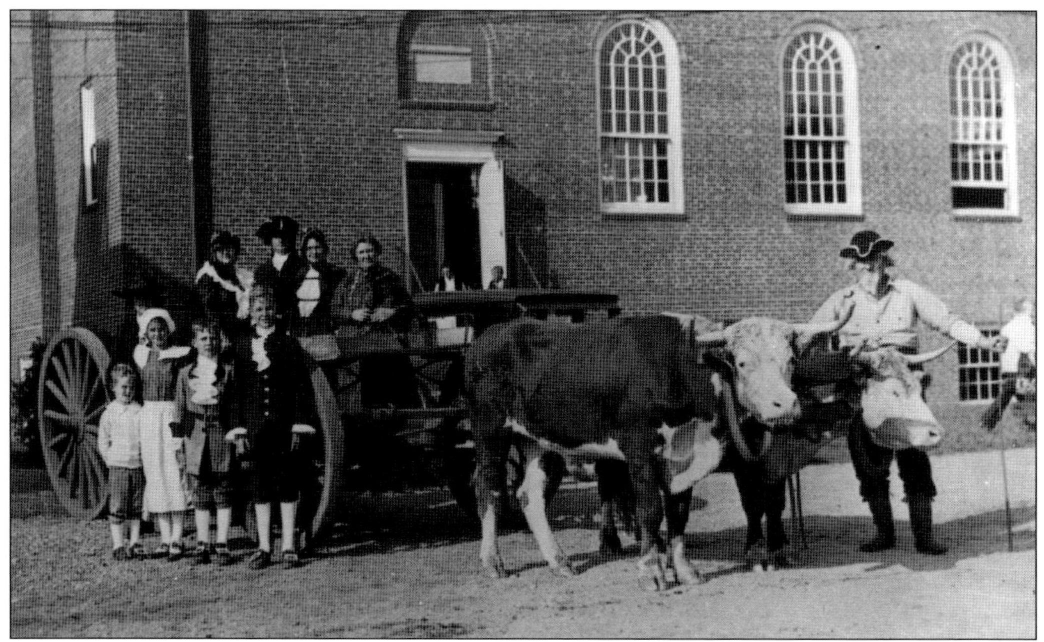

Ready to march in the parade, the French family is seen with oxen and a wagon lined up beside the Town Hall. They proudly represent colonial times in Tewksbury when farming was prevalent. Records say that the French family settled in Tewksbury in the early 1700s, and the family-owned large tracks of farmland in the vicinity of French, Astle, Whipple, and North Billerica Roads.

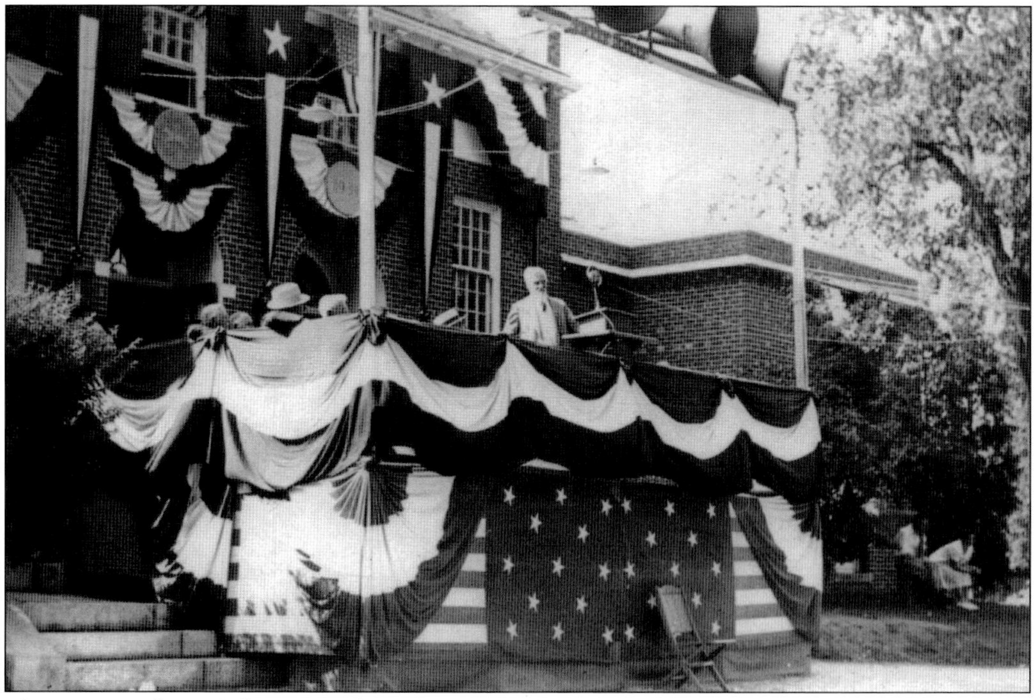

The Town Hall was fully outfitted for the weekend with patriotic buntings and signs of the years 1734 and 1934, representing the 200th anniversary. The speaker on the stage was Albert Stackpole, who was a Civil War veteran.

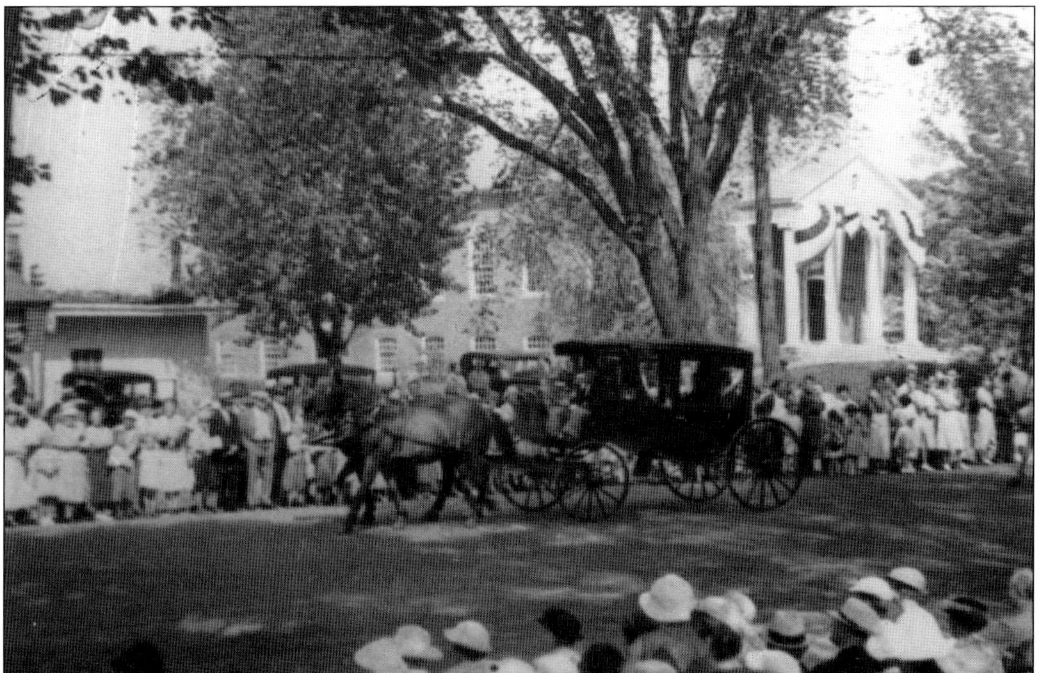

A horse and buggy strut along the parade route in front of the Congregational church in Town Center. Notice the large shade trees on both sides of the church as well as the celebration buntings on the church. The town and church were closely tied in 1734 when founding a church was a requirement to fulfill the act to incorporate Tewksbury as a separate town from Billerica.

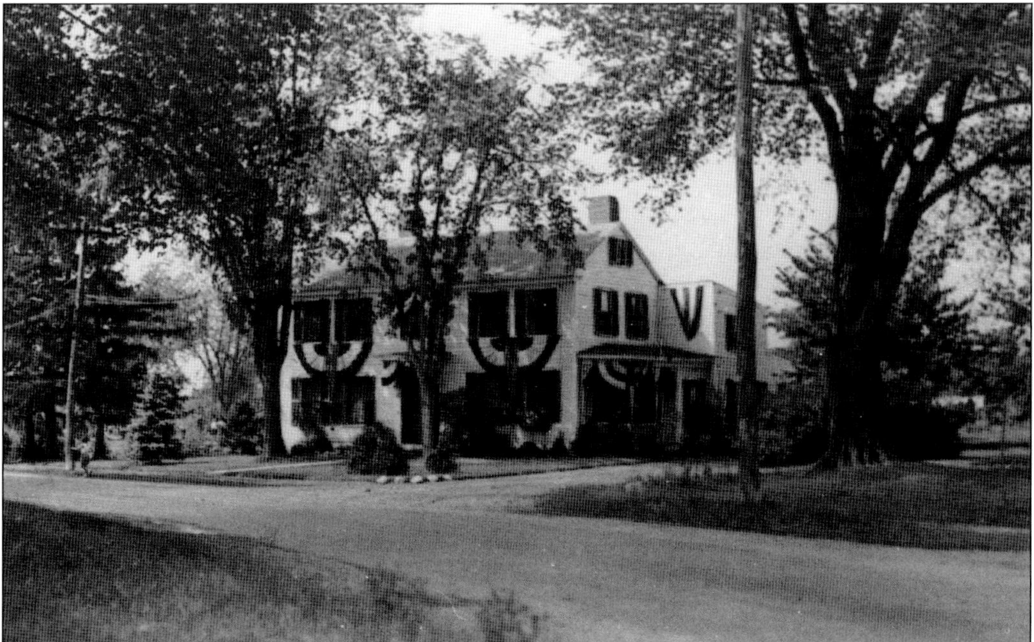

The Preston House, later known as the Pillsbury House, on Pleasant Street, was decorated for the 1934 commemoration. Built in the late 1700s, the home still stands next to the driveway of the Center Elementary School.

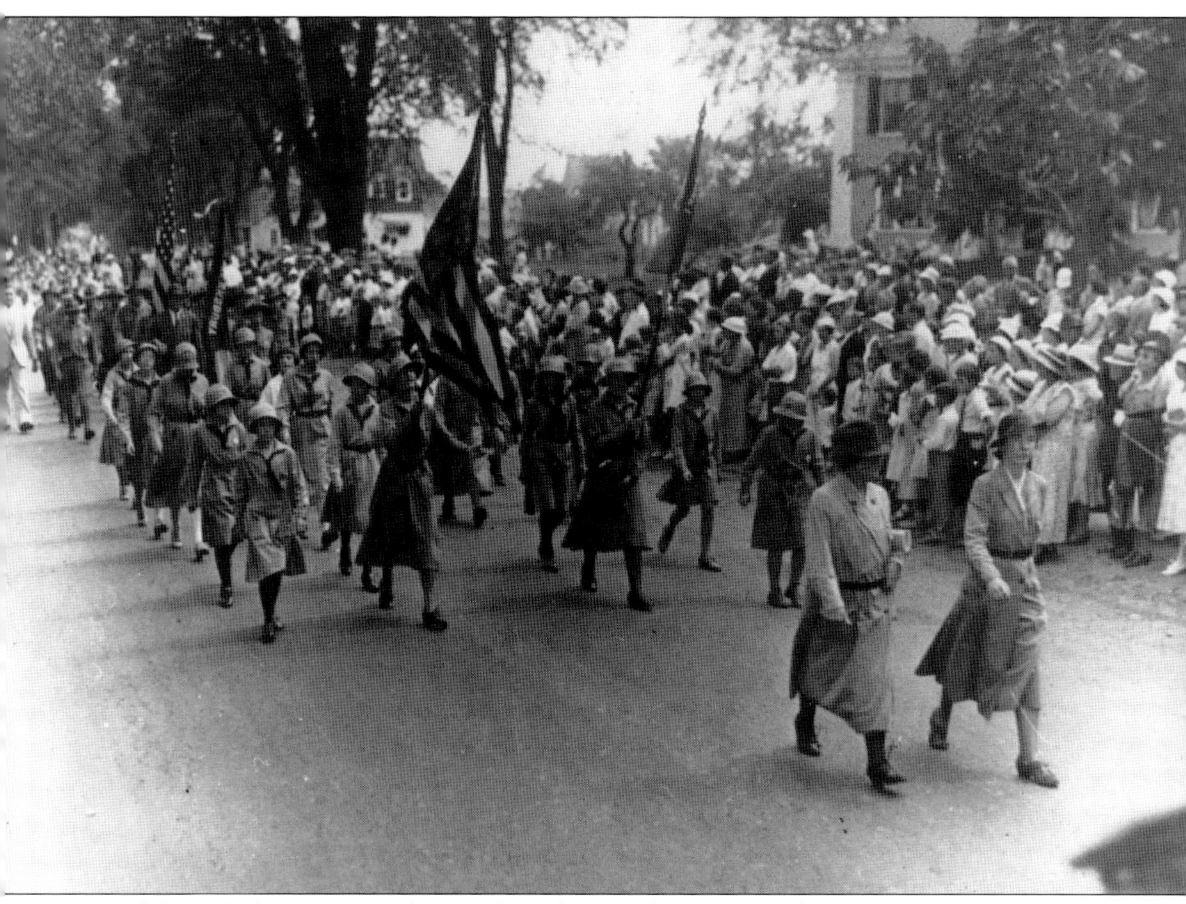

Tewksbury Girl Scouts proudly march in the parade of 1934. These young women rise to the occasion, evoking a clear patriotic theme. Marching through Town Center, across from Sycamore Hall on Main Street, their spirit, loyalty to country, and resolve shine through, especially in the young lady holding strong and gazing at the American flag she commands.

Two

Farms and Carnations

Tewksbury's farming and timber businesses originated long before the town's incorporation in 1734. Being the northern part of the mother town of Billerica, established in 1655, agriculture was the primary trade. Other forms of workmanship were often performed on those farms, such as blacksmithing and sewing. In the late 1700s, Zephaniah Clark purchased Aaron Beard's 1750 homestead on what is now Main Street, near Heath Brook and the current post office. Clark was in the timber business. His granddaughter married Jonathan Folsom, and his other son, Charles, stayed and ran a blacksmith business. By 1907, the heirs of the Jonathan Folsom family owned the homestead and large farm with a barn across Main Street. Two pairs of oxen pulled heavy loads, and they tilled the farm many years before a shopping center was built on the property in the mid-1900s. This is just one story of the longstanding family tradition of farming and cultivation in the town. Another example, built upon generations of work and decades of ingenuity, are the many florists, greenhouses, and carnation-cultivating businesses that became the signature of the town. Due to high production numbers and the quality of stock, Tewksbury was named the "Carnation Capital of the World" by *Yankee* magazine in 1976.

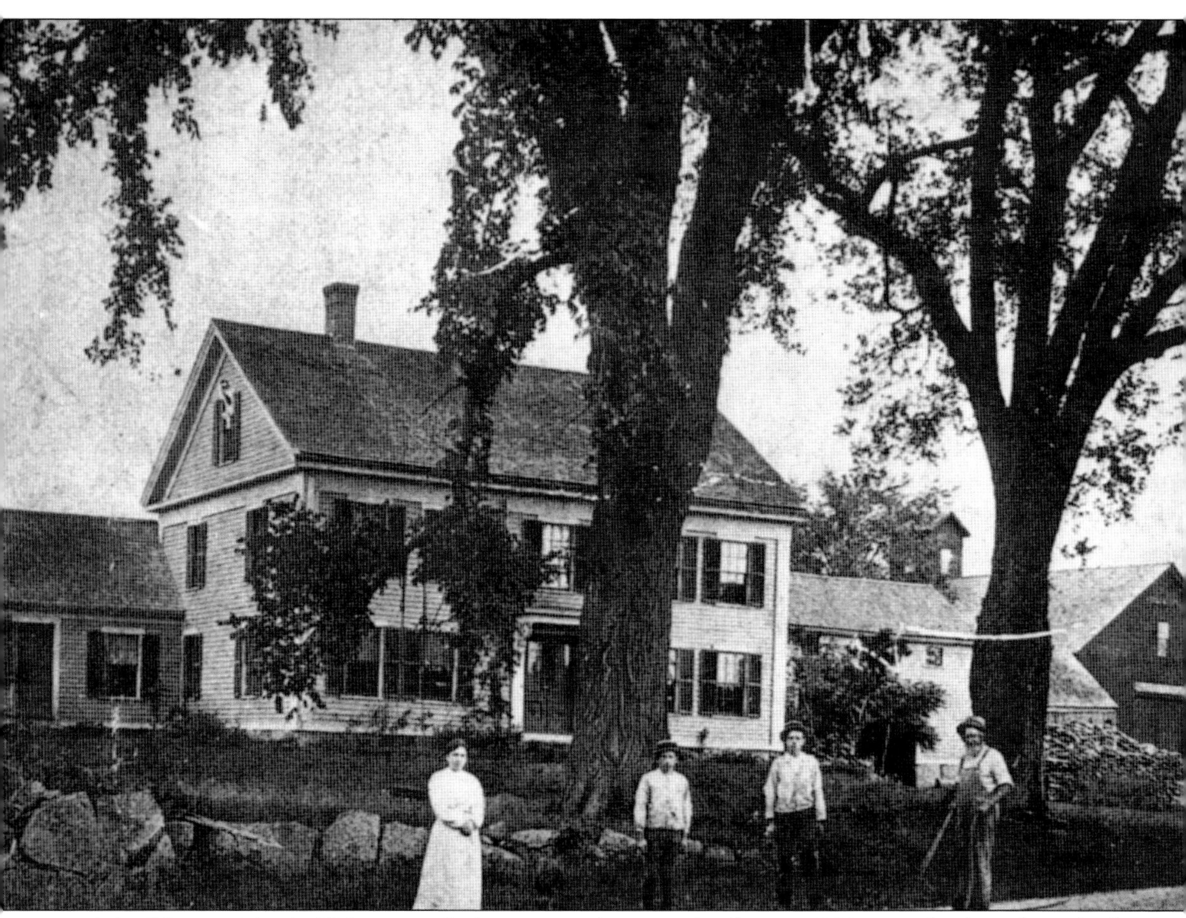

The Thomas Marshall Homestead, shown in a photograph taken in 1889, is said to have been built in 1728. The Marshall family resided there for several generations. The 200-acre farm extended behind the home to what is now Marshall Street. Pictured left to right are Etta Marshall and her two brothers James and George with their father, George A. Marshall. James's son, James "Jimmy" Marshall, 1933–2013, served in the US Army and as a heavy equipment mechanic for the Tewksbury Department of Public Works until 1978. He lived his entire life at the Homestead. The setback center portion on the right side of the house is the original home structure of the large farm. Today, the homestead has been refurbished, and the center portion remains in its original state.

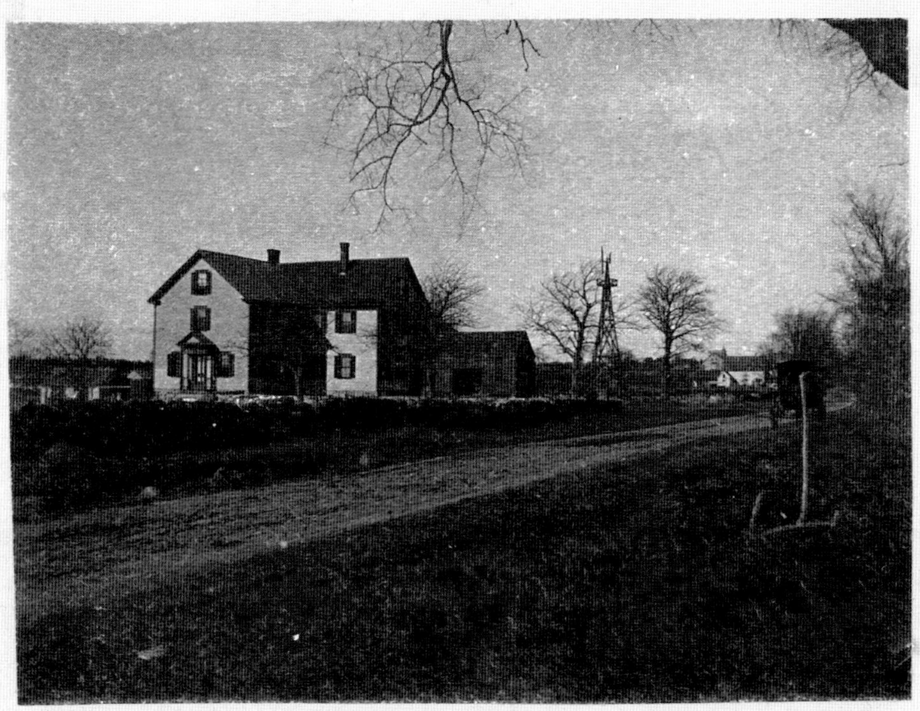

The Town Farm, seen here around 1900, was established by the town in 1828 at the Kittredge Farm property on North Street, on the west side, next to what is now the Interstate 495 overpass. For almost 100 years, the Town Farm served paupers and the needy elderly of the town in the best way possible during those times. In 1918, it was closed and sold. In the early 1960s, An Wang purchased the 85-acre property for his Cambridge, Massachusetts, company, Wang Laboratories. The company prospered there from 1964 to 1976, when it moved its headquarters to Lowell.

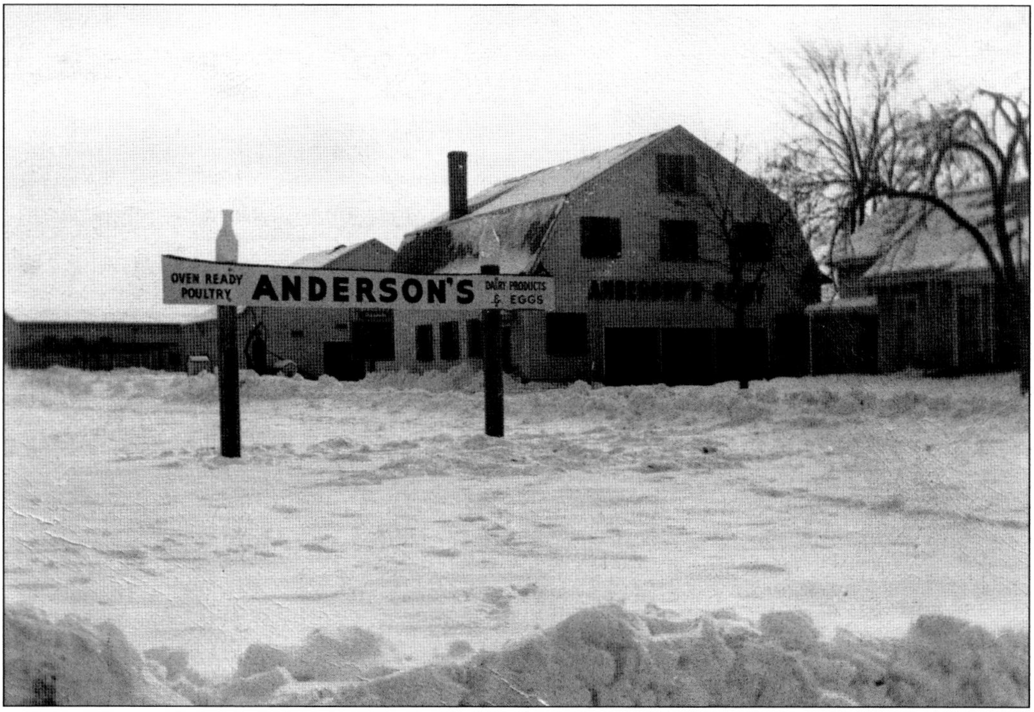

Anderson's Dairy on French Street was founded by Nils Martin Anderson, born in Sweden in 1864, and emigrated to Lowell in 1883. In 1889, he married his wife, Hanna, and they bought the property and founded the poultry and orchard business. Their sons, Anthony and Ralph, continued the farm and added cows and dairy to the establishment, thus forming Anderson's Dairy.

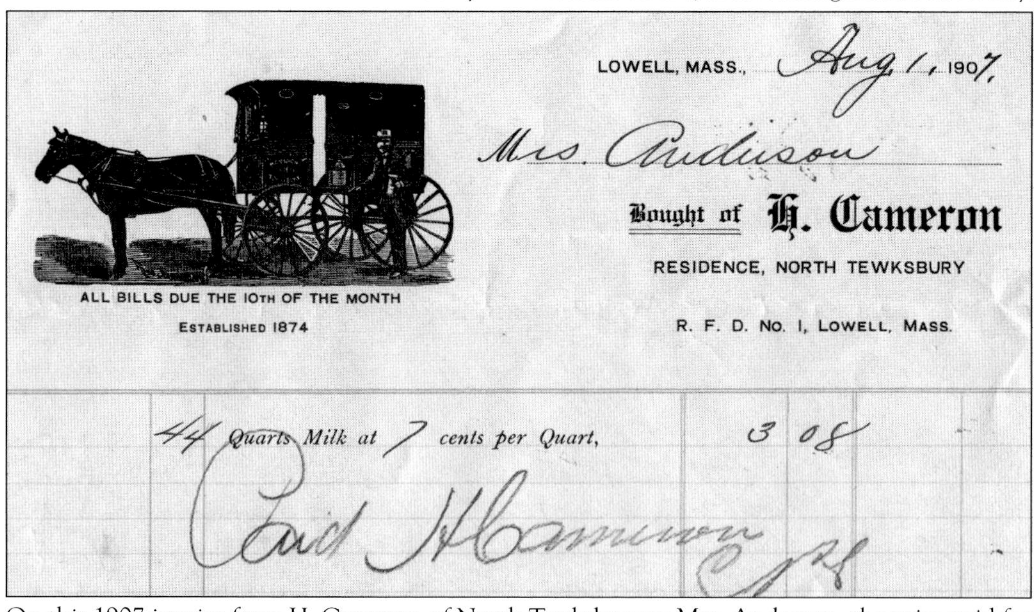

LOWELL, MASS., Aug. 1, 1907

Mrs. Anderson

Bought of H. Cameron

RESIDENCE, NORTH TEWKSBURY

ALL BILLS DUE THE 10TH OF THE MONTH

ESTABLISHED 1874

R. F. D. NO. 1, LOWELL, MASS.

44 Quarts Milk at 7 cents per Quart, 3 08

Paid H Cameron

On this 1907 invoice from H. Cameron of North Tewksbury to Mrs. Anderson, the price paid for a quart of delivered milk was 7¢. The note also mentions that the dairy was established in 1874. It is amazing to think that one enterprise raised the cows, sourced and bottled the milk, and delivered it to their customers for such a low price.

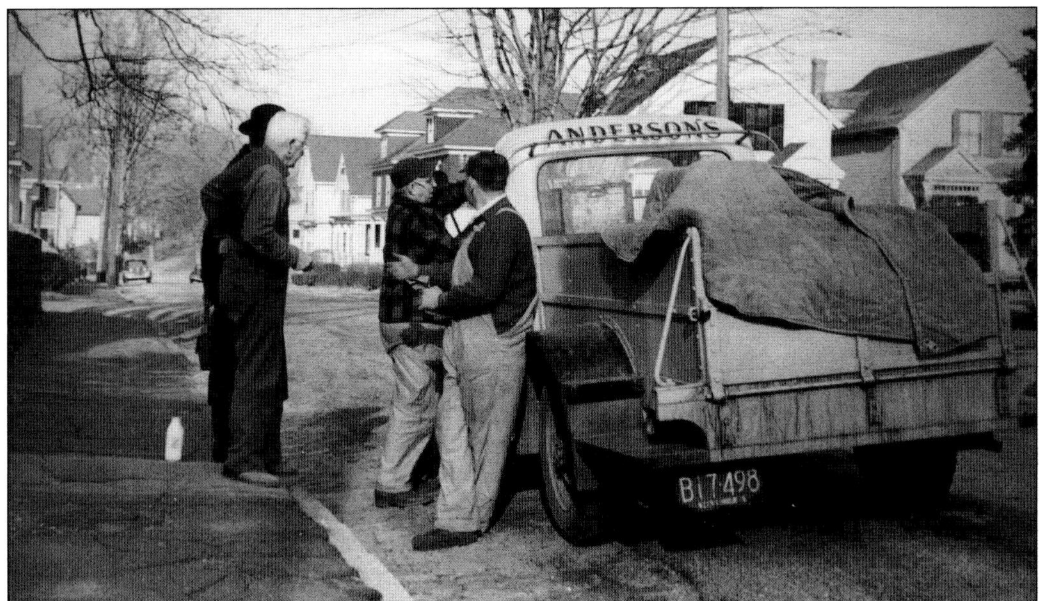

Anderson's Dairy milk truck is pictured making deliveries in a nearby neighborhood, possibly in Lowell. Notice the glass bottles, which were placed in an insulated box on the porch or cubie on the house. The empty bottles would be picked up by the milkman, and customer payments were made based on the number of empty bottles collected.

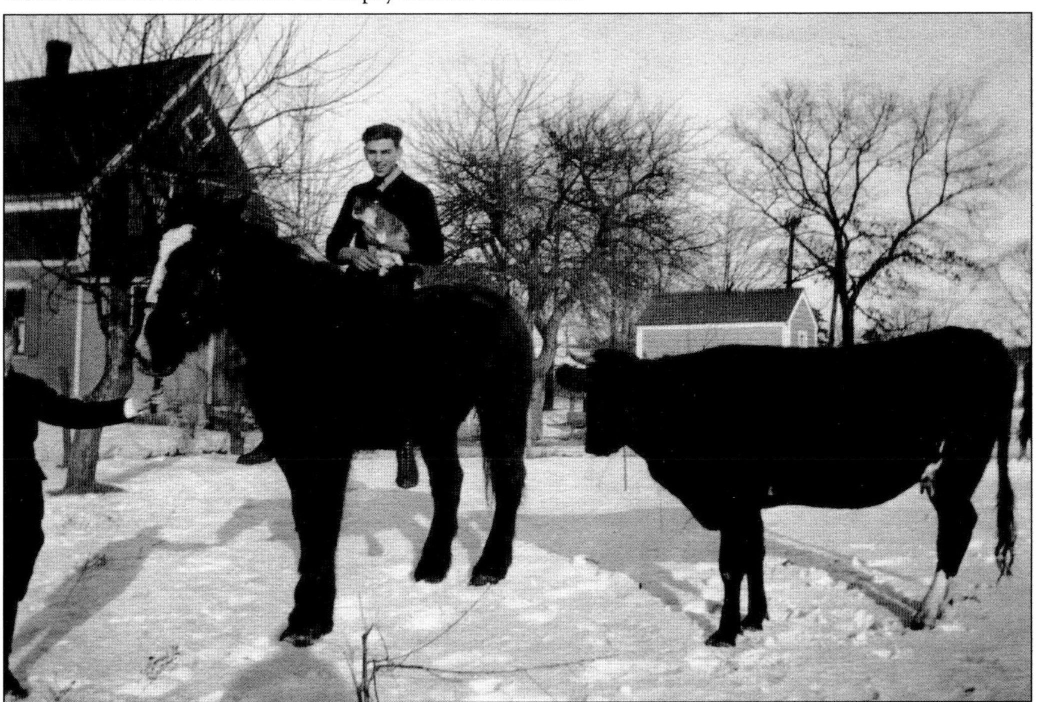

Anthony "Tony" Anderson sits on a horse at his family's dairy farm. This photograph dates to around 1925. The farm was across the street from the one-room West School, which dates to 1865. Tony took photographs of the school, which were later given to Marie Georgia Rutledge, author of the booklet *Just One Room But Many Memories, the West School*, published in 2004.

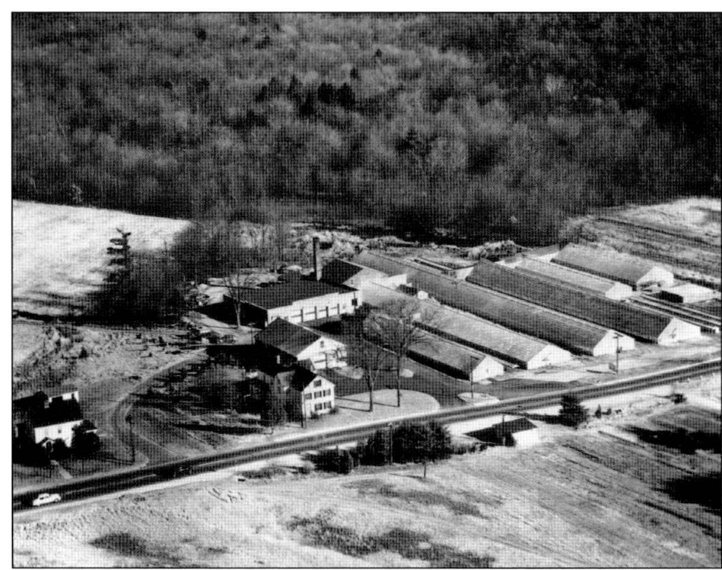

This aerial view of Carter's Greenhouses on Main Street shows the expanse of the farm and greenhouses. Also seen is the former David Carter House, a Cape-style home at 1574 Main Street, built around 1788 and recently demolished. The left side of this site is home to Carter Green Condominiums, built in the late 1970s following a spike in oil prices that caused many greenhouses to close because the cost to run the greenhouses was greater than the profits.

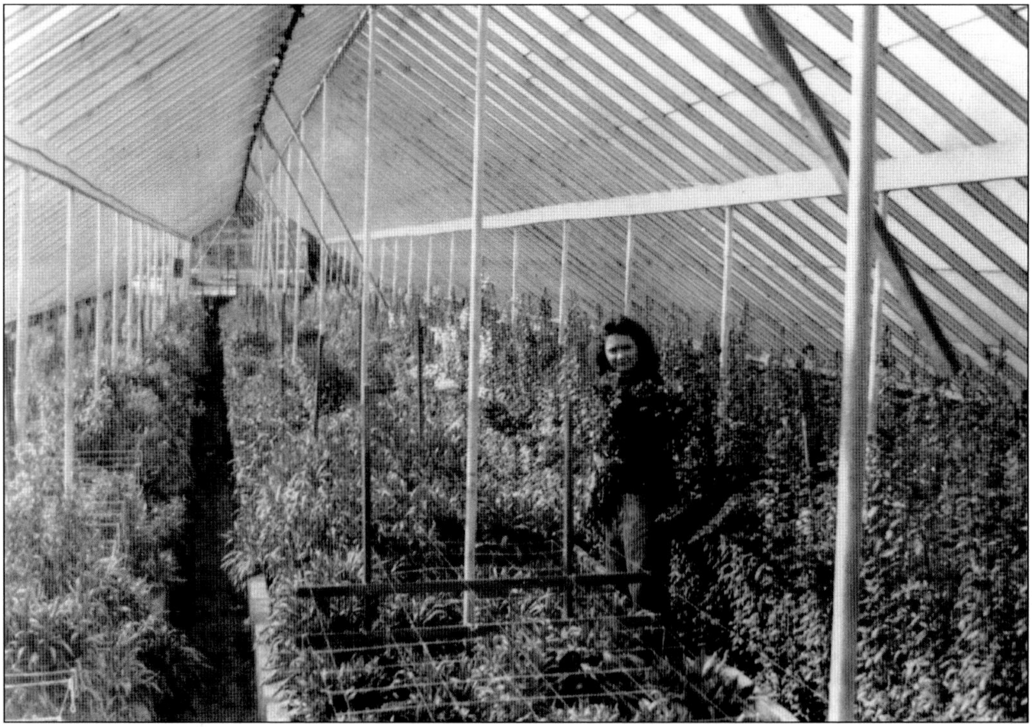

Mary Garland is seen in the Garland Greenhouses, in the area of John E. Smith Drive on Chandler Street, in about 1950. Mary graduated from Lowell Normal School, now University of Massachusetts Lowell (UMASS Lowell), in 1929 and taught in Tewksbury schools until her marriage to Ralph Garland in 1937. She and Ralph ran greenhouses and a florist's shop for many years. Mary was also a founding member of the Tewksbury Historical Society in 1993.

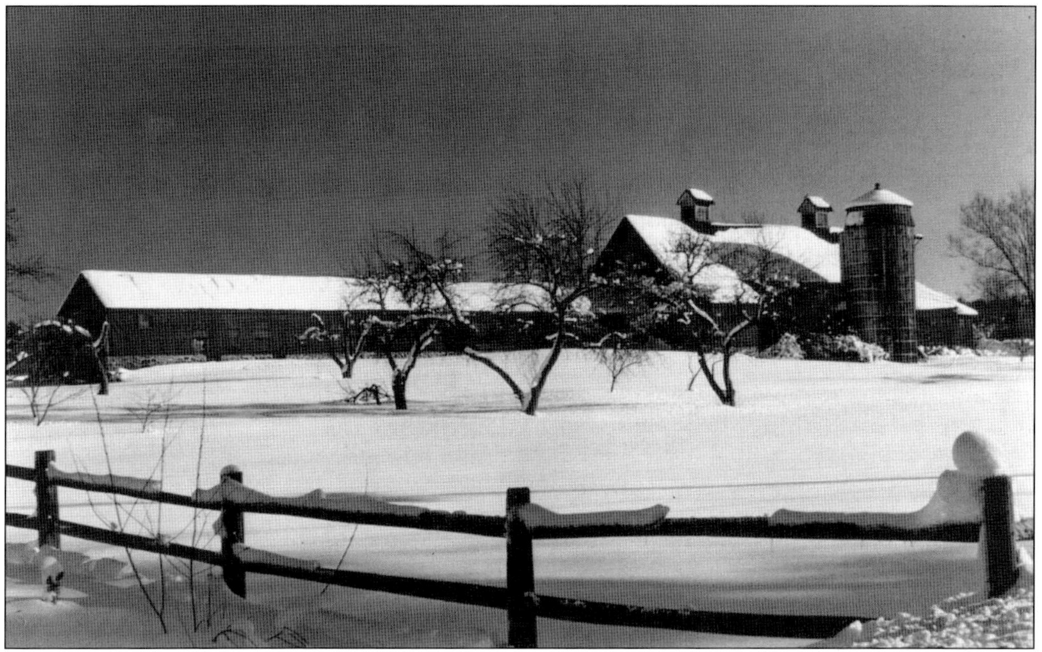

Heidenrich Guernsey Farm on North Billerica Road was founded by Karl and Ottilie Heidenrich. Karl had come to Lawrence, Massachusetts, from Austria and then married Ottilie in 1907. They purchased the farm on North Billerica Road in 1920 and raised Guernsey cattle. Their sons Karl Jr. and Frank continued the work at the dairy until it closed in the 1960s.

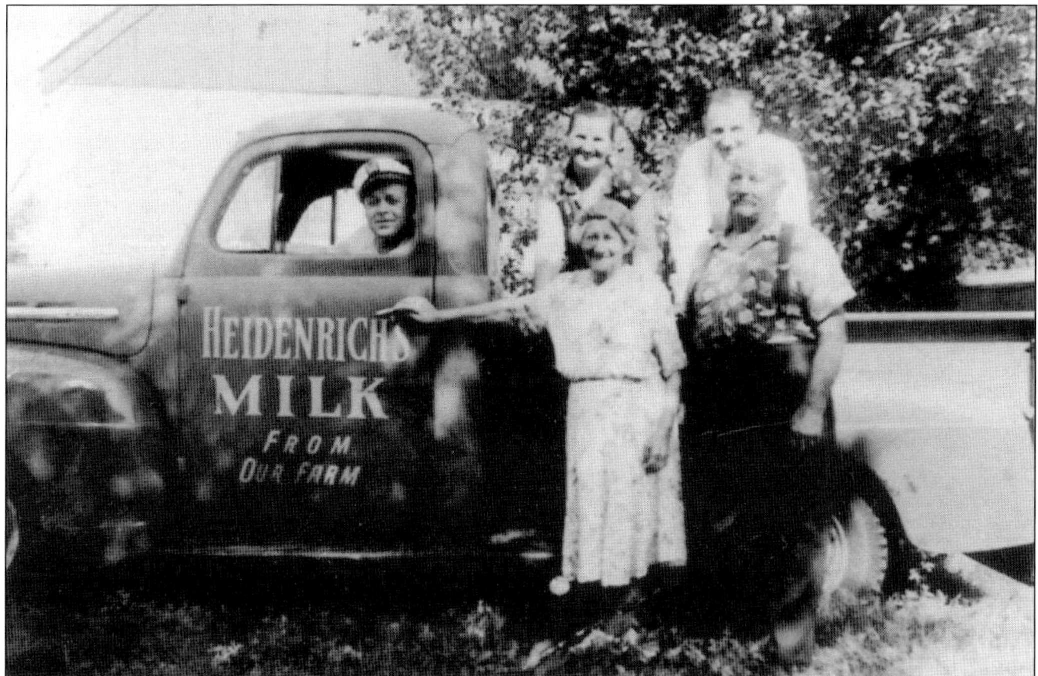

The Heidenrich Dairy truck was a familiar sight in West Tewksbury delivering its distinctive rich milk, high in protein, fat, and beta-carotene from the Guernsey cows at their farms. These unnamed workers are most likely members of the Heidenrich family, Karl Sr., and his wife "Tillie."

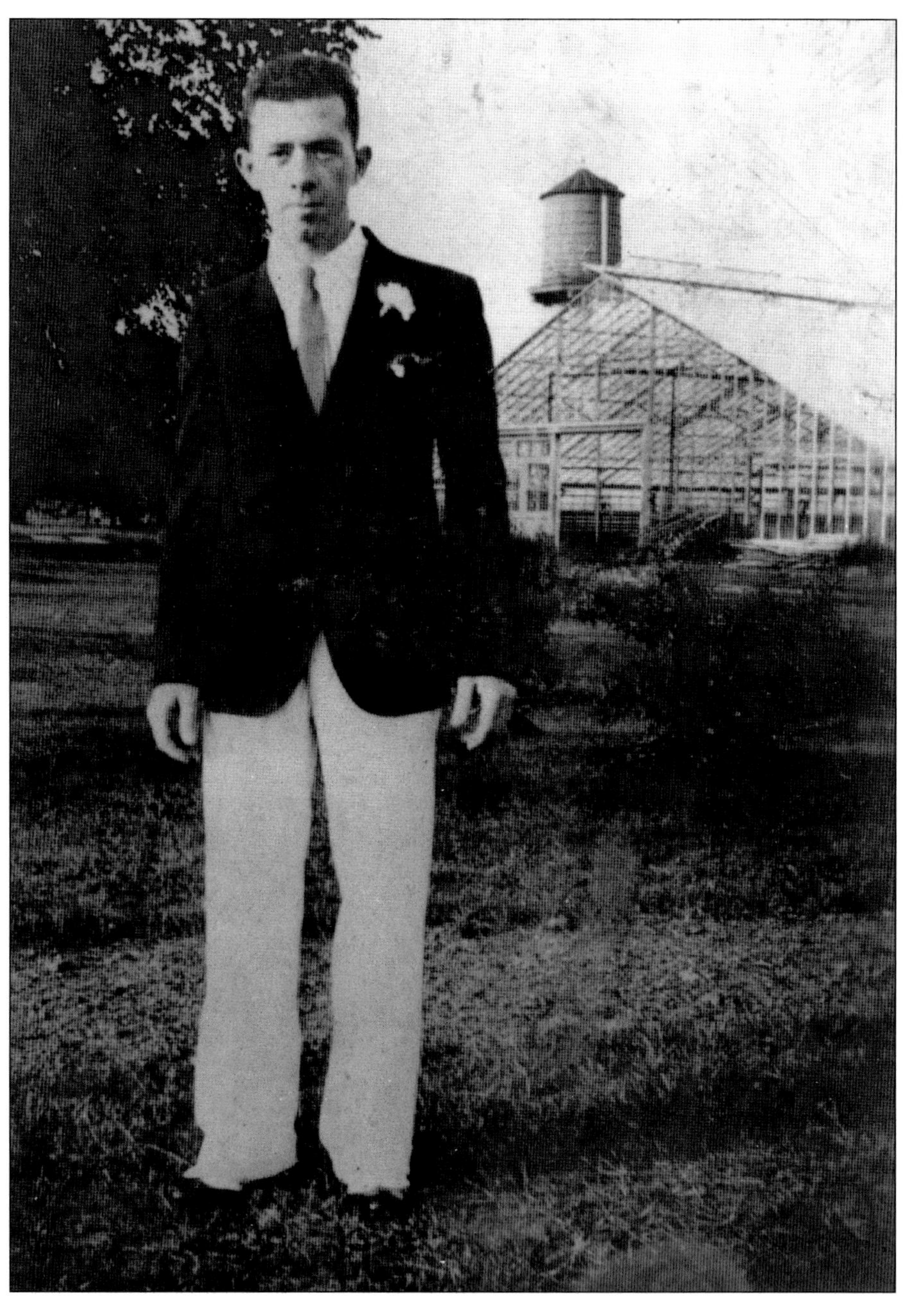

Mark "Red" W. Roper is pictured here around 1930 in front of the greenhouses and florist business his father, Mark Roper, founded on Pleasant Street. As a family business, Mark Roper & Sons was a member of the American and New England Carnation Growers Associations. Red's father served in World War I and was a member of the town finance committee and the 1934 200th Anniversary General Committee. Born in 1915, Red served in World War II. His son Mark W. Roper Jr., born in Tewksbury in 1939, was decorated for his 23-year service in the armed forces and saw combat duty in Vietnam. Mark Jr. went on to be the crew chief of Air Force One under Presidents Nixon, Ford, and Carter. He shuttled Secretary of State Henry Kissinger all over the world and back.

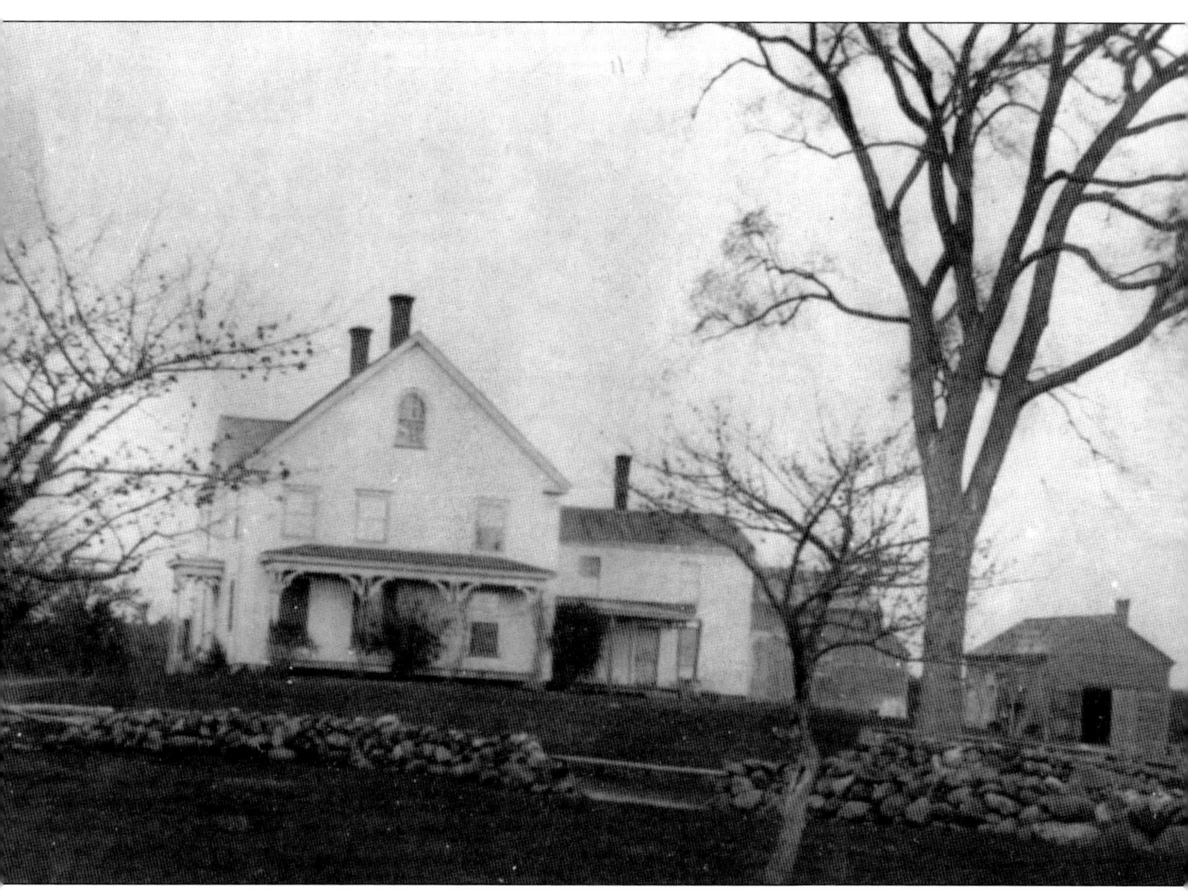

Folsom Farm on Main Street was a mainstay in the community. Before the town was incorporated in 1734, the Beard family owned the property. In the late 1700s, Zephaniah Clark purchased the land for a timber business. Being in the floodplains of Heath Brook, the soil was quite fertile. By the early 1900s, one Clark family member had married into the Folsom family, and they took over running the farm until the Lacy family purchased the property around 1940. The Lacys uncovered Native American arrowheads over the 25 years they turned over the soil on the farm.

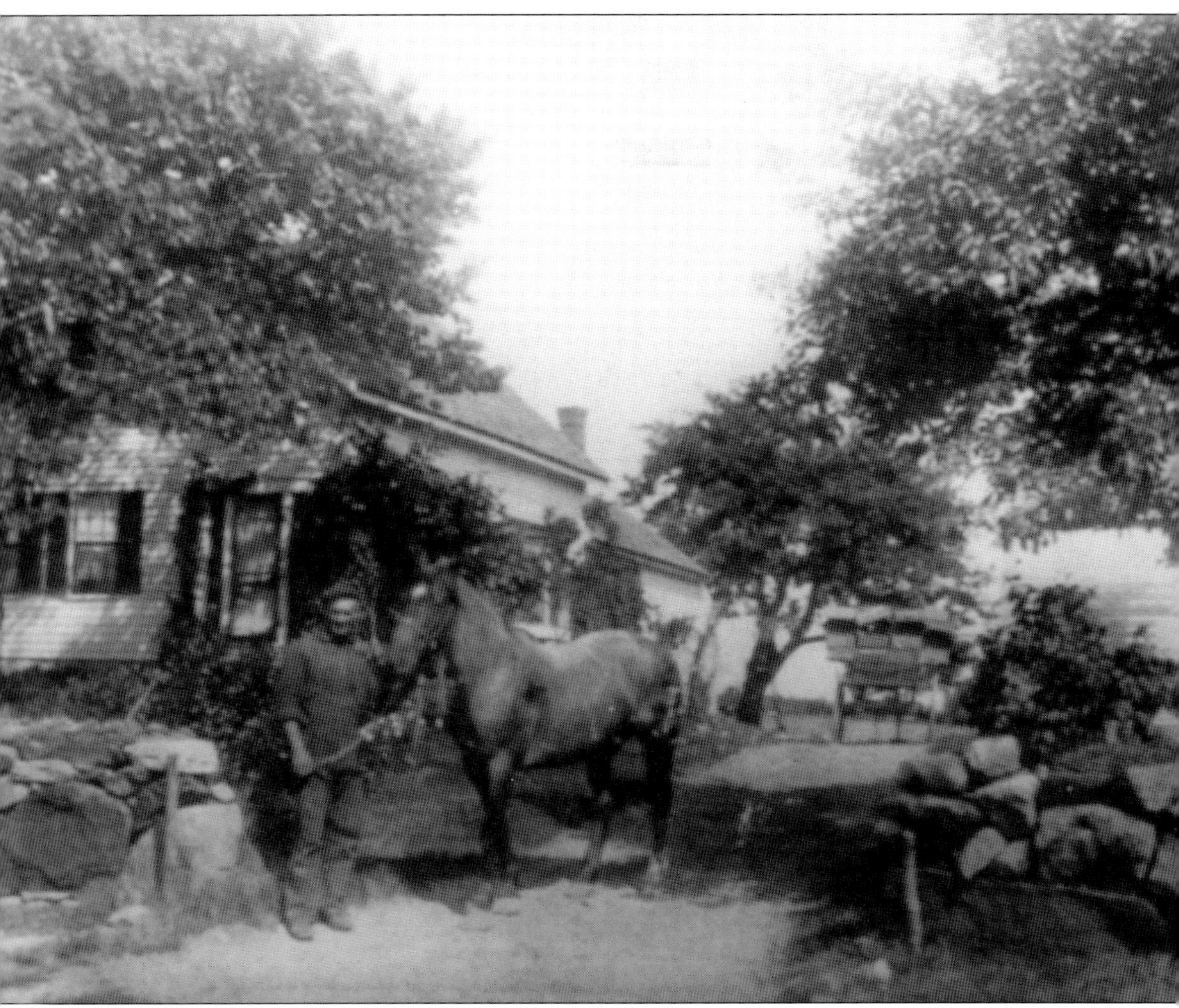

Hiram Littlefield House, also known as Friendship Farm, was a poultry business on Main Street in the Wamesit area. The Littlefields also owned several houses in the area during the mid-1800s, with Hiram's sons building homes nearby. After 1925, the Kalems ran the farm. In this undated photograph could be either owner. In 2013, the home and barns were demolished to make way for Cumberland Farms.

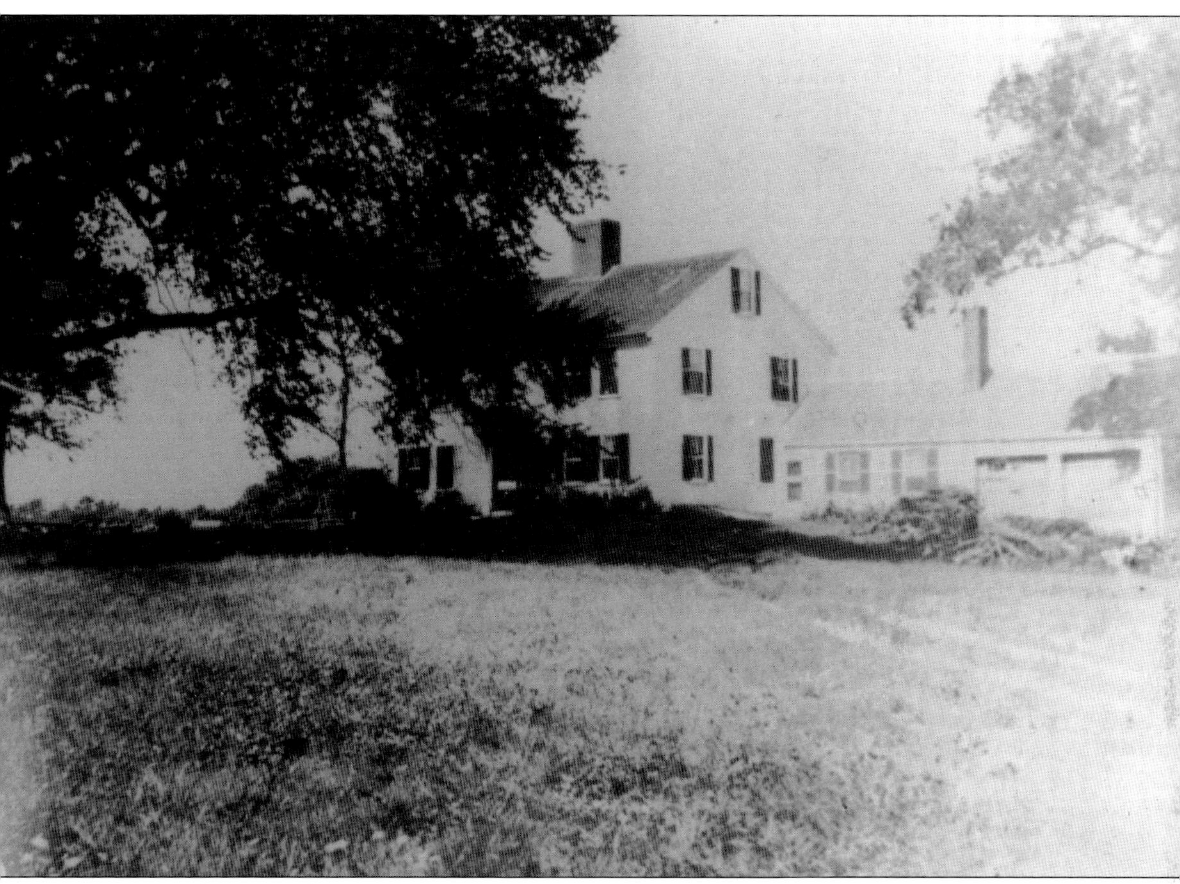

Bridges Farmhouse, built in 1745 on Main Street, was located approximately where McDonald's Restaurant is today. It was destroyed by fire in 1916. The farm extended over many acres on both sides of Main Street, parallel to the Shawsheen River. Before 1900, the Lowell Bicycle Club would ride to the site from Lowell. They would stop there to take a drink of the "best of water that could be drawn up," according to Patten's *Ask Now of the Days That Are Past, A History of Tewksbury, Massachusetts, 1734–1964*. It eventually became the land where Tew-Mac Airport and then Tewksbury Country Club, a golf course, and Eagles Landing Condominiums were built.

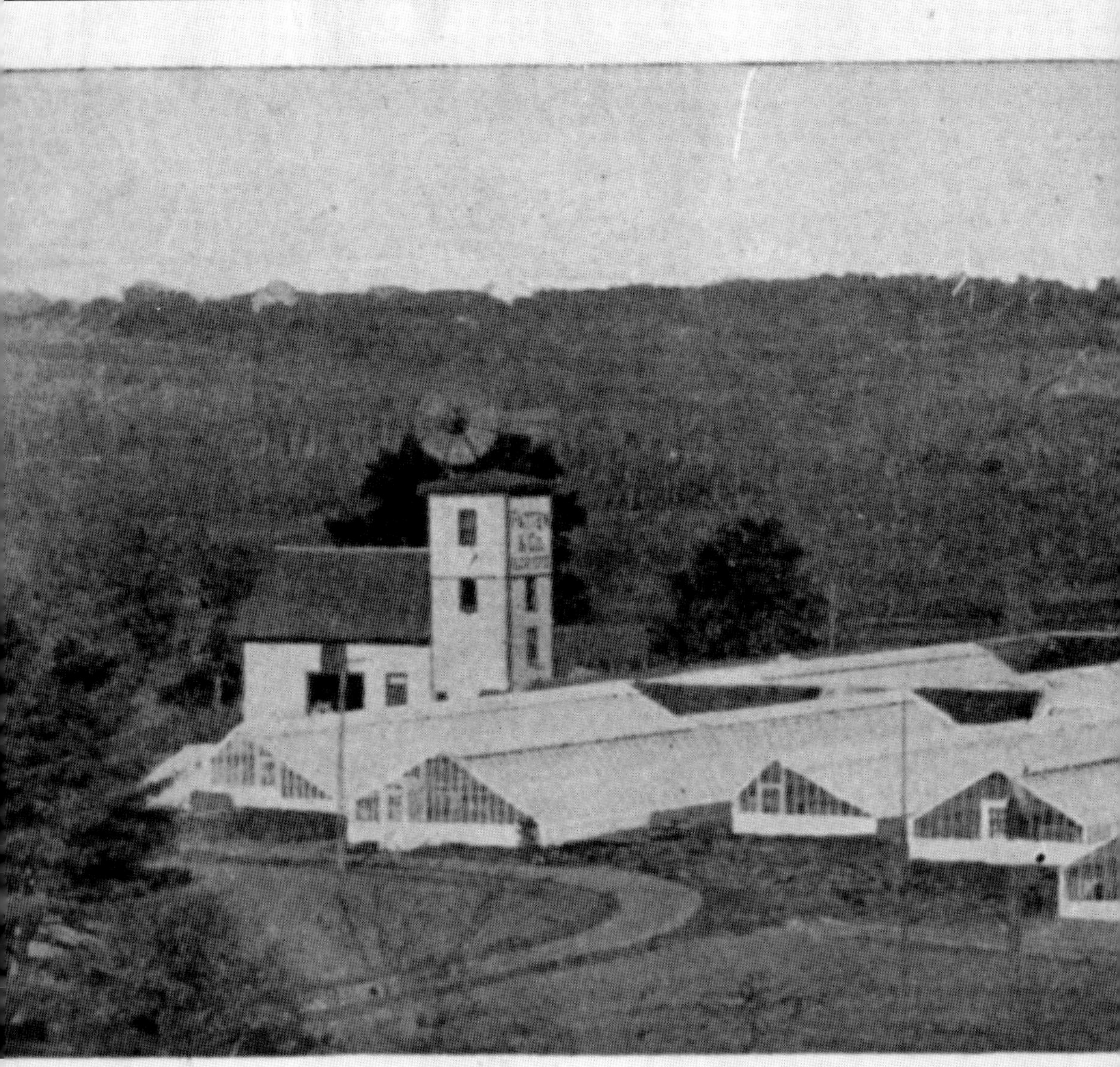

Patten & Co. Florist greenhouses on North Street are seen in a Stearns Cypress Greenhouses, Neponset, Massachusetts, advertisement booklet from around 1930. Marcellus Patten had moved the greenhouses he established in 1870 from Lowell to Tewksbury at North Street in 1886. The company remained a family business for three generations until the 1970s, when the

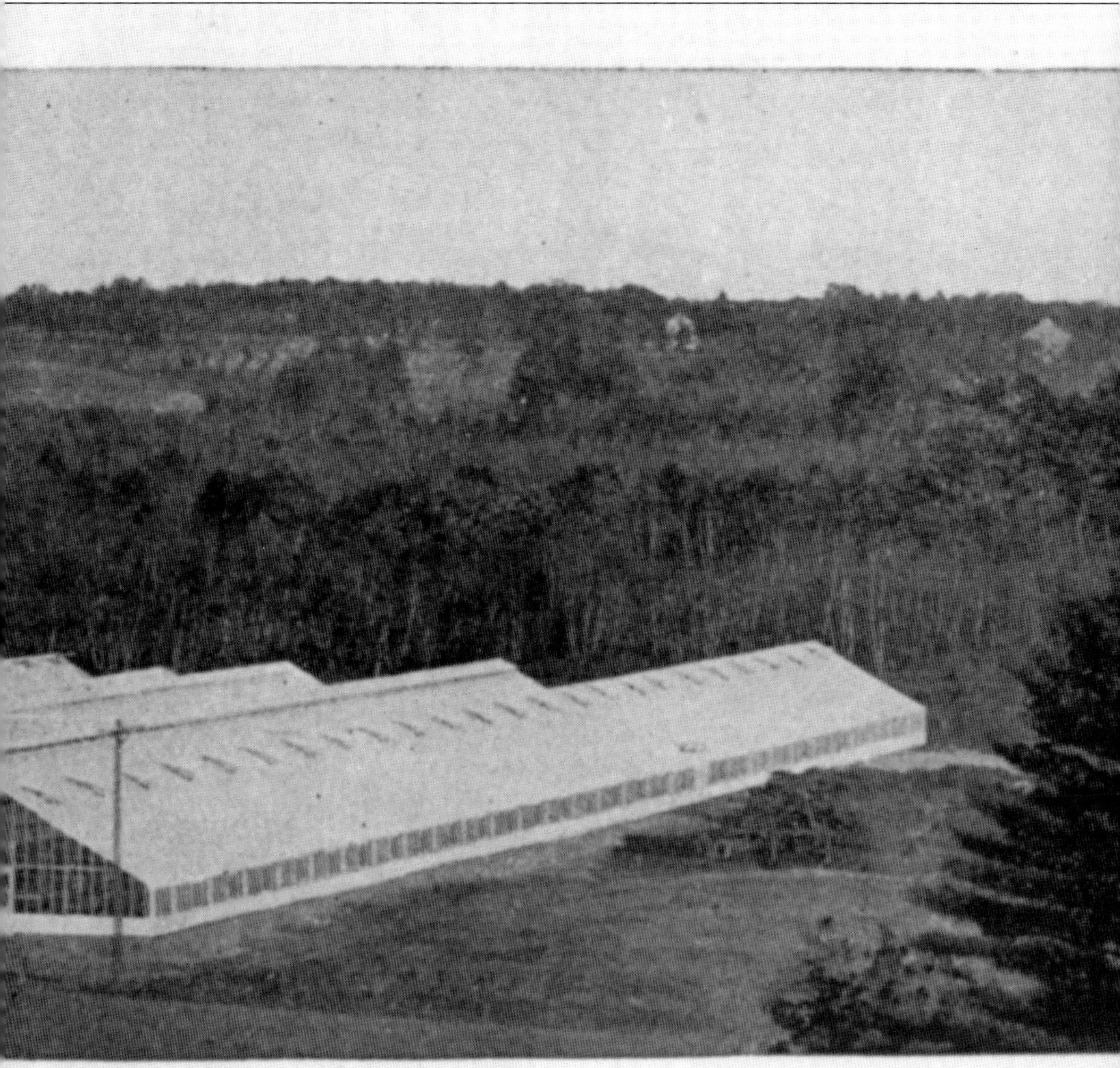

site was redeveloped as Patten Green Condominiums. Marcellus's son Harold succeeded in the hybridization and cultivation of carnations, contributing to the town being named the Carnation Capital of the World in 1976 by *Yankee* magazine. Harold Patten is also the author of the "*Ask Now of the Days That Are Past," A History of Tewksbury, Massachusetts, 1734–1964*.

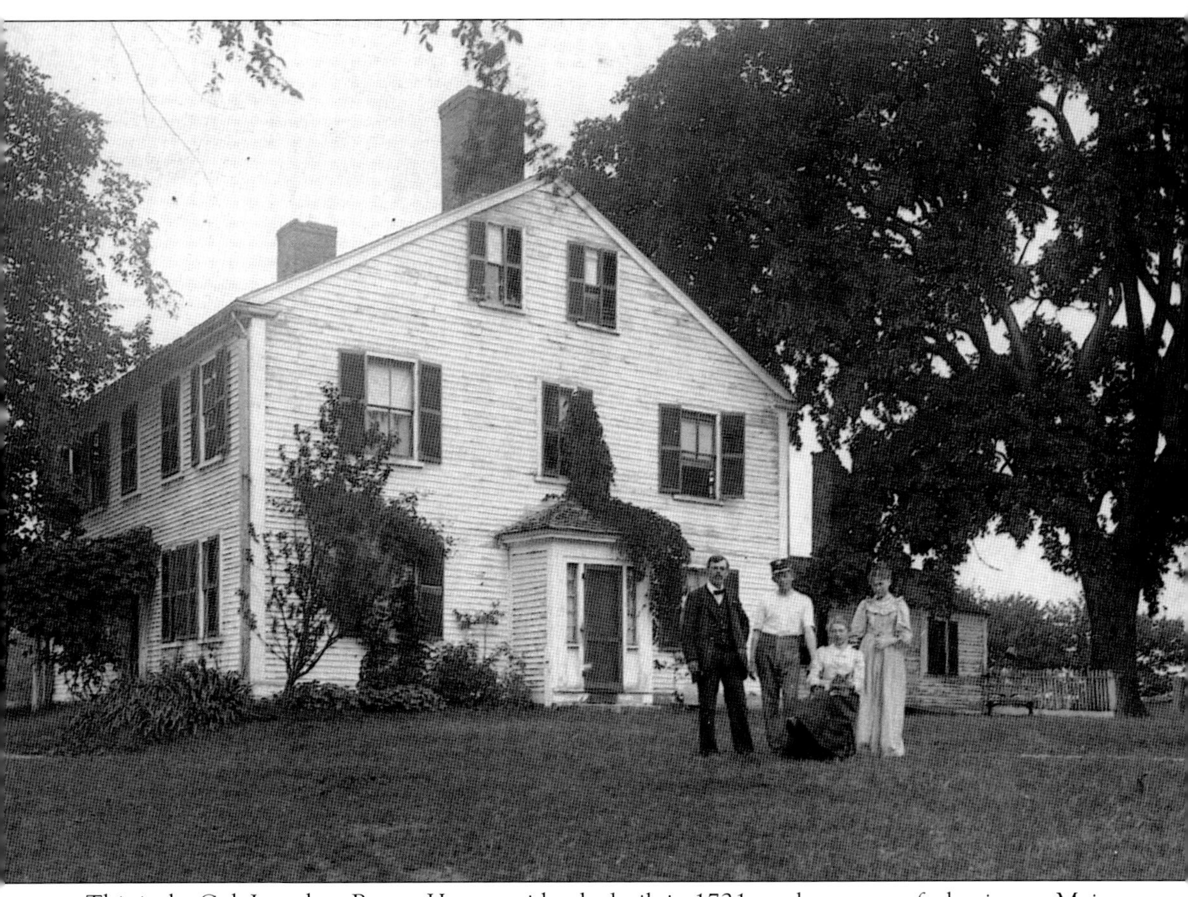

This is the Col. Jonathan Brown House, said to be built in 1721 on the corner of what is now Main and South Streets, where the current Tewksbury United Methodist Church is located. It was also the home of Enoch Warren Foster for several decades. This was also known as Foster's Corner at one time. Some of the Foster family are shown in this undated picture. The home was taken down in 1958 to make way for the church. (See page 100.)

Three

Homes and Landmarks

Historic homes and places tell the story of how Tewksbury and its early families were established and grew. There are also a few landmarks here that note significant events from those early times. After the Massachusetts General Court approved the incorporation of the town on December 23, 1734, the first town meeting was in January 1735. It was voted that Daniel Kittredge, John French, Joseph Hunt Jr., and Joseph Kittredge would serve as selectmen, Nathan Pattin as town clerk, and Nathan Shed as town treasurer. In March 1735, they voted that the town's first meeting house would be 48 feet long and 36 feet wide. In May 1735, they voted to find the center of town and assigned chainmen to assist with this mapping. In September 1736, it was voted that Rev. Sampson Spaulding of Chelmsford would be the first minister and his homestead was built on East Street that same year. In these early days, the residents of the town were interested in all that pertained to the church. At town meetings, the first item of business was to set the minister's salary. This remained so until 1834, when the union of church and state matters were dissolved. With a plan and site for the first meeting house and the church covenant establishing the First Congregational Church in Town Center in 1735, Tewksbury was on its way to fulfilling the Act of 1734, incorporating itself as a separate town from Billerica.

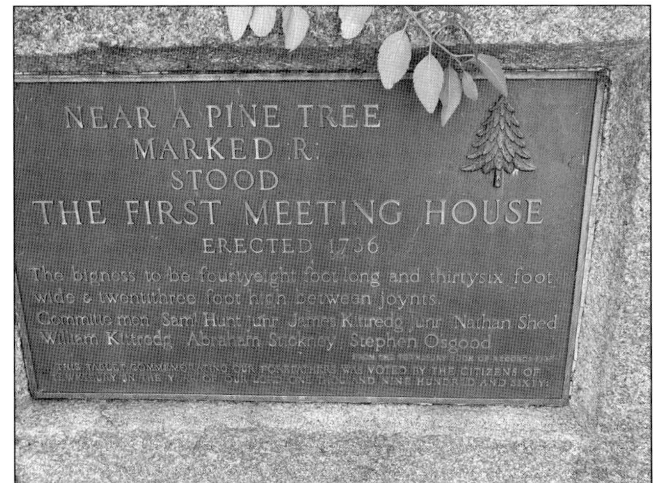

The first Town Hall marker on Town Common was placed in 1960 by an appointed committee of Harold Patten, James Gaffney Jr., and Fredrick M. Carter. They were set forth to locate the spot where the first meetinghouse stood. This was done upon examination of a 1796 map of Tewksbury. The spot is marked on that map across the street from the Tewksbury Congregational Church on East Street. The monument is still on Town Common and can be read from the East Street side.

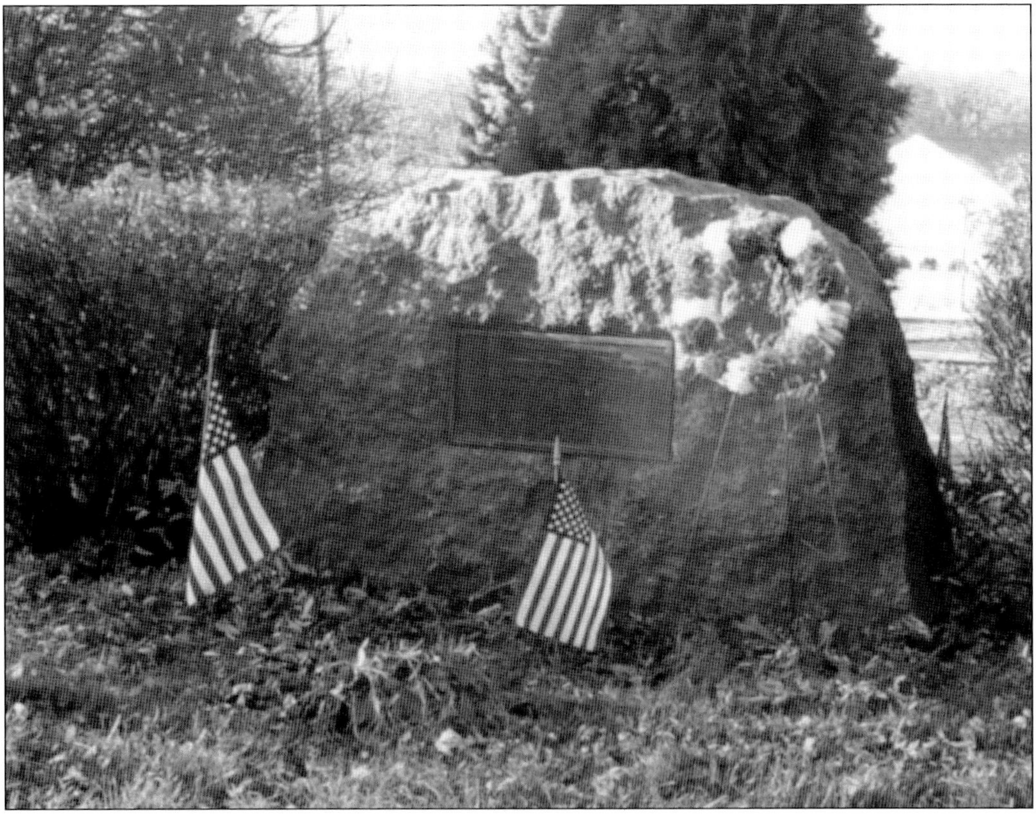

Capt. John Trull of North Tewksbury was given notice by one of Paul Revere's riders that the march of the British Regulars had begun and the battles in Lexington and Concord were imminent. Trull's monument commemorates his action as planned; he fired three shots across the Merrimack River to Captain Varnum of the Dracut Minutemen to signal the British Regulars' march. It was the early morning of April 19, 1775. The marker reads, "This stone is placed here at the direction of a grateful descendant to perpetuate the memory of a patriot of the American Revolution of 1775, Captain John Trull, Captain of the 8th Regt. Mass. Vol. Infantry who led his company of Minutemen into action at or near Lexington on that memorable day."

Once all of Tewksbury's militia were notified of the skirmish at Lexington on April 19, 1775, they met in Town Center and proceeded along East Street, Lee Street, and Chandler Street and onward to Lexington and Concord. This marker stands with others along the Tewksbury route taken that day. On their way, Tewksbury's militia and others engaged the British Regulars returning from the North Bridge battle in Concord, heading back to Boston. It was at Meriam's Corner where the companies from Reading, Chelmsford, and Tewksbury had arrived and took cover when they saw the British infantry on their way back to Boston. Seeing the British vulnerable to attack, they opened fire and started the 16-mile battle that was the start of a war that would last eight years.

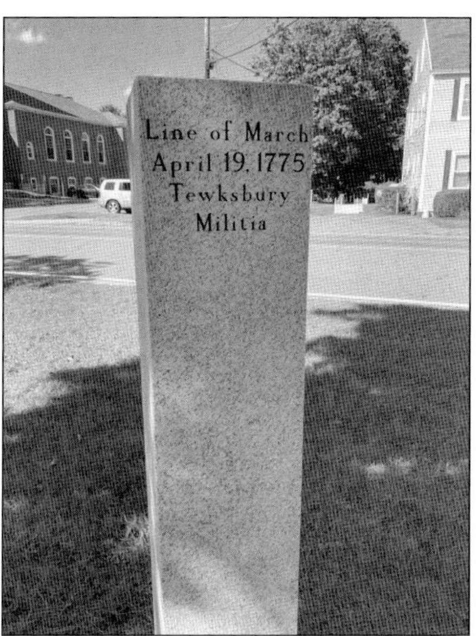

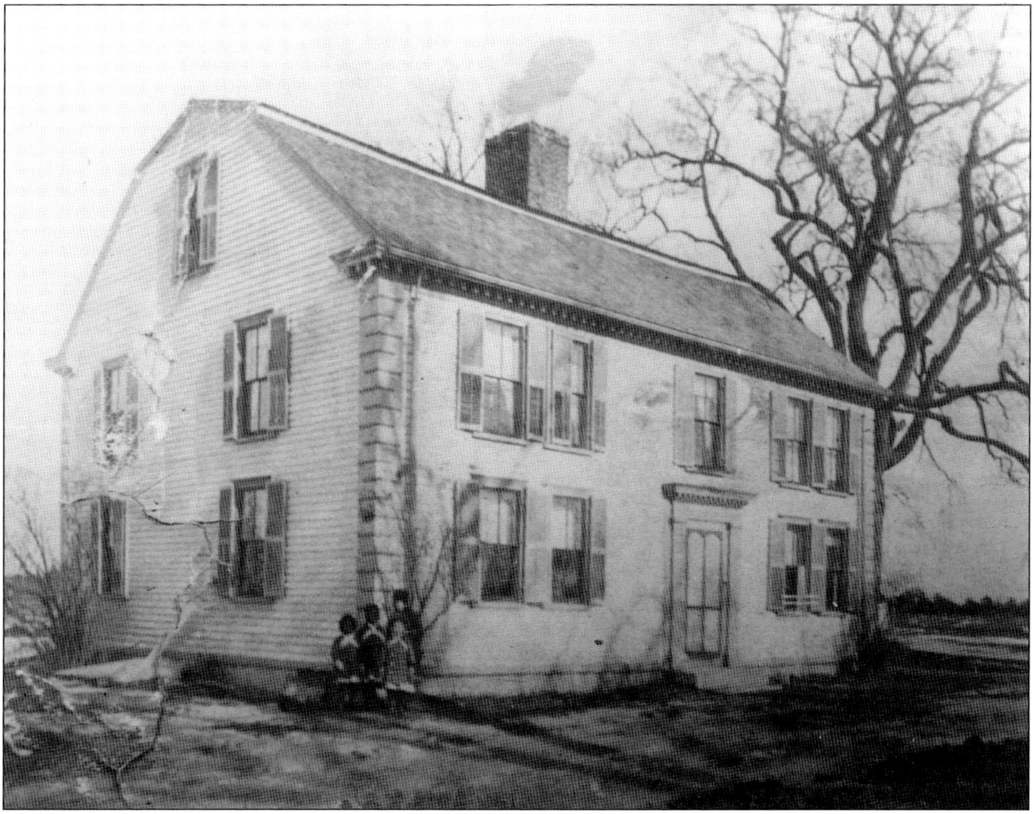

Rev. Sampson Spaulding's house, located on East Street in Town Center, was built in 1736, most likely by the townspeople, as was customary at the time. Originally, the farmland extended over to the Foster School on Main Street and north along North Street. The farm included a home, barn, pig house, hen house, smokehouse, and well house. The west front parlor served several purposes, including post office, worship, and wedding room.

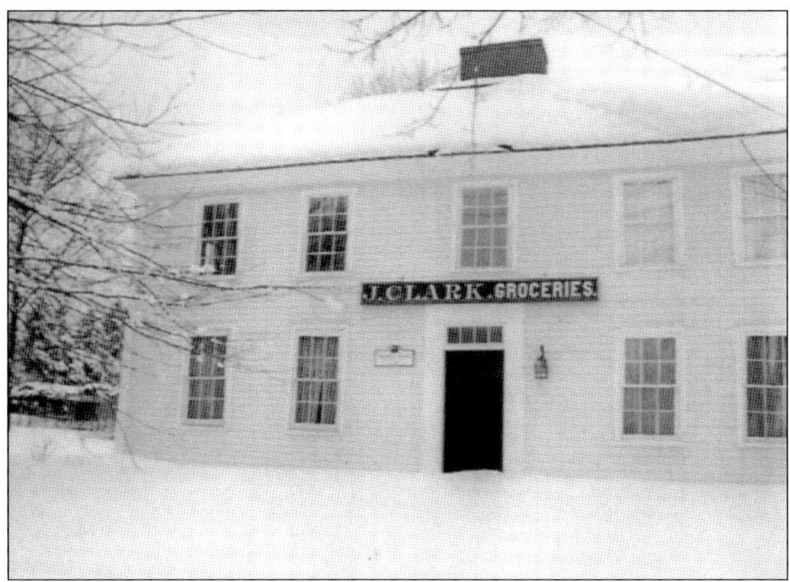

The Jonathan Clark Homestead on Andover Street is believed to have been built in 1746. The home stayed in the Clark and Kittredge families through marriage until the 1960s. The original homestead property included a barn, 60 acres, and another 33 acres of separate lots.

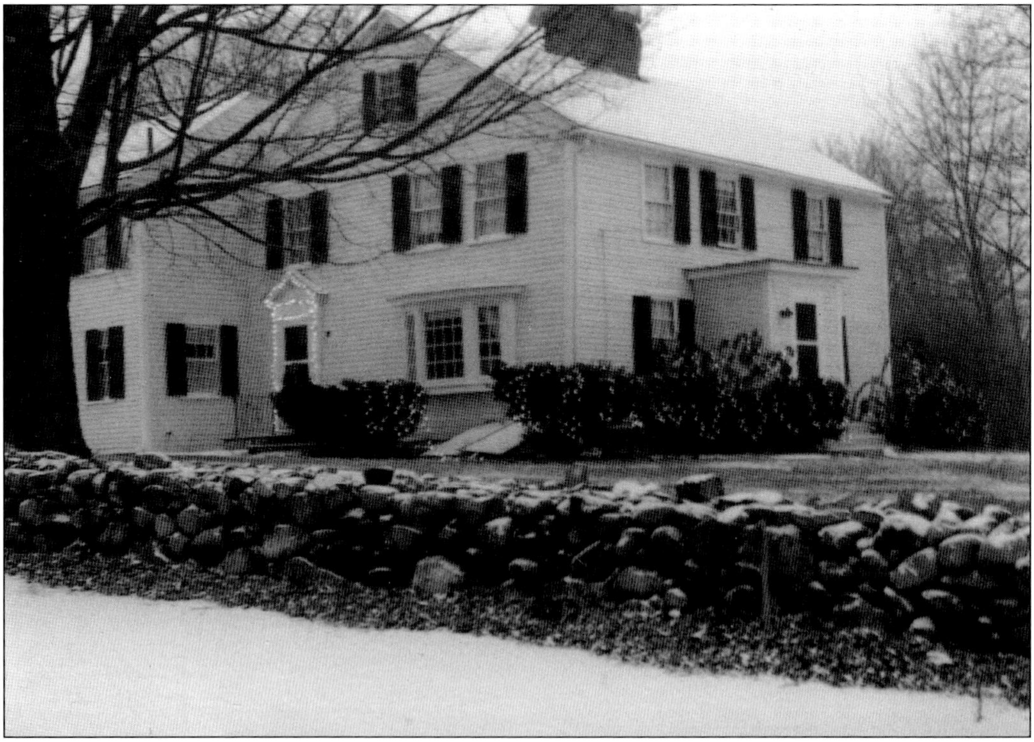

The Battles Homestead on North Street, as records state, is a rare example of Georgian architecture in Tewksbury and an early square-plan house of timber-frame construction that remains standing in Massachusetts. The homestead, built around 1740, also included 40 acres of farmland used until the mid-1960s as prize-winning apple and peach orchards. The farmland is now the site of Raytheon Integrated Defense.

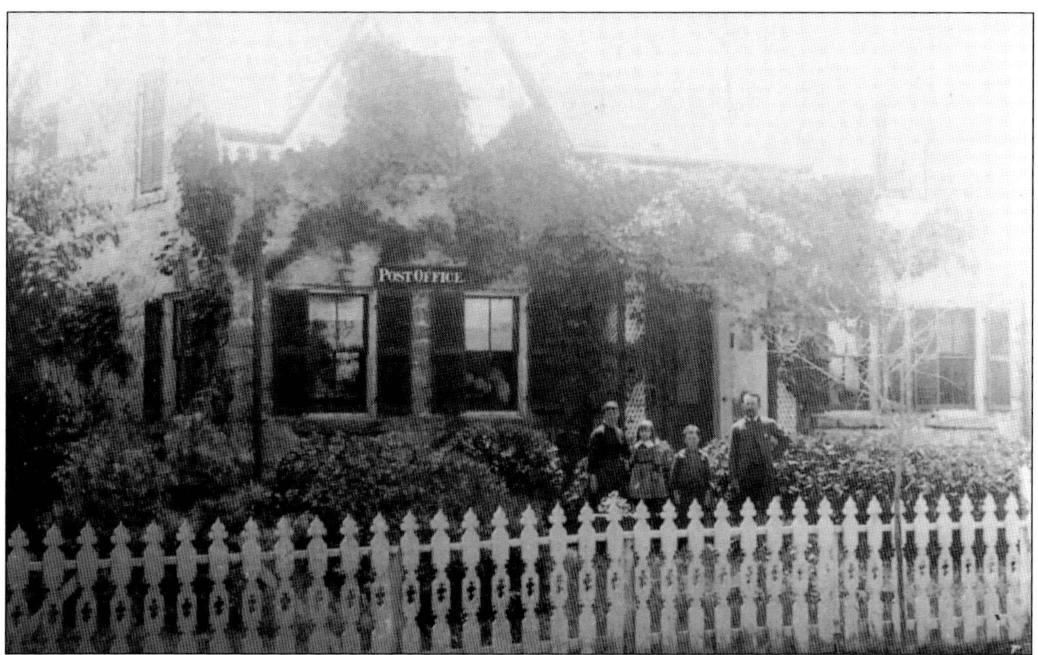

The Stone House on East Street, built in 1841 and shown here around 1900, was the home of James Fairgrieve, pictured with his wife, Penelope, and children Arthur and Ethel. James had been the station agent for the Tewksbury Center Railroad Station around the corner on North Street, telegraph agent, and postmaster in the late 1800s. The post office was in his home, as the sign indicates. His son Arthur followed him as postmaster and acting station agent in the early 1900s. Arthur also worked at the family grocery store, Fairgrieve & Co. in Town Center. James's daughter Ethel Fairgrieve Jackson made a significant donation toward the construction of a new town library in the 1960s. A library trust fund in her name remains to this day.

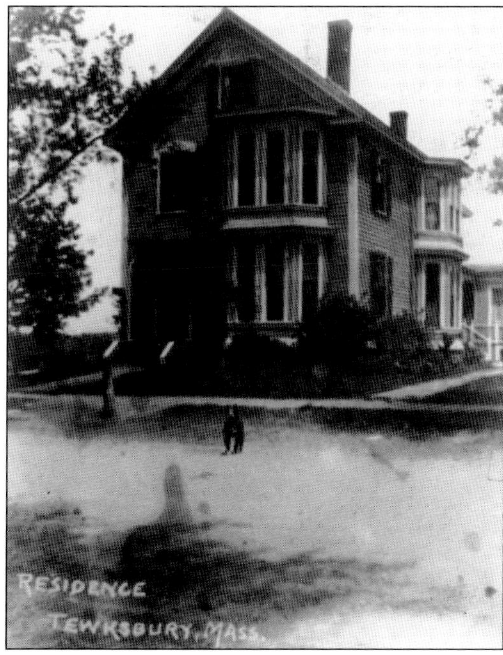

The Darby House, also on East Street, was built in about 1875, owned by the Kelsea family, and sold to the Mears family in 1883. In 1890, the 14-acre property, extending to Main Street, included the home, a mill building, and a blacksmith shop. Homer and Myra Darby bought the home in 1929, and the family remained there until 1989.

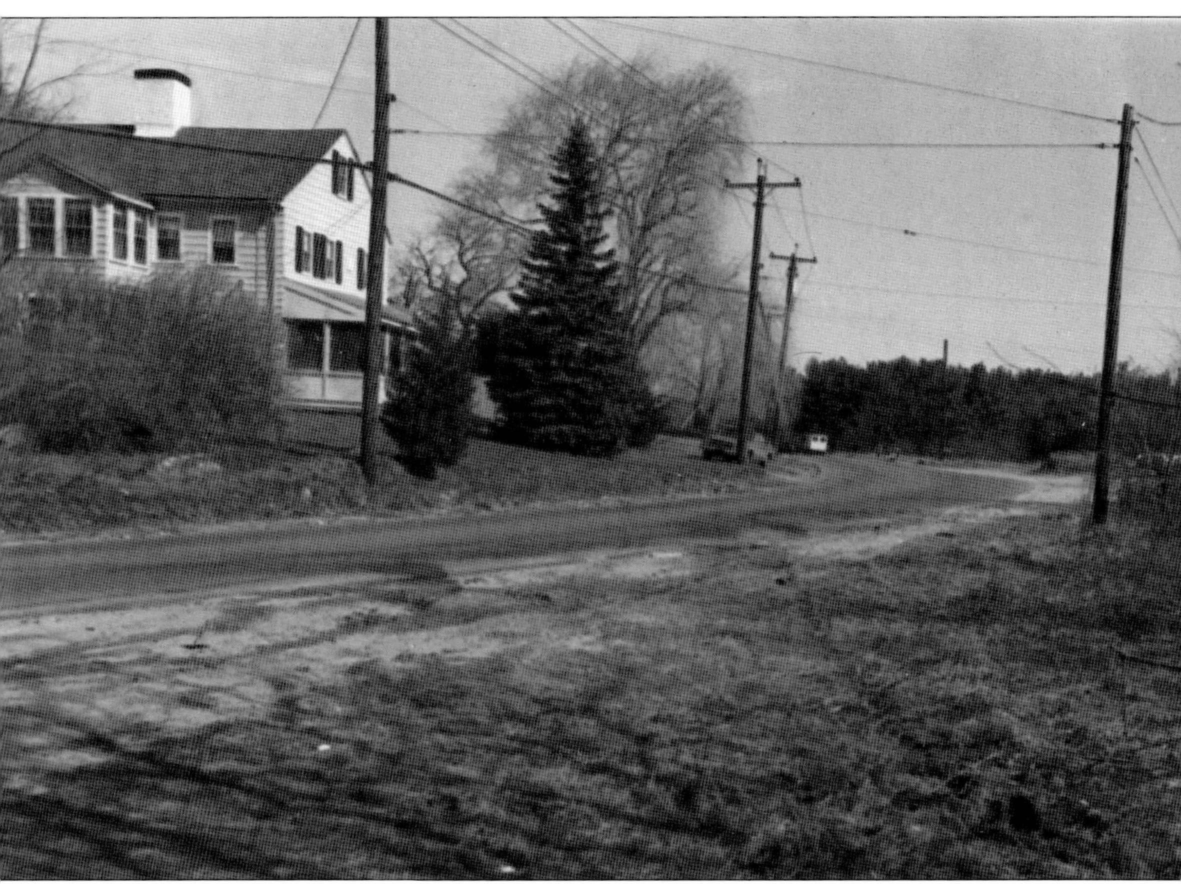

The Kittredge Homestead on Shawsheen Street is situated on property that was deeded in 1660, when Tewksbury was still part of Billerica, to John Kittredge. The land extended over both sides of Shawsheen, with over 30 acres on each side of the street. One of the family, Dr. Henry A. Kittredge, was a surgeon in the Civil War and died in 1862 in a Civil War hospital in New Orleans. Henry's father, Dr. Benjamin Kittredge (1740–1836), famously had eight sons who became physicians.

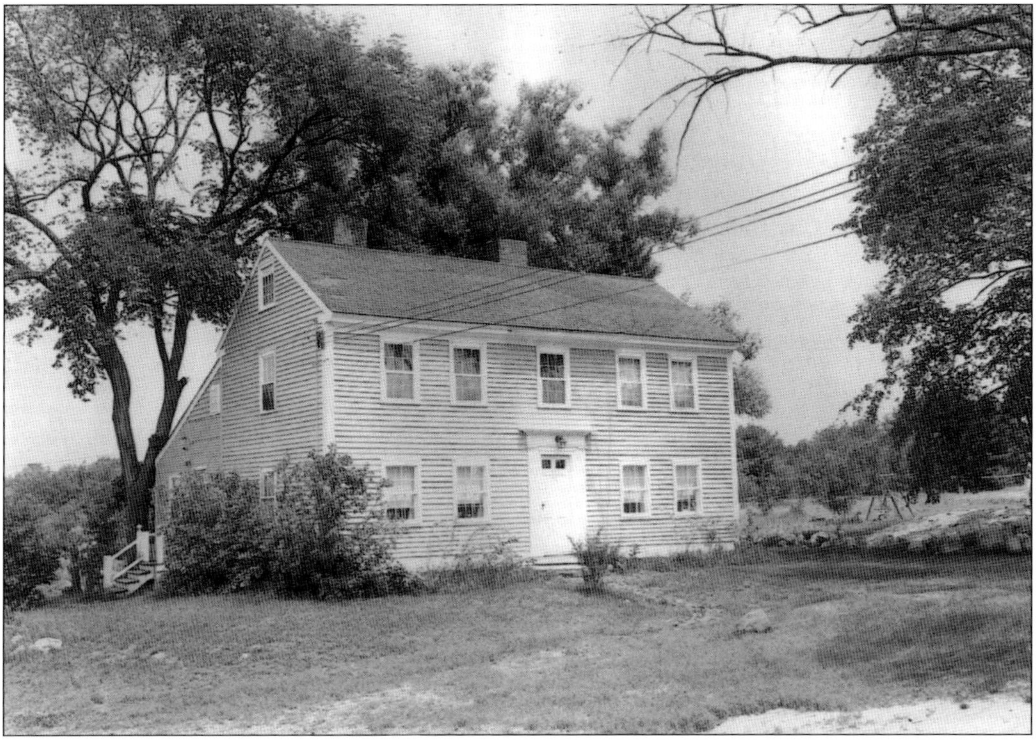

The Burtt House, on South Street near the Andover line, is recorded as being built around 1800. Benjamin Burtt purchased the 100-acre property from Enoch Foster. South Street extended into Andover. Over the years, the Burtt family expanded their land ownership to a total of 215 acres to the banks of the Shawsheen River and into Andover. The Burtts had business interests in lumber and sawmilling. In 1890, upon his death, Benjamin had 400 cords of cut wood and 40,000 feet of lumber on the property.

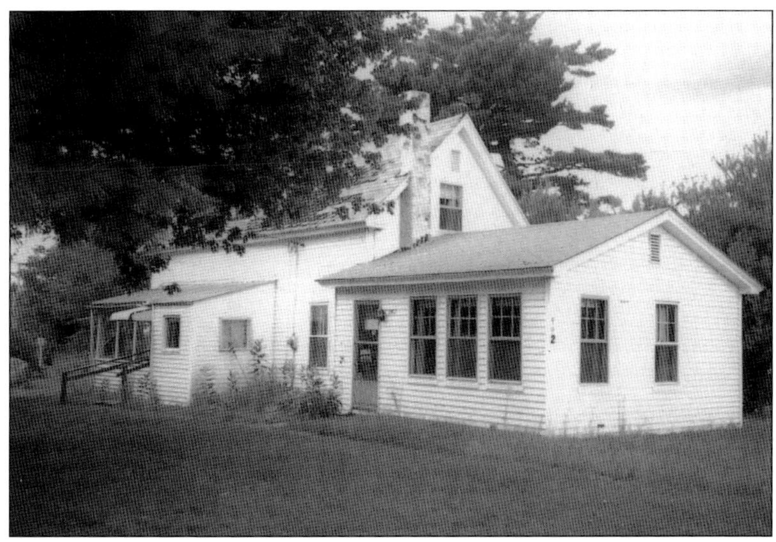

Col. Russell Mears House, on Main Street at the corner of Old Boston Road, was built in 1780. Colonel Mears was a Tewksbury Revolutionary War veteran. The home was built on 80 acres that extended over both sides of Main Street and was owned by his parents, who lived near Town Center at that time. It was demolished in 2024.

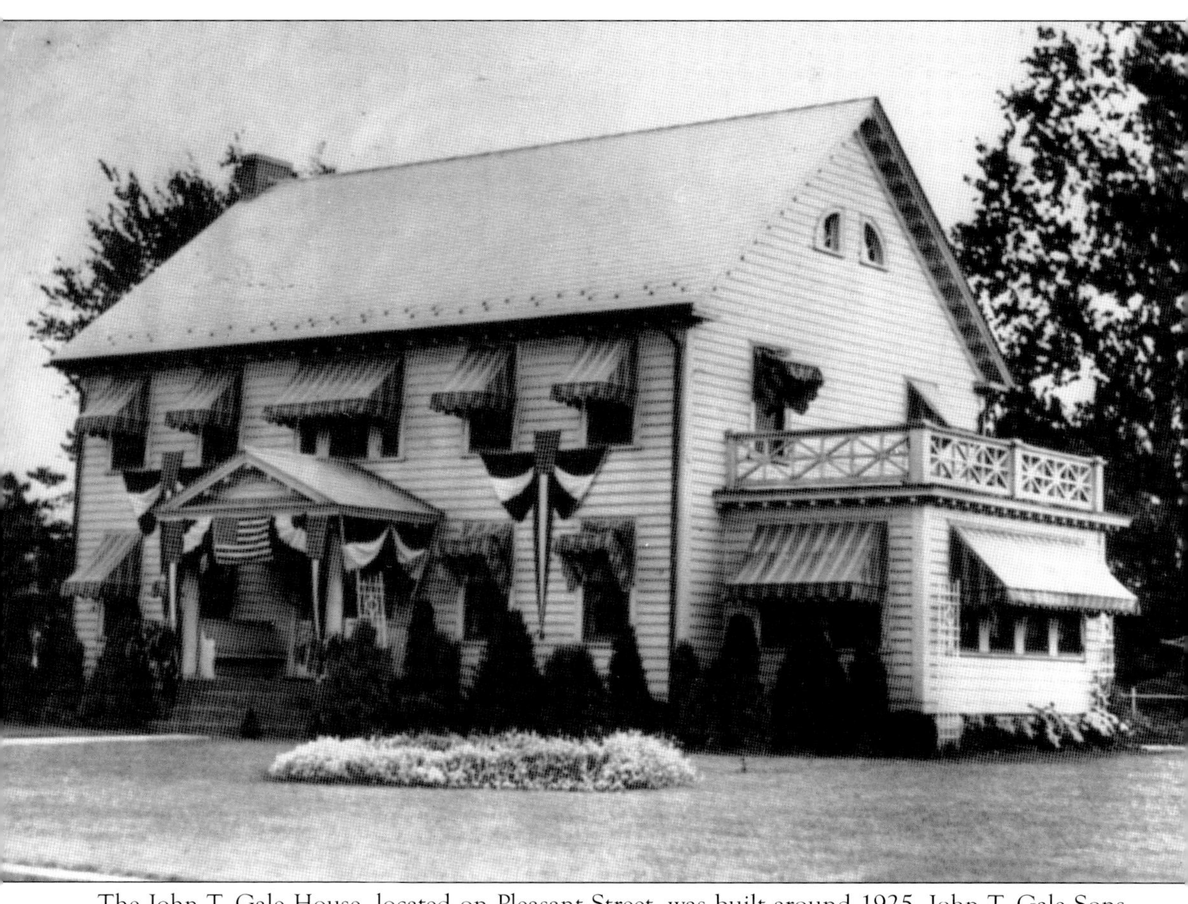

The John T. Gale House, located on Pleasant Street, was built around 1925. John T. Gale Sons Wholesale Florist was established on Helvetia Street in about 1905. While many greenhouses were demolished in the middle to late 20th century, the Gale greenhouse operation is still active.

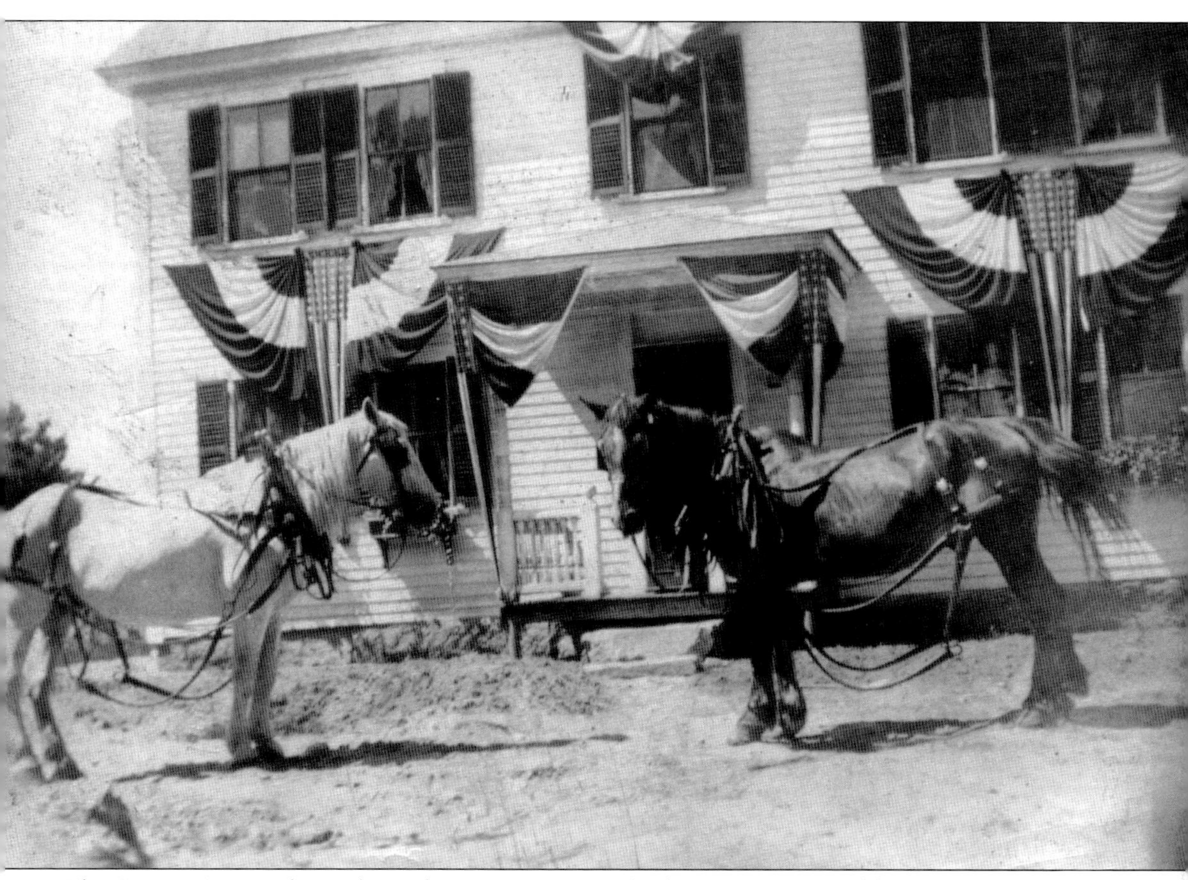

The Preston House, located on Pleasant Street, was built in 1790. Owned by Henry Preston in 1834, who had a merchant shop on Main Street near the Foster School and was postmaster in the mid-1800s. The property had 40 acres in 1869. Herbert Pillsbury owned the home in the early 1900s; thus, it is sometimes called the "Pillsbury House." It was decorated in this image for the 200th Anniversary of the town's incorporation in 1934.

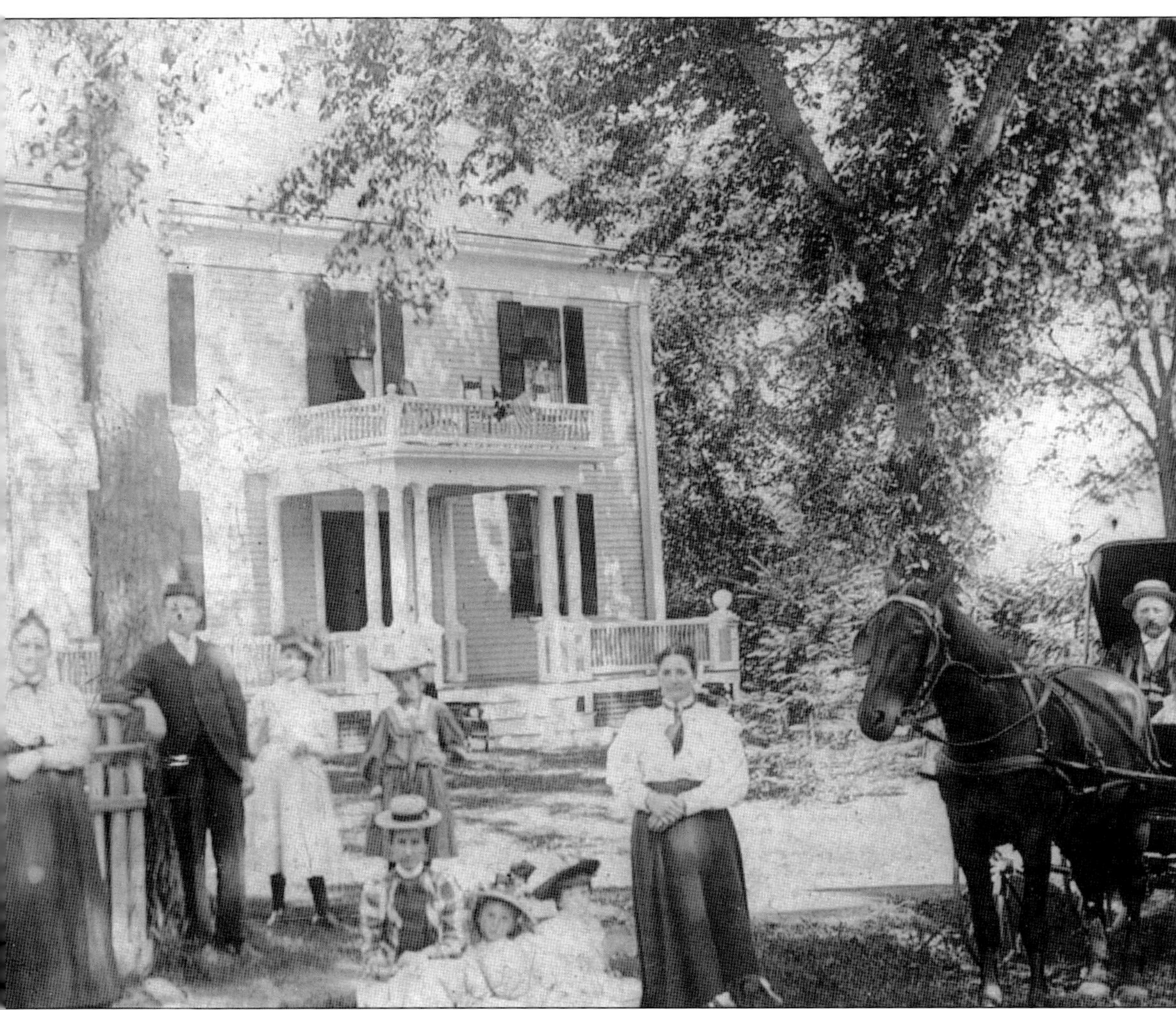

The Frank Farmer House, situated on Lee Street, is pictured in the summer before it burned down in November 1898. The house was built in 1870 by William Lee, son of George Lee, who had established a tannery on the same street. Frank Farmer was the town undertaker, police chief, and selectman. Frank's son Henry was also an undertaker with his father at the house. The business is now called Farmer and Dee Funeral Home, noted as being in continuous business since 1878.

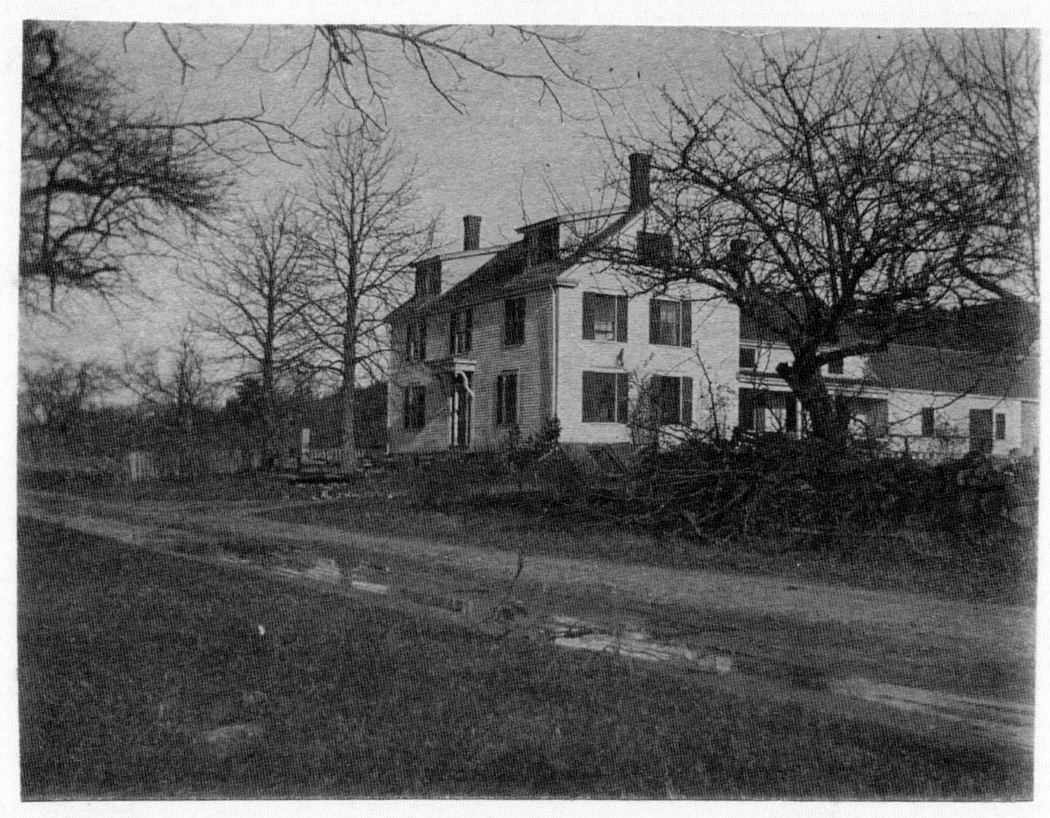

The Charles Clark House on North Street was purchased by Charles from Cyrus Battles in 1886 and included 87 acres on the east side of North Street and 20 acres on the opposite side of North Street. The land and buildings were eventually purchased by Adelbert Ames, who purchased a total of 700 acres on Prospect Hill and built Ames Castle.

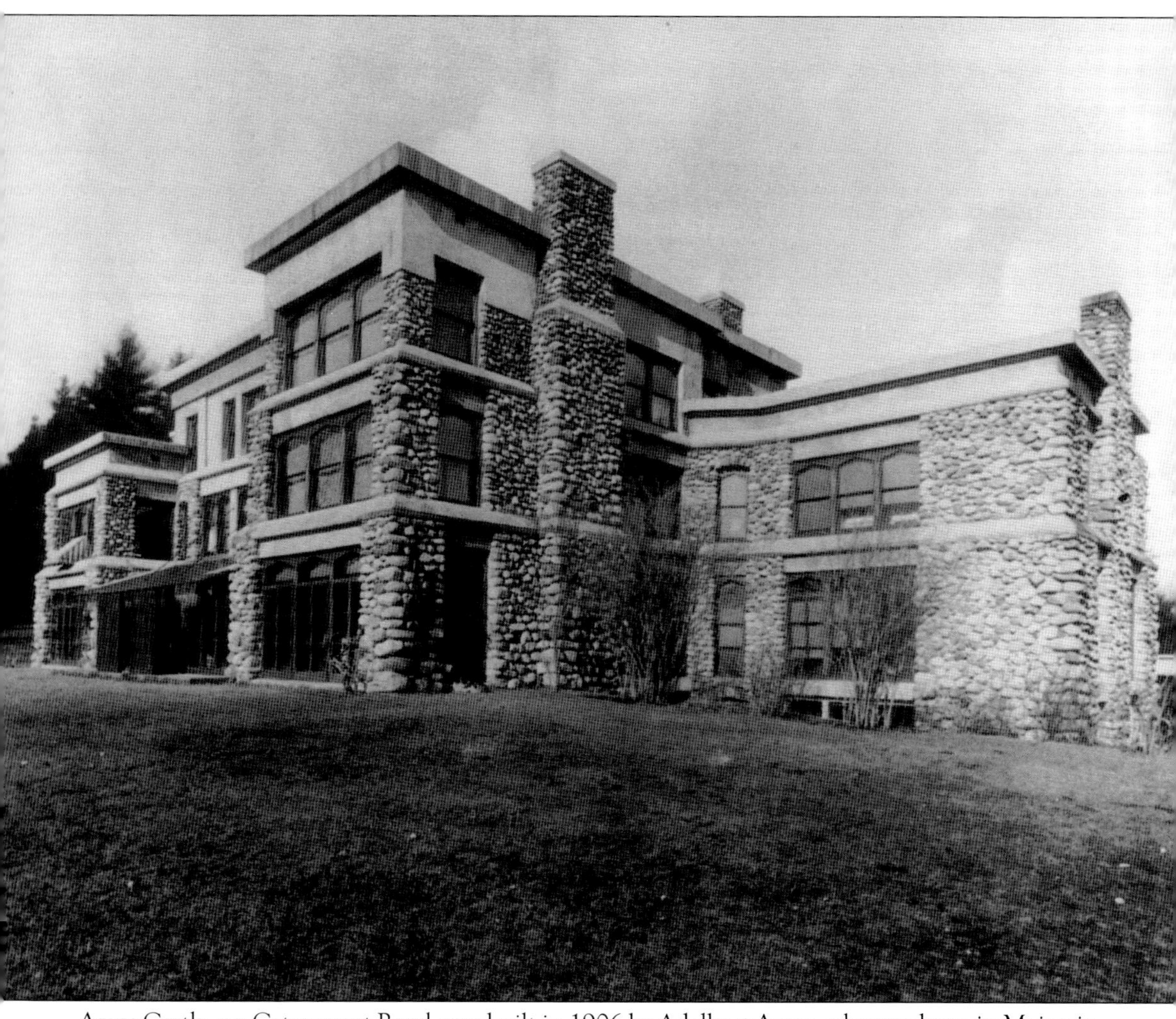

Ames Castle, on Catamount Road, was built in 1906 by Adelbert Ames, who was born in Maine in 1835. He graduated from the US Military Academy at West Point in 1861 and was commissioned to the Union army of the Civil War in 1861. After the war, he was appointed as governor of Mississippi in 1868 and later elected in 1874. Ames married Benjamin Butler's daughter Blanche of Lowell, Massachusetts, and they returned to the area for business, purchasing 700 acres on Prospect Hill in Tewksbury in 1906 and building the 17-room fieldstone castle.

The Ames Castle staircase was a grand focal point of the three-story home. In his service during the Civil War, Adelbert received the Medal of Honor for his efforts in the Battle of First Bull Run. He continued to contribute successfully throughout his career in battles during the war, rising to the rank of brigadier general in 1898. Adelbert was a staunch supporter of equality for African Americans.

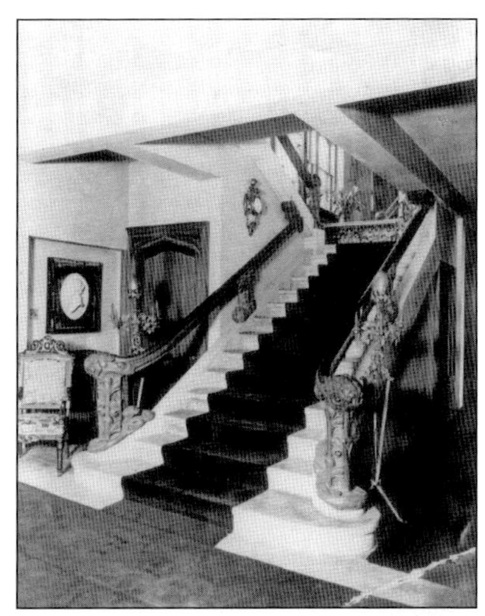

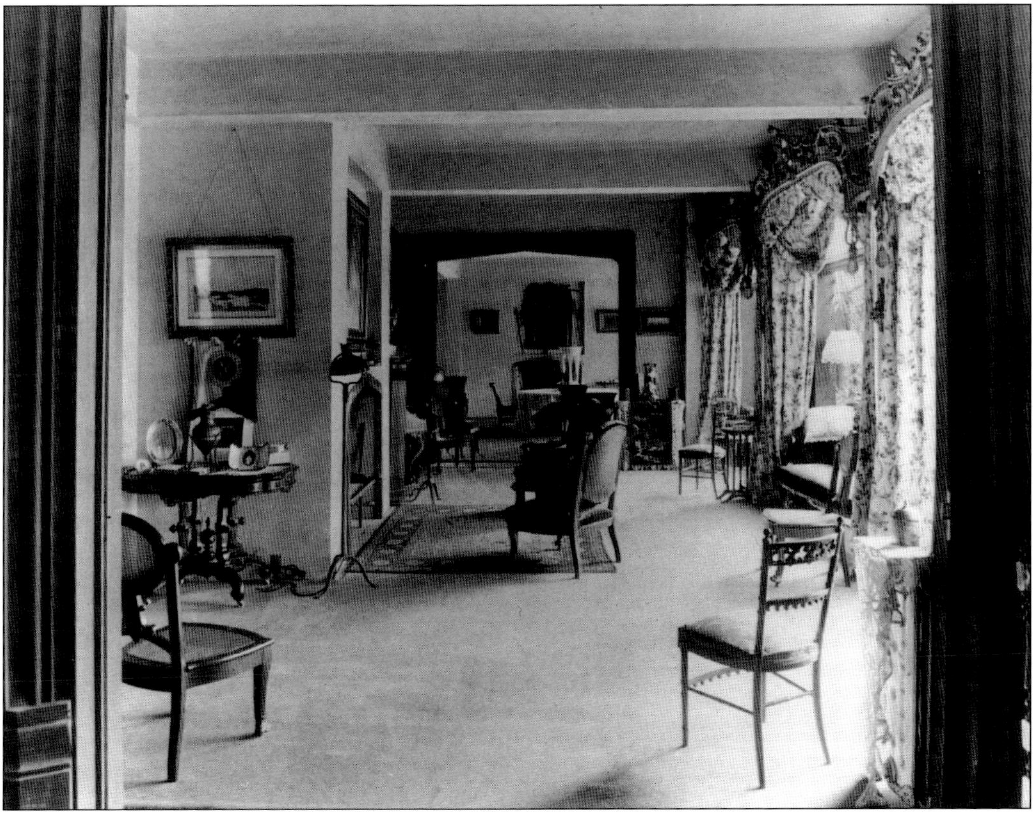

Ames Castle's ample living room shows the floor-to-ceiling windows providing light to the stylish furnishing of the home. After arriving in Tewksbury, Ames worked as an East Coast executive for his father's Minnesota flour business and became an investor in the Boston-Lowell Interurban Railway, an electric line that went from Lowell to Boston and through Tewksbury. Adelbert Ames's son Adelbert Jr. was a noted ophthalmologist, psychologist, and artist. In 1912, he created the American Indian bust that the Shawmut Bank of Boston adopted as its trademark. Adelbert's daughter Blanch was an activist for women's suffrage and birth control reform. Adelbert passed away in 1933 at the age of 97 in Florida. He was the last surviving full-rank general of the Civil War.

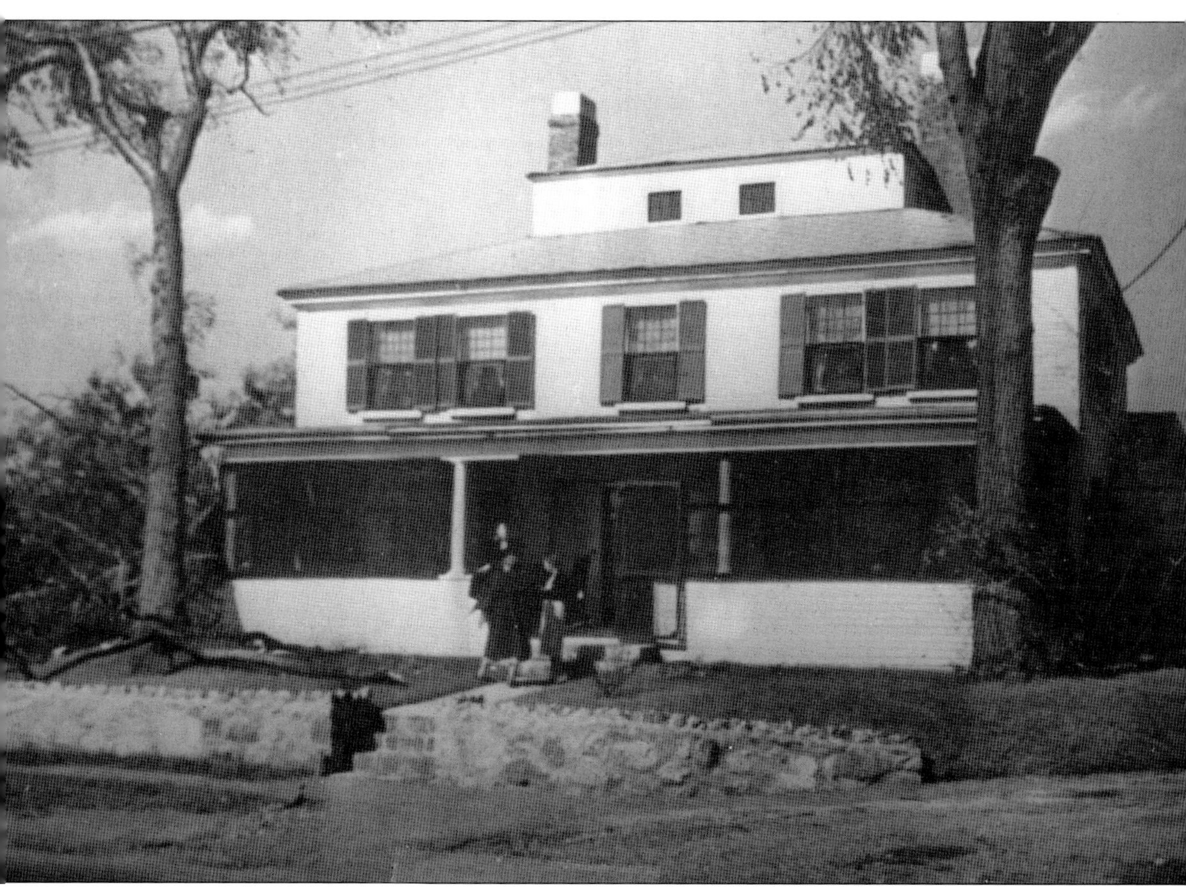

The Hardy-Pike House on Main Street, pictured in 1938, was the home of Zachariah Hardy, who built the house around 1740. The site has been said to have been a halfway stop for stagecoaches traveling between Boston and Nashua, New Hampshire, in the 1800s. It was later owned by Samuel Pike, who owned a 93-acre farm on Pike Street and the 40-acre Hardy place in 1890. Samuel's son Daniel married Alice, and they took ownership of the Hardy spot in 1934. Alice Pike, who might be one of the women in this picture, was the town clerk for Tewksbury, serving from the home for many years; she stayed there until 1976.

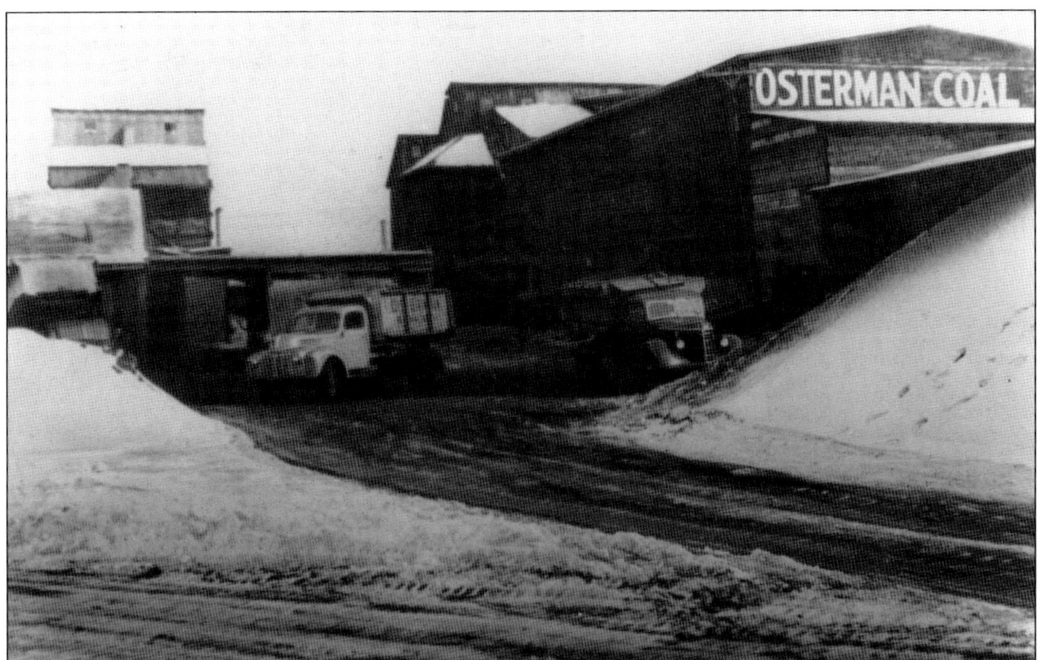

Osterman's Coal in West Tewksbury was a coal, coke, and oil company where Frederic Osterman, son of Aaron Osterman, worked. Aaron was a dairy farmer in the late 1800s, operating the Osterman Dairy Farm on the corner of North Billerica Road and French Streets. Three generations of the Osterman family continued to run the dairy until the mid-1900s.

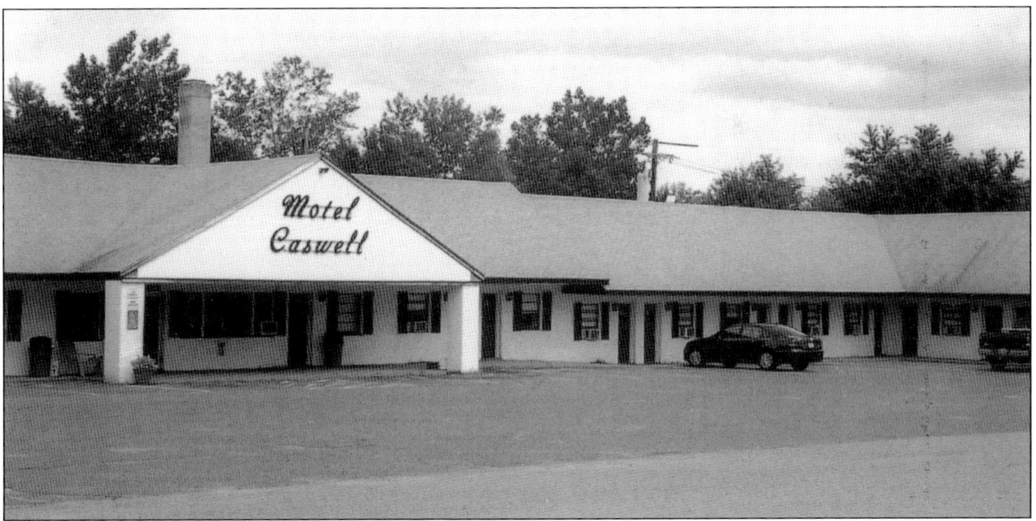

Motel Caswell on Main Street was a town landmark founded in the 1950s by Russ Caswell Sr. In the early 2000s, the 56-room budget motel was often a site connected to narcotics investigations. In 2009, the federal government filed a case against the owner, saying that he could have done more to stop the drug use on the premises. The US District Court for Massachusetts in *the United States vs. 434 Main Street, Tewksbury* (2012) held that the federal government's attempt to seize the property under 21 US Code § 881(a)(7) was excessive. This was a landmark case in limiting the power of the federal government to confiscate property. The motel was demolished in 2014. The property is now the site of Wamesit Lanes.

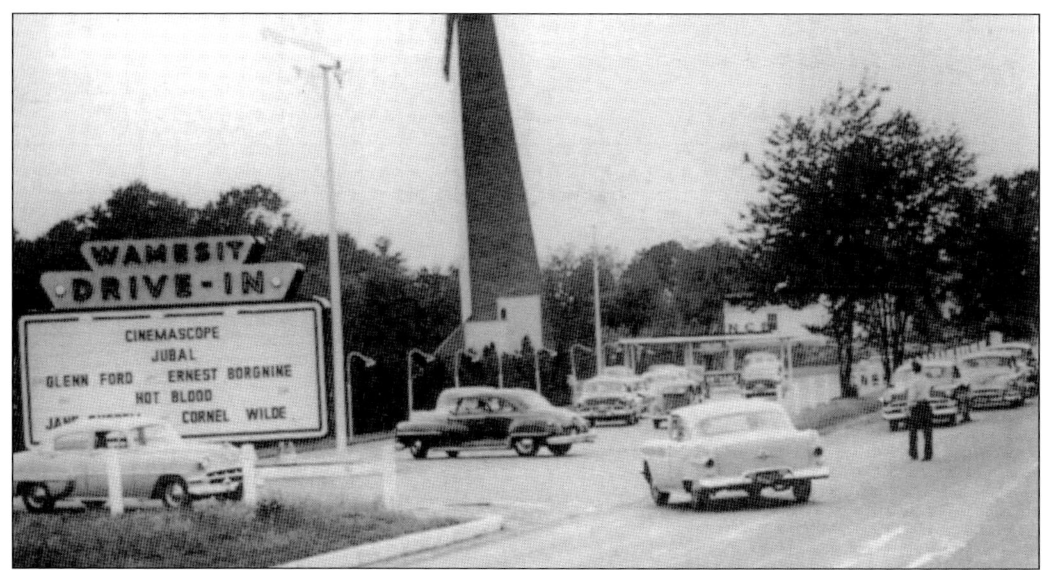

Wamesit Drive-In was at the intersection of Route 38 and Interstate 495 and opened in the 1950s. There was room for six hundred cars and there were three movie screens. The Wamesit Drive-In neon sign was an iconic image preserved after the demolition of the site in 1992 and was part of a sign exhibit at Lexington National Heritage Museum in 2003.

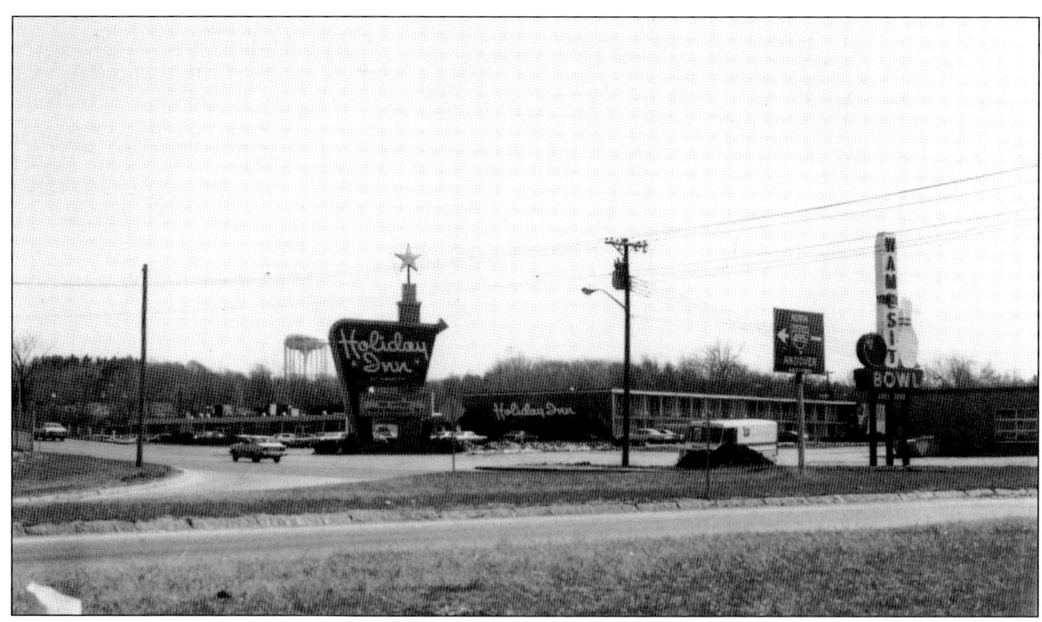

Holiday Inn and Wamesit Bowl-O-Matic are shown here at the intersection of Route 38 and the new Interstate 495 in the 1960s. The Holiday Inn of America was opened in 1965 with 120 rooms, a swimming pool, and a dining room for 300 people. Wamesit Bowl-O-Matic and the Wamesit Drive-In were already landmarks in the area, opened in the 1950s.

Four

Town Center

The character of Town Center in the early years of Tewksbury can be seen in photographs from over a century ago and even in the remaining buildings of today. The Village Improvement Association Inc., established in 1891, was a private group of residents who looked after improving the look and feel of the Town Center. They installed gas streetlamps, sidewalks, trees, and other plantings and kept the landscape trimmed. In 1934, it was voted to end the association, with the town taking over the care of the center. Main Street, once called the road to Lowell, is the route that crosses the entire length of the town, from east to west, and at the center, it intersects with East and Pleasant Streets. At times, the only way to get across town is to go through the Center. Where there were once dirt roads for horses and buggies, then train stations and trolleys, a gas station and automobiles, the Town Center has remained the vital crossroads of the town. It is where the town government, safety, and emergency services, as well as the first church, are located. The Town Common, with its bandstand, has been and is still the place our community gathers for Memorial Day parades, Veterans Day memorials, winter holiday festivals, community exhibits, and vigils. From scenes of the Town Center before the fire of 1918 to the new Town Hall and Congregational church that were both rebuilt after World War I, the town has kept its New England charm, patriotism, and community feeling.

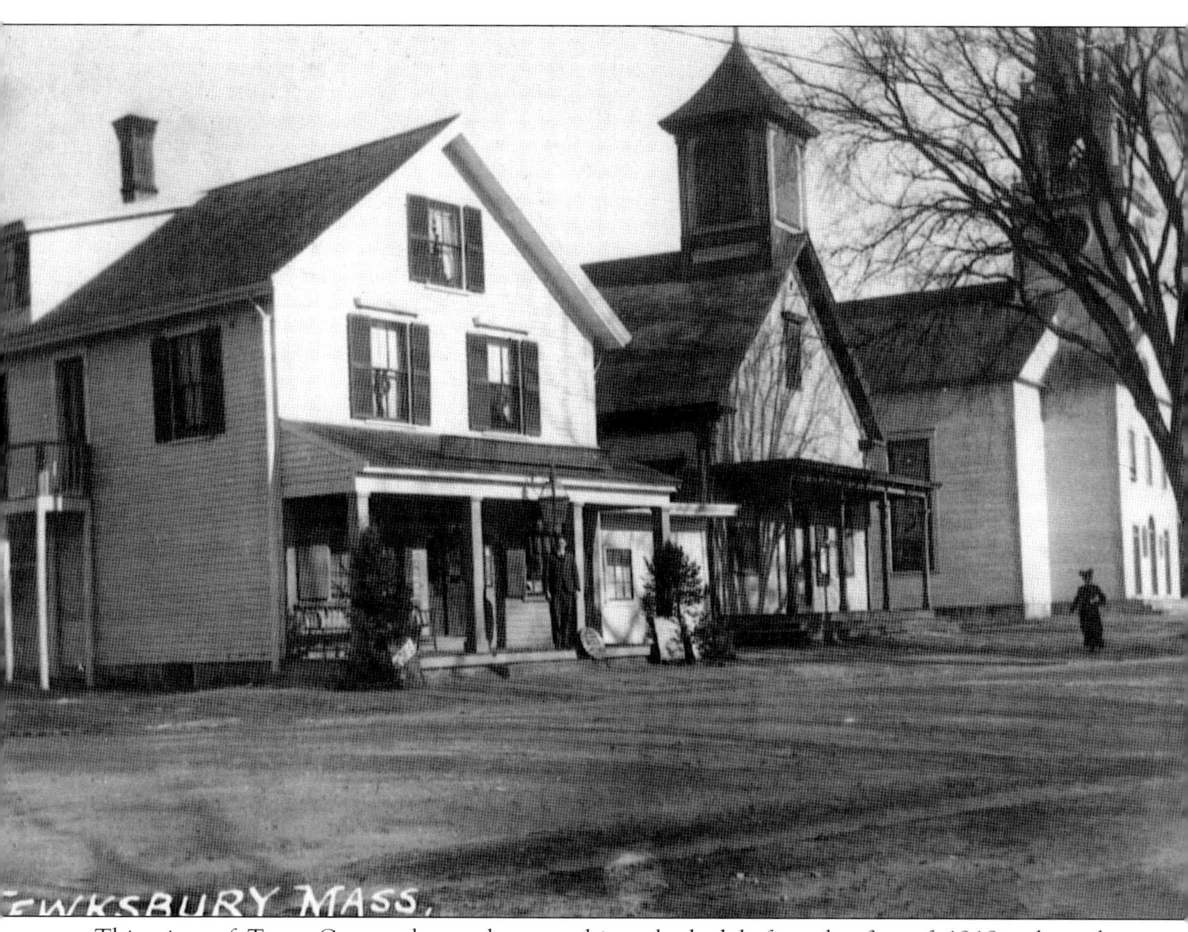

This view of Town Center shows the way things looked before the fire of 1918, when the Congregational church (right) and the Town Hall (center) burned down in a devastating fire. It was Sunday morning on October 13, 1918, when the church and the horse sheds in the back, along with the Town Hall, were destroyed. They are seen here with Fairgreive's Store on the far left.

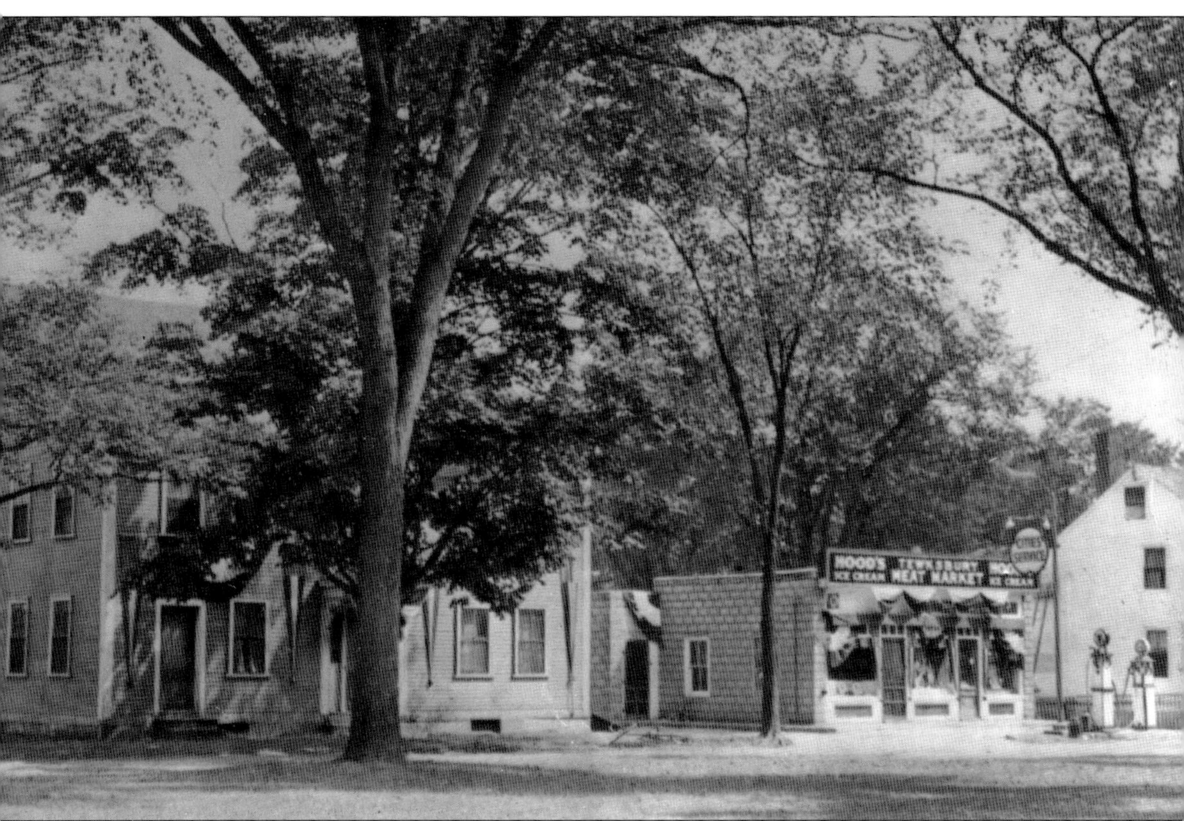

This is another view of the Town Center at the beginning of East Street in about 1934. The same buildings stand there today. The middle building was the Tewksbury Meat Market. Signage includes Hood's Ice Cream and Cities Service Gasoline, along with the gas pumps. Cities Service Gasoline became CITGO in 1965. In 1972, CITGO launched its first Quik Mart that combined the sale of food with the sale of gasoline. It appears the Tewksbury Center gas station was ahead of its time.

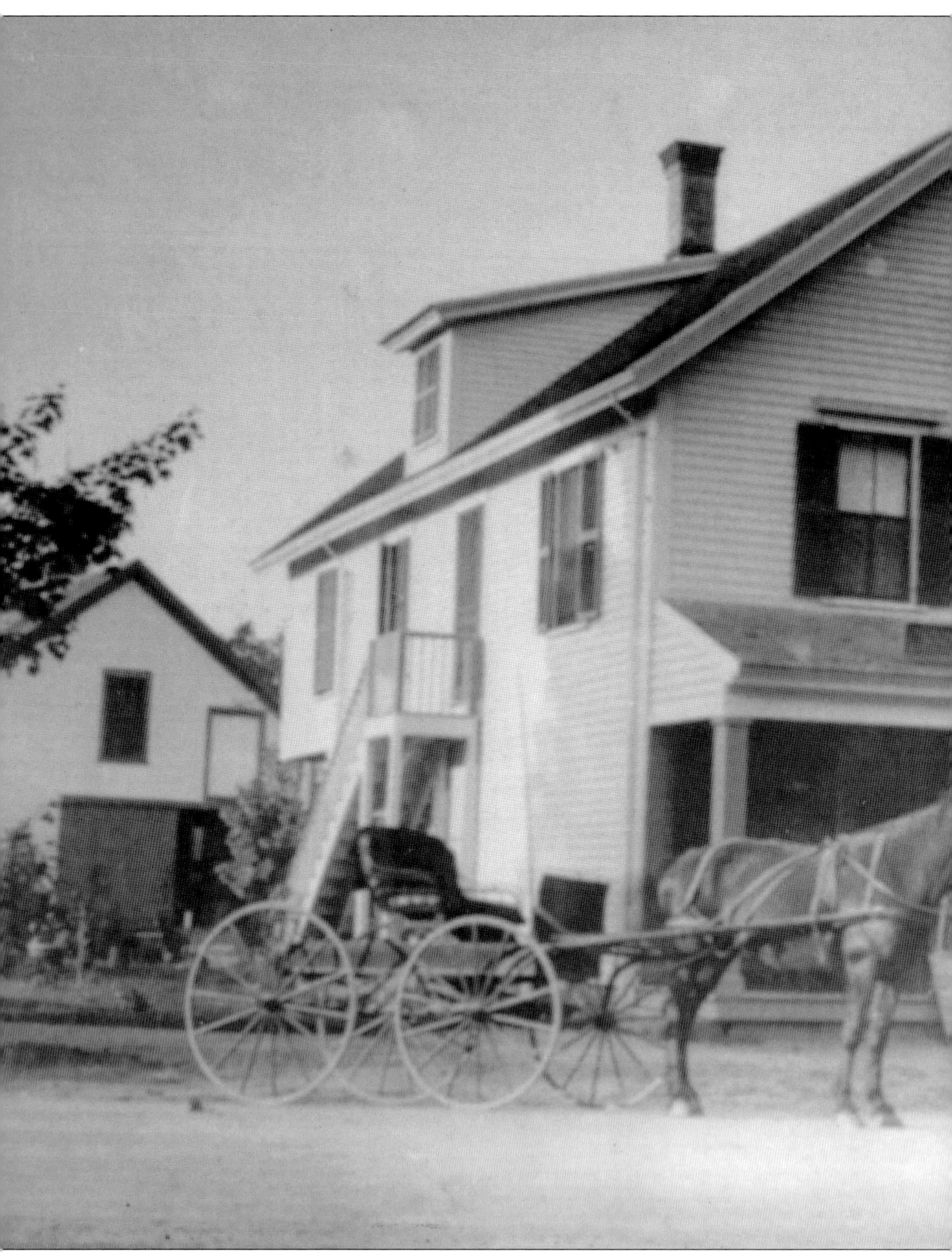

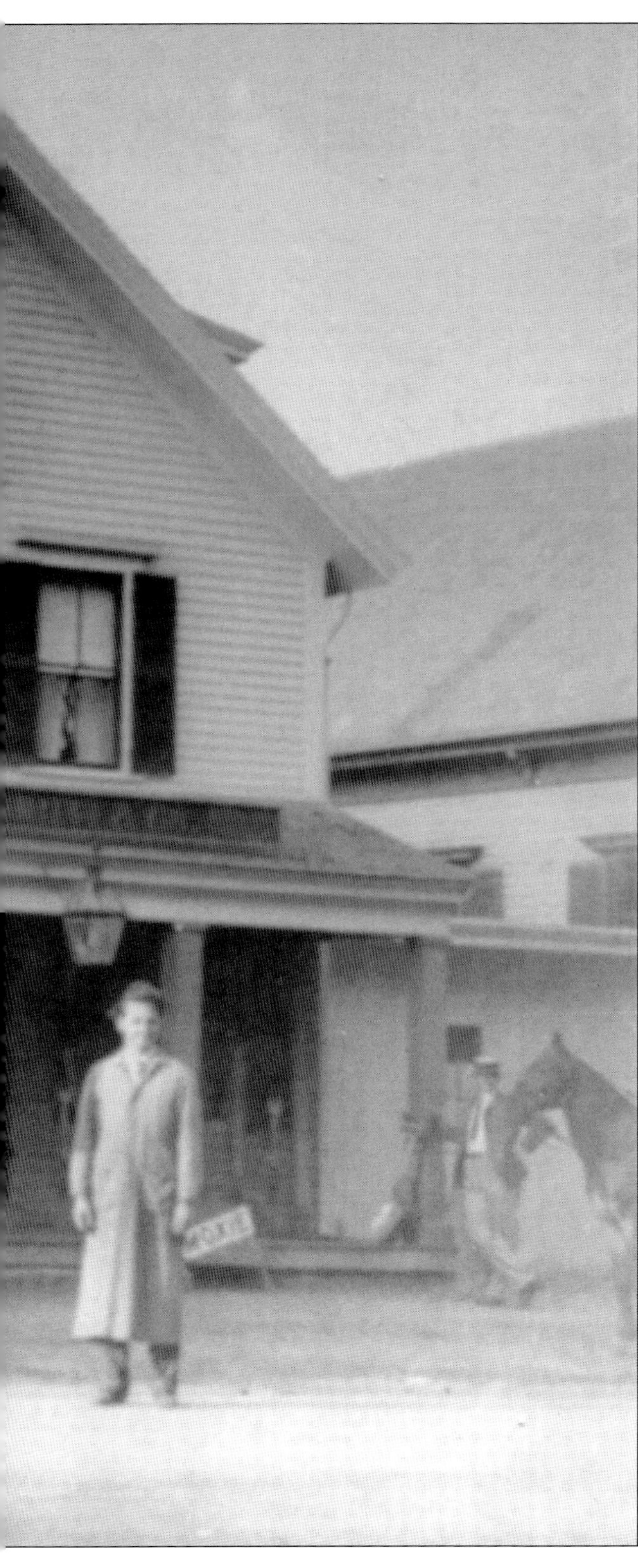

Fairgreive's Store was in its glory days, complete with horse and buggy in the late 1800s. The family lived a block away on East Street at the Stone House, page 43. The general store and post office had been run by James Fairgrieve and later by his son Arthur. The former Town Hall is on the right.

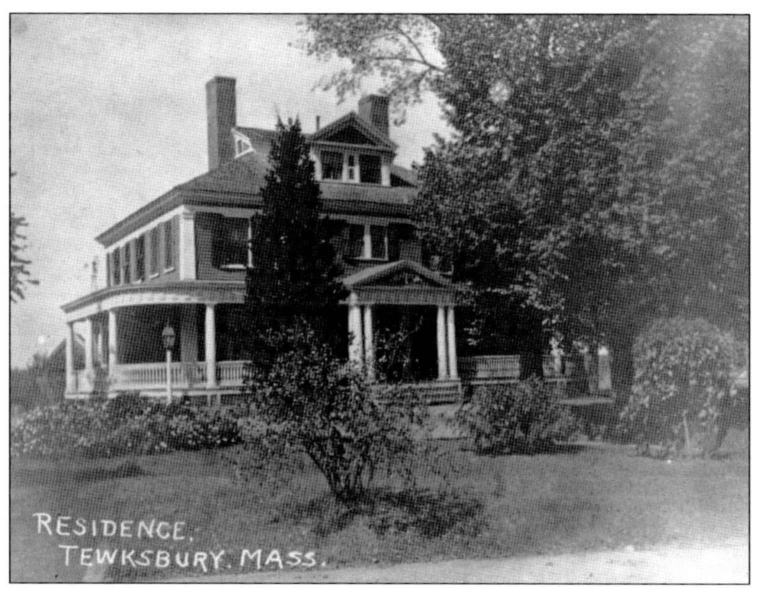

Brown's Tavern stands at the right of the 1920 Town Hall and was built in about 1740. It was the home of Jonathan Brown (1735–1822), a member of the town's militia who responded to the alarm in April 1775 and marched to Meriam's Corner at the start of the American Revolution. Brown went on to be a selectman and Massachusetts state representative serving the Town of Tewksbury.

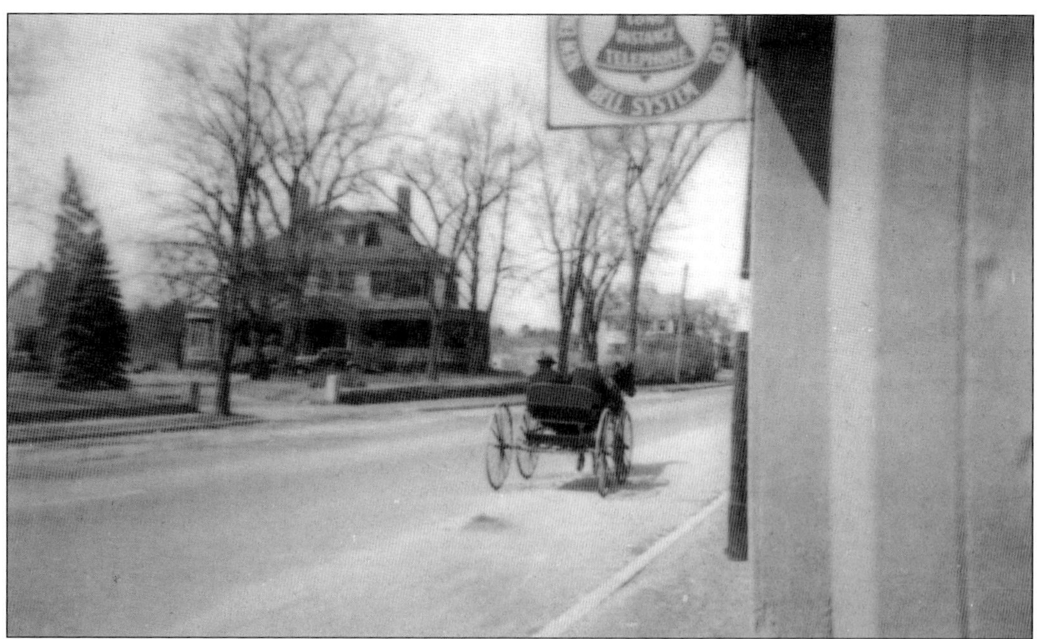

This scene is a reminder of times gone by, before the automobile, with Brown's Tavern on the left and the horse and buggy taking its time traversing through Town Center in the late 1800s. A trolley line was soon running on Main Street, as approval had been granted in 1895.

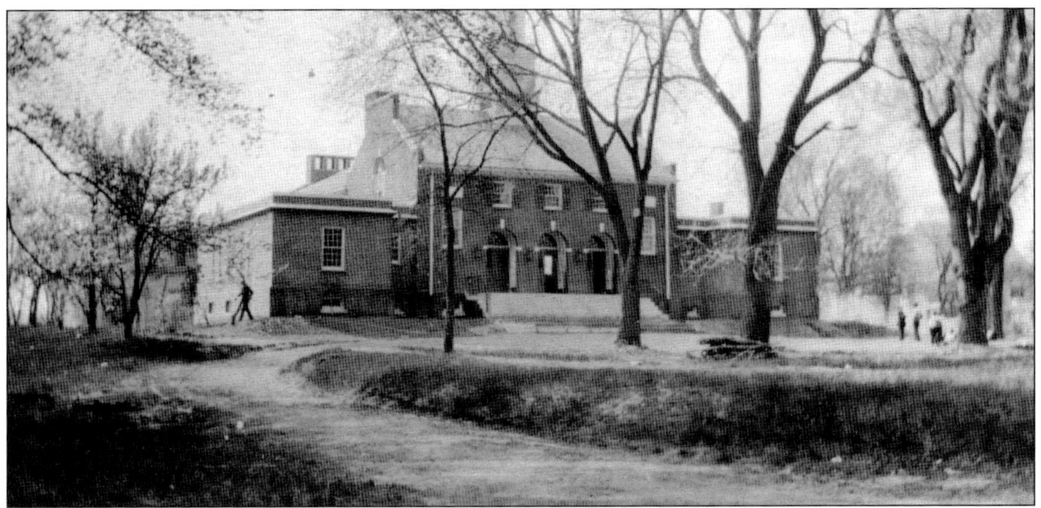

This image is of the 1920 Town Hall soon after it was built. Inside, there are two marble tablets listing the names of Tewksbury's World War I veterans. The design of the Town Hall had been used by architects after the war to assist other towns in their efforts to build community buildings that would embrace the soldiers coming home from the war and be places of gathering for townspeople.

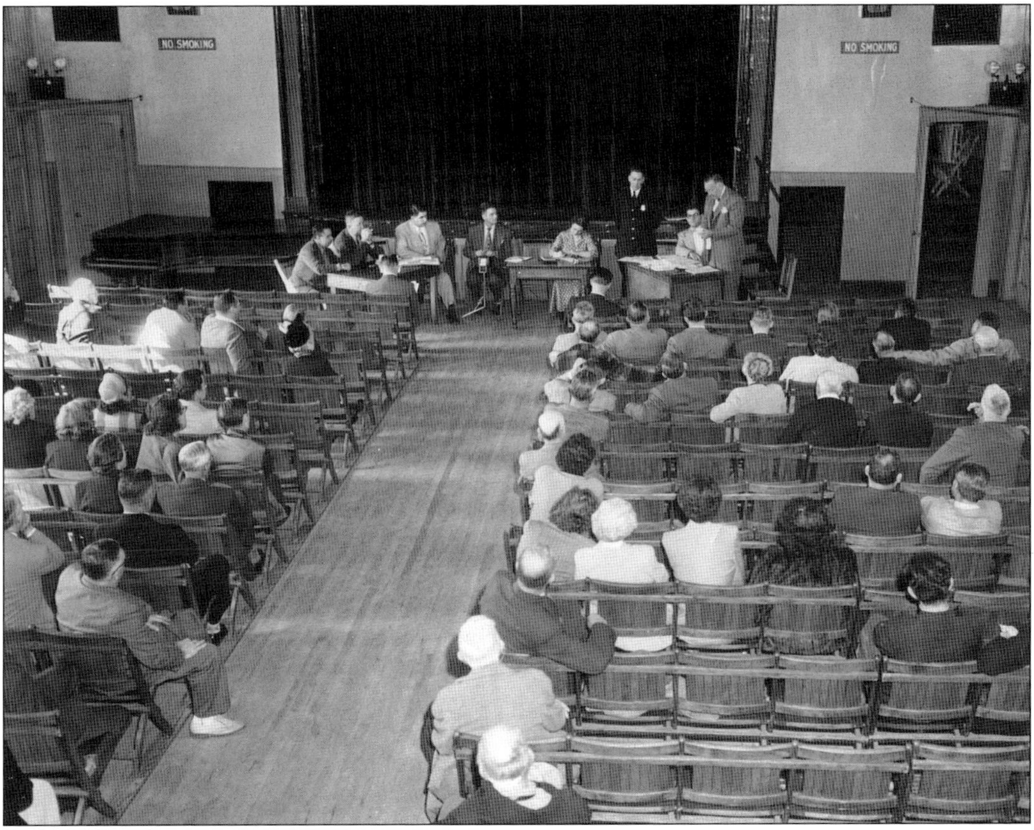

The Town Hall auditorium shown is of a hearing in the 1940s. Before the 2016 renovation, the auditorium originally included a fully functioning stage and a balcony in the rear. The room could hold 500 people and extended to the front lobby of the building.

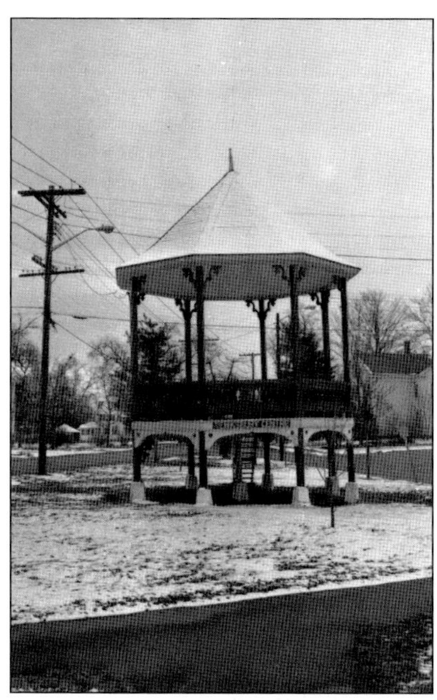

The former bandstand on the Town Common was built in 1891. It was renovated in the late 1900s to lower the floor height and include a ramp for handicapped access. It stands as a reminder of band concerts, Gold Star Mothers, Memorial Day, and Veterans Day ceremonies that occur there annually.

The Benjamin Spaulding house on North Street, near the corner of East Street, was built around 1890. The land for the home was broken off from his family's parcel at the Reverend Sampson Spaulding homestead on East Street. Benjamin founded the Village Improvement Association for the Town Center in the early 1880s. He headed up the planting of elm trees along East Street and the Town Common, the construction of the bandstand in 1891, and other beautification efforts in the Town Center. In 1959, Dr. John Lu and his wife, Pauline, moved into the home. Dr. Lu (1920–2006) was born in China, came to America to complete his studies, and was the chief surgeon and medical director at Tewksbury Hospital before entering distinguished private practice.

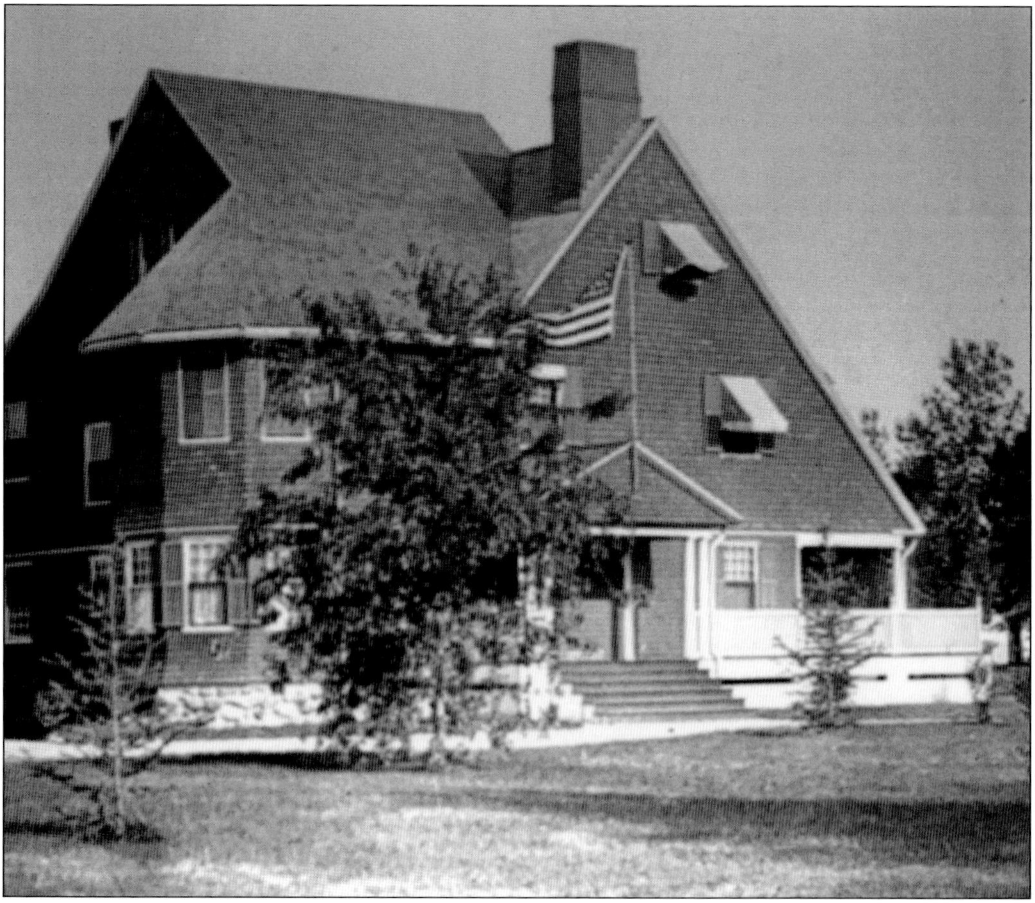

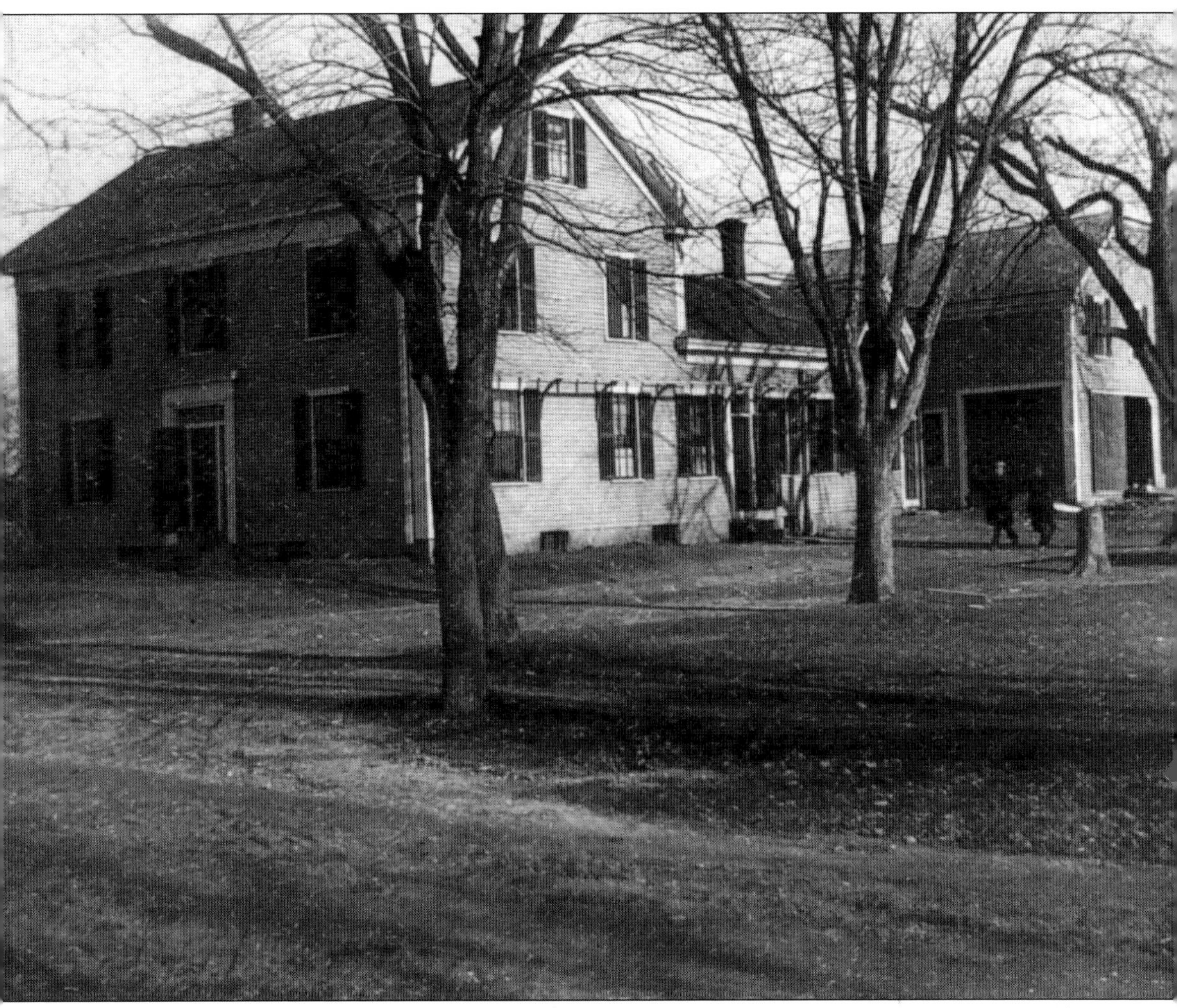

The Tremblay House on Pleasant Street was built around 1840. It had been owned by Joel Foster, Enoch Foster's brother, who lived at the home at the site of the current Town Hall. In the late 19th century, Perry Jefferson owned the home and had a soap factory in the far back, where Robinson Avenue is now. He produced long brown bars of soap until 1904, when he sold the company to Lowell Rendering Co. The Tremblays owned the home beginning in the 1970s.

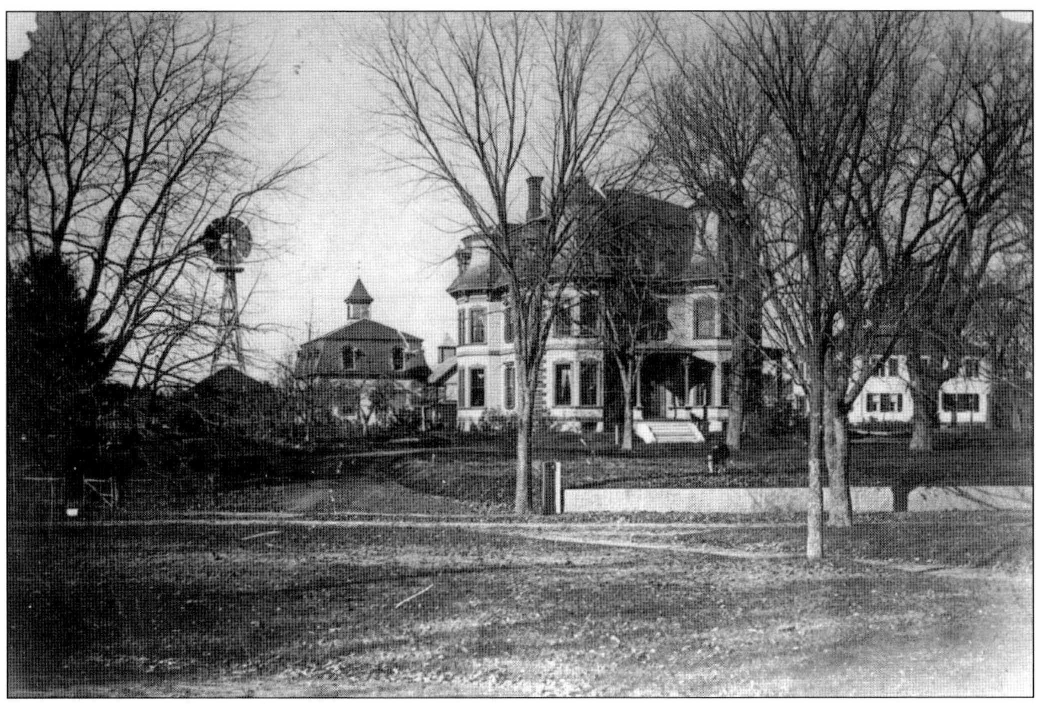

Enoch Foster's home stands as it did before this site became the home of the new Town Hall in 1920. The rear portion of the home was moved to Dewey Street, and the barn, shown in the back, was used as the fire station once the new Town Hall was built. Enoch was born in 1831 and had been in the furniture manufacturing business, starting in 1851. He was also a deacon at the Tewksbury Congregational Church and a descendant of Amos Foster, a signer of that church's covenant in 1735. Brown's Tavern is shown on the right.

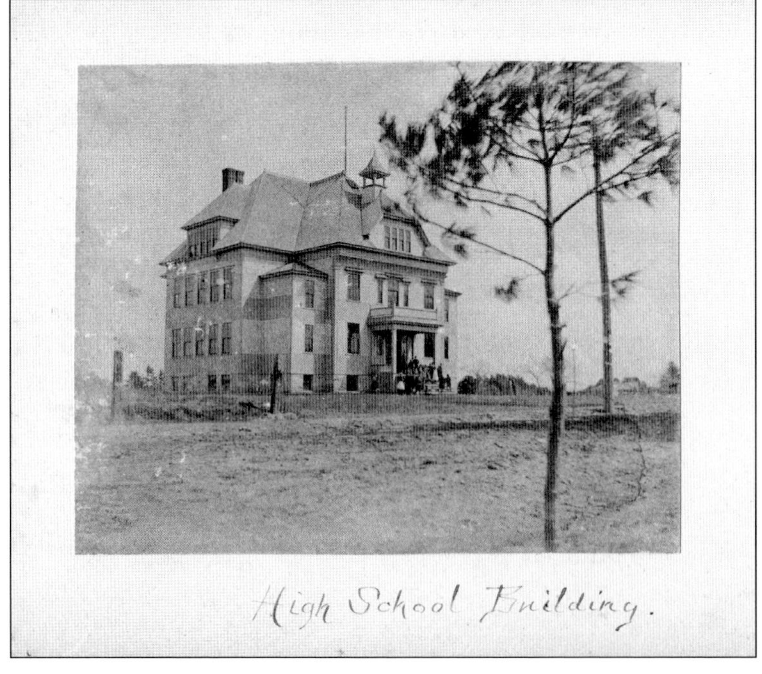

This is the Foster School after its construction in 1894. It served as the town's high school until 1900, when students went to Lowell for high school, and the Foster School was used for elementary school students. Pickering Hall on the third floor was named after J.C. Pickering. Both Pickering and Enoch Foster had assisted in funding the construction of the school.

This is the Tewksbury Congregational Church before it was destroyed by fire in 1918. There were horse stall sheds across the rear yard for parishioners' horses to stay during services. It was the second church built there and was dedicated in 1824.

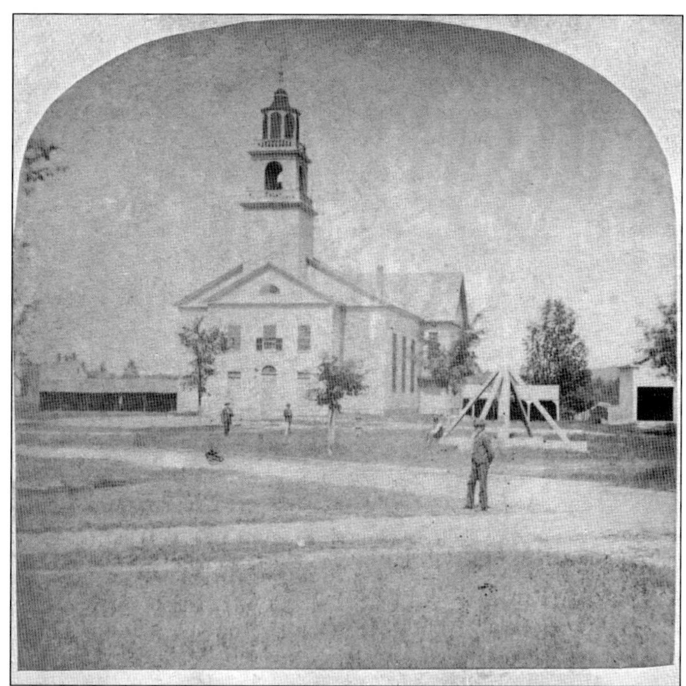

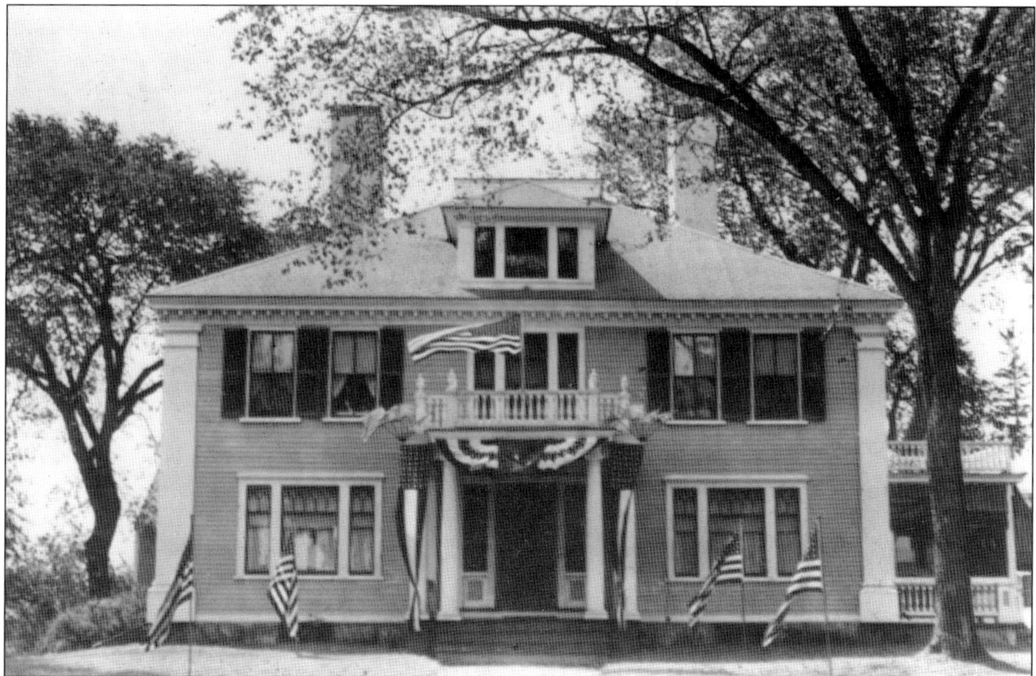

Sycamore Hall, also known as the Reverend Jacob Coggin House, was built in 1806. Coggin was the third pastor of the Congregational Church across the street. He instructed young men in the home, and it was known as Sycamore Hall for the large tree in the yard. Coggin's son Jacob inherited the house upon his death in 1854. It stayed in the Coggins family until 1900, when the Billings family took ownership until 1941. It was during the Billings' tenure that the sycamore tree was taken down.

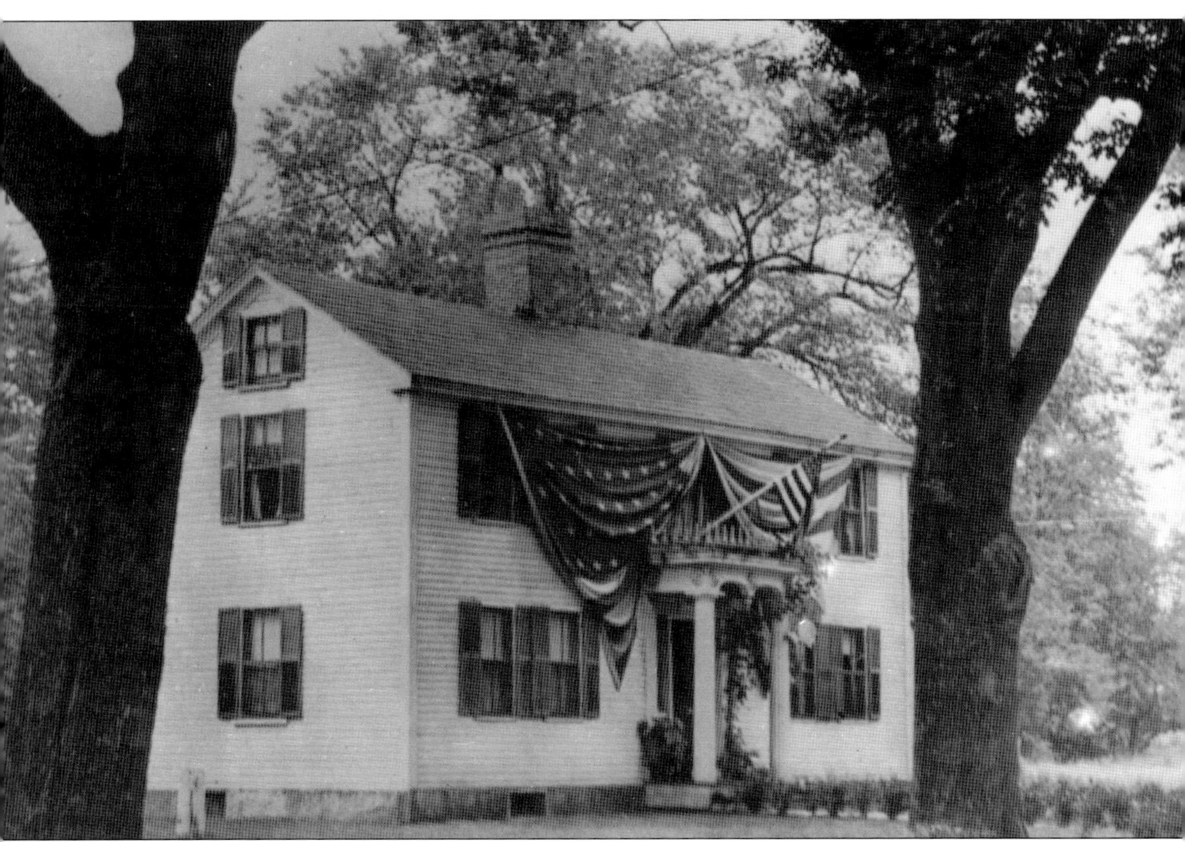

The Chapman House at the corner of East and North Streets is noted as being built in 1803 by John Chapman, who lived there with his wife, Clarissa. Here it is in 1902, with buntings for the Old Home Week event. The house was owned by the Albert Briggs family from around 1900 to 1934. Albert was a carpenter at the state infirmary.

Five

People

There are many interesting people who have formed the history of Tewksbury. From the State Almshouse in the late 1800s, there is the legacy of Anne Sullivan, her impact on Helen Keller's life, and her studies at the Perkins School for the Blind in Boston. From the Civil War, there is the courage and battle success of Maj. Gen. Adelbert Ames, who would later become the governor of Mississippi and, with his wife, build "the Castle" on Tewksbury's Prospect Hill. From surviving World War II concentration camps as a child in Romania, Tewksbury sculptor Mico Kaufman has left an enduring presence with his works displayed in town. His sculptures represent various themes like "Toughing Souls" and "Muster" and historical town icons such as the "Wamesit Indian" and "Water" as well as war memorials on the Town Common. Over the years, other people in the town have found their niche, each in their own way. Whether it was military service here or overseas, being the first Black police officer in the town, writing a town history book, cultivating first-class carnations, dairy farming, mail delivery, public works, and automotive repair, or advocating for Black suffrage, they all took pride in doing their best for their country and community.

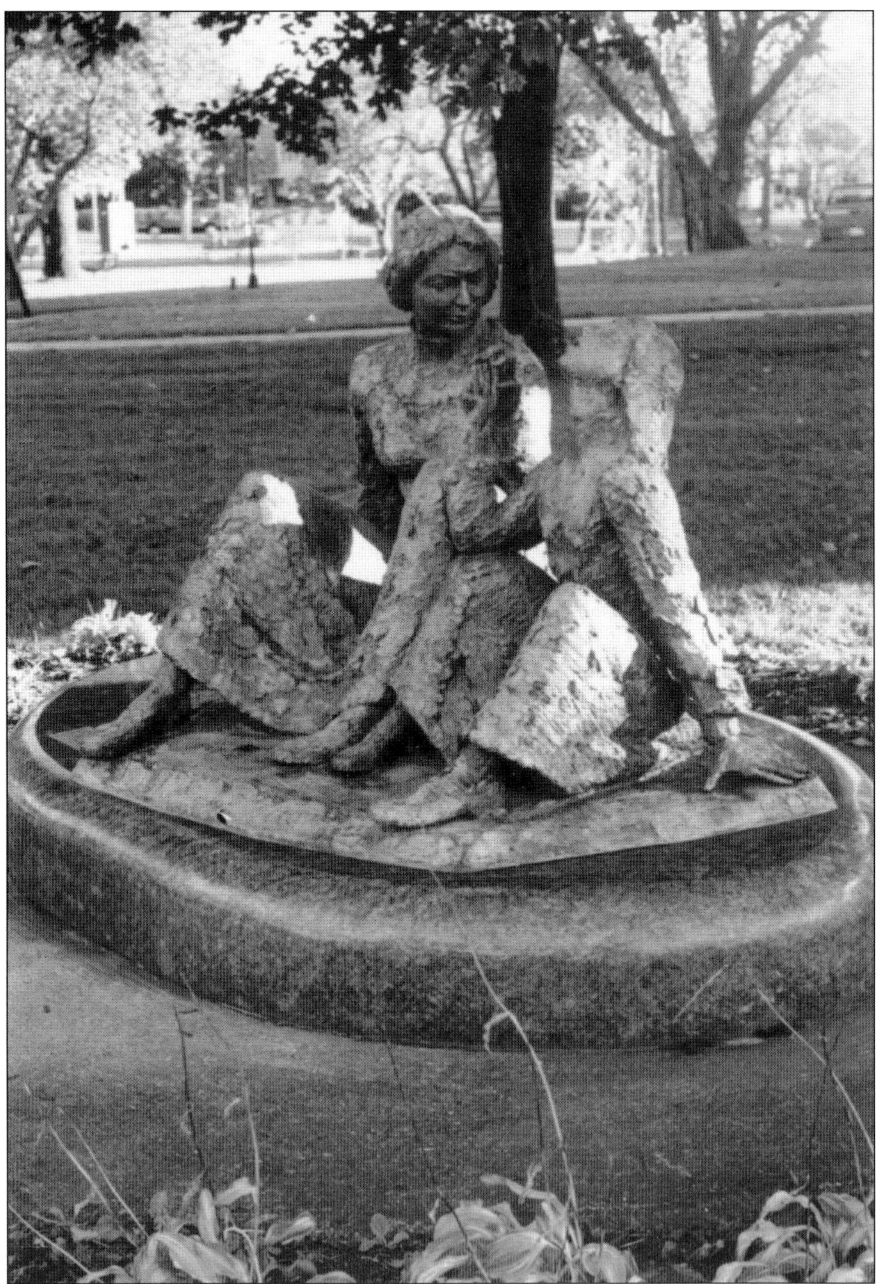

Sculptor Mico Kaufman's statue named "Water" is shown on the right side of Town Hall in Town Center. The 1985 statue captures the moment when teacher Anne Sullivan spilled water over Helen Keller's hand and spelled out the word "water," and thereafter, Helen and Anne continued for many years to improve on this innovative method of communication for the deaf and blind. Anne had been placed at the Tewksbury Almshouse in 1876 with her brother Jimmie. Anne was partially blind due to a childhood eye infection. She rose from her hospital experiences and, in 1880, transferred to the Perkins School for the Blind in Massachusetts. After graduating, Anne was recommended to teach the seven-year-old deaf and blind Helen Keller in Alabama, after Helen's father had contacted the director of the school.

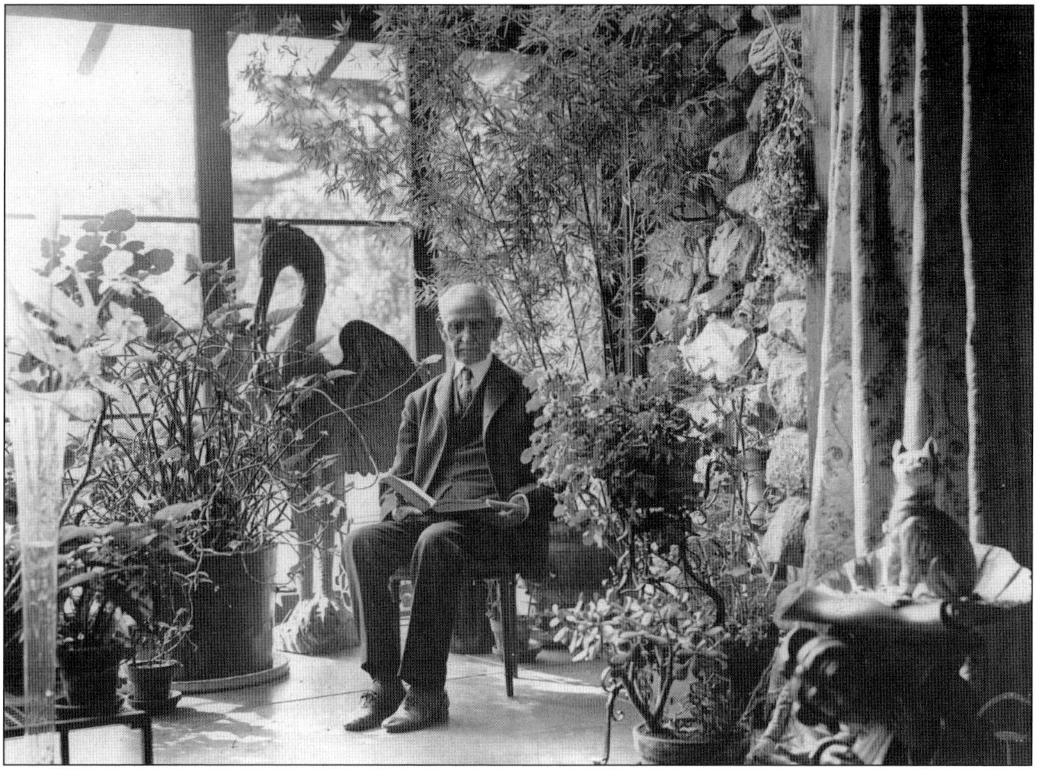

Adelbert Ames (1835–1933) reads in the greenhouse room of his 17-room estate on Prospect Hill, locally known as "the Castle," in about 1930. Ames was governor of Mississippi; he was the 27th military governor from 1868 to 1870 and the 30th civilian governor from 1874 to 1876. When Mississippi was readmitted to the Union, Ames served as a US senator in the seat formerly held by Confederate president Jefferson Davis (1872–1874). Ames was a highly vocal advocate of Black suffrage who became enormously popular among the formerly enslaved. He appointed the first Black officeholders in the state's history. He rapidly rose to the leadership of Mississippi's newly established Republican Party. Formerly slave-holding Democrats plotted their revenge, forcing him to resign as governor, hastening his move back north to the Lowell area.

This is a rear view of Ames Castle, showing the many large windows and the greenhouse room. One reason Ames moved to the Lowell area was that his wife, Blanche's father, Benjamin Butler, had ties with Massachusetts. Butler and Ames had also connected during the Civil War and in business in Massachusetts. In 1883, Gov. Benjamin Butler famously accused the management of the Tewksbury Almshouse of malfeasance, theft, and patient abuse for political reasons, with most allegations being dismissed.

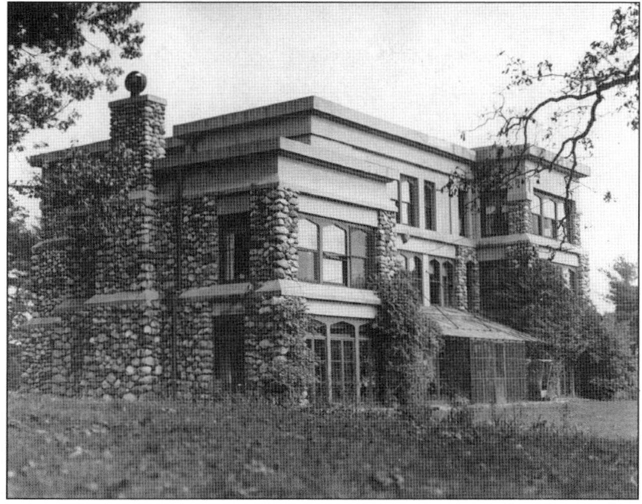

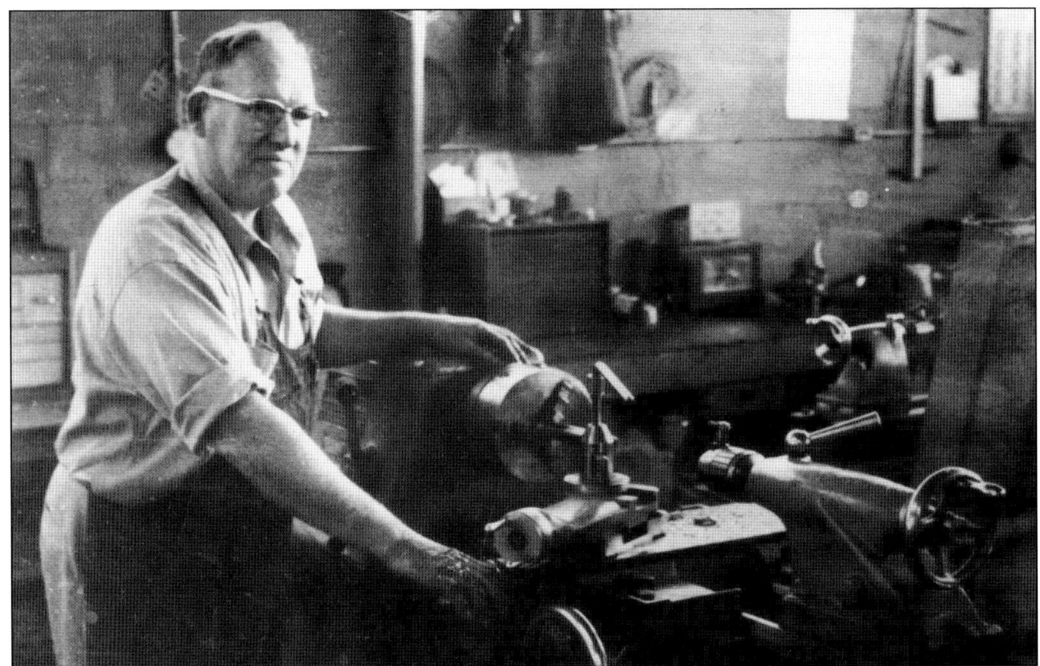

William "Irving" Bailey is working at his craft in his automotive service garage on Andover Street prior to 1950. The service and gas station were built in about 1918 and were mainstays for the automotive needs of North Tewksbury residents for decades. Irving lived at the home, which was built around 1820, and he was the son of Edward Bailey, the previous owner. Irving also was the janitor from 1920 to 1941 at the District No. 3 School, later known as the Ella E. Flemings School.

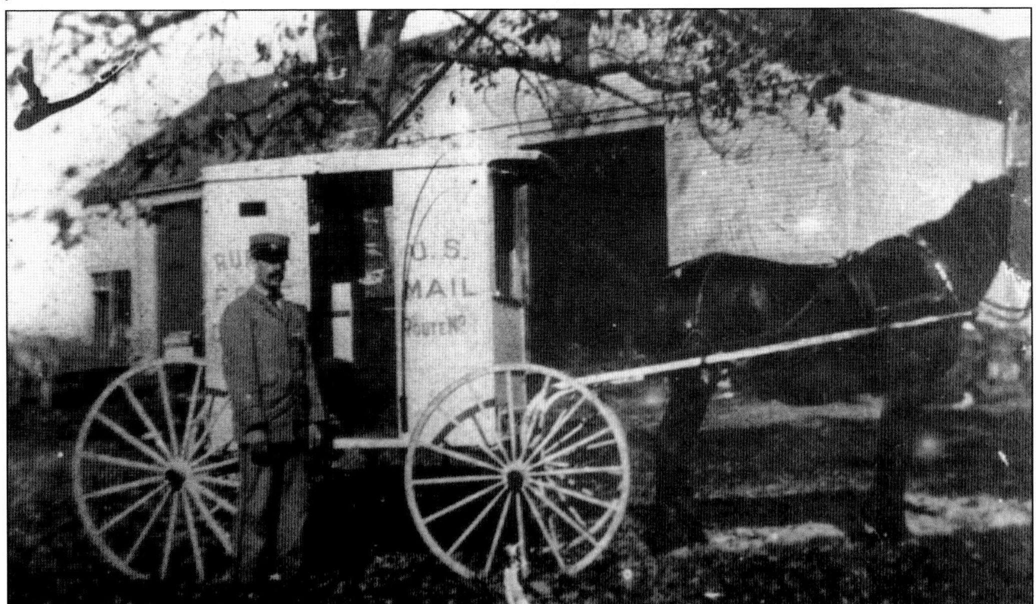

Edward Bailey of Andover Street is standing with his mail wagon in about 1900 on the former Mail Rural Route No. 1 that covered Lowell, Tewksbury, and Andover. This photograph is noted as being taken on Hackett's Pond Road, Andover, a section of the route. Edward was the father of William "Irving" Bailey.

Francis "Taddy" Brown, born in 1915, is riding his wagon in front of Enoch Foster's home in Town Center, where the new Town Hall was built in 1920. Taddy grew up to be a World War II Army veteran and Tewksbury town historian. Many photographs in the Tewksbury Historical Society's collection are from Taddy.

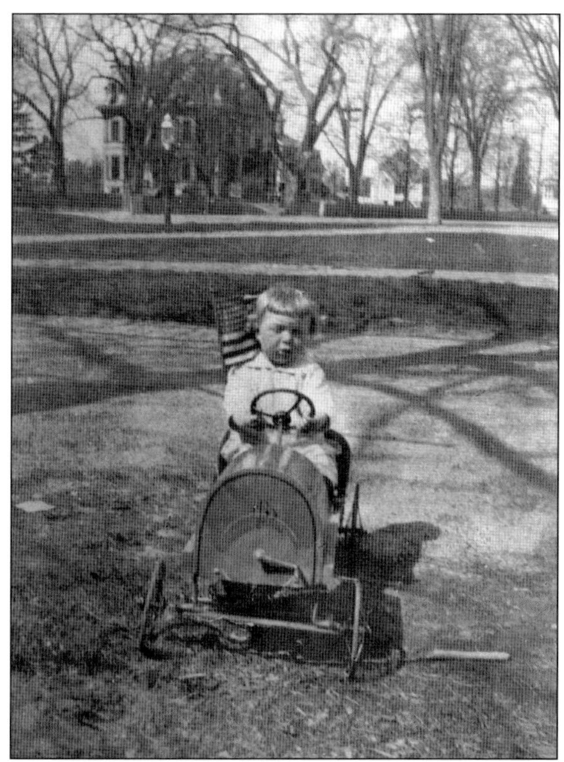

Taddy Brown stands on the left as a Tewksbury Highway Department Foreman in about 1950. He and his wife, Mary, lived in Town Center on Summer Street. Taddy always had a passion for all things Tewksbury. When his father was killed in a trench collapse while working for the town, his job was given to Taddy on the condition that he pay rent to his mother. The job was seen by the town as a way of compensating the Brown family for their loss. Taddy passed away in 2001.

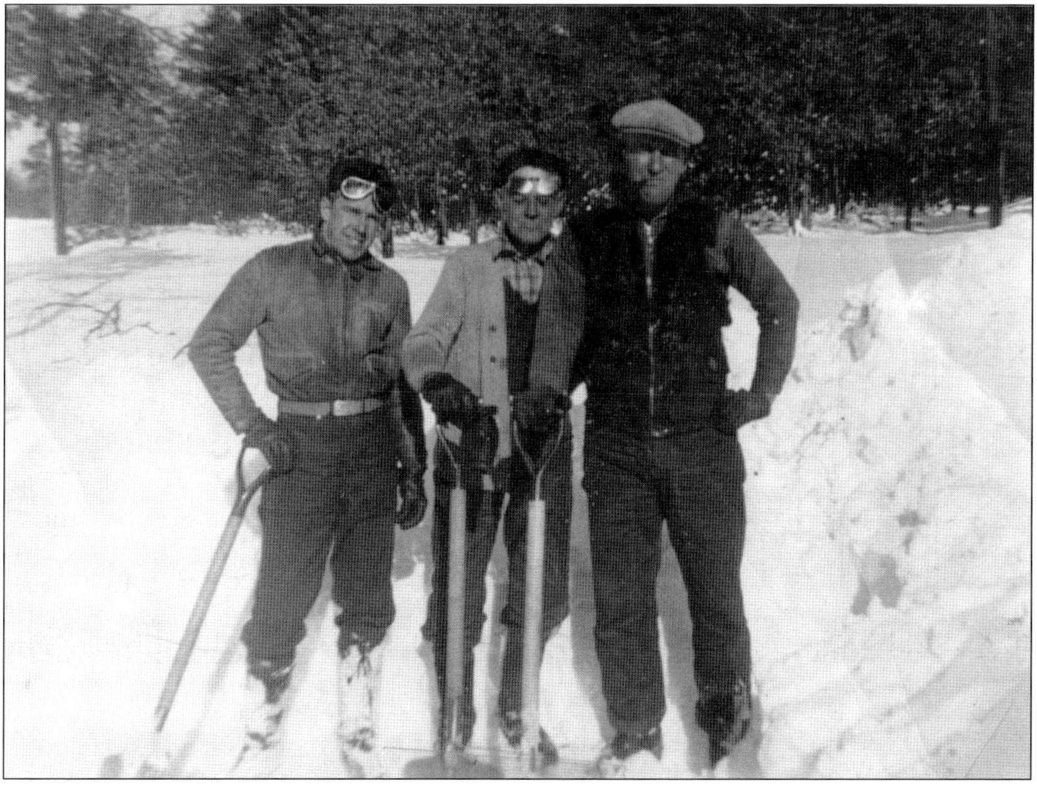

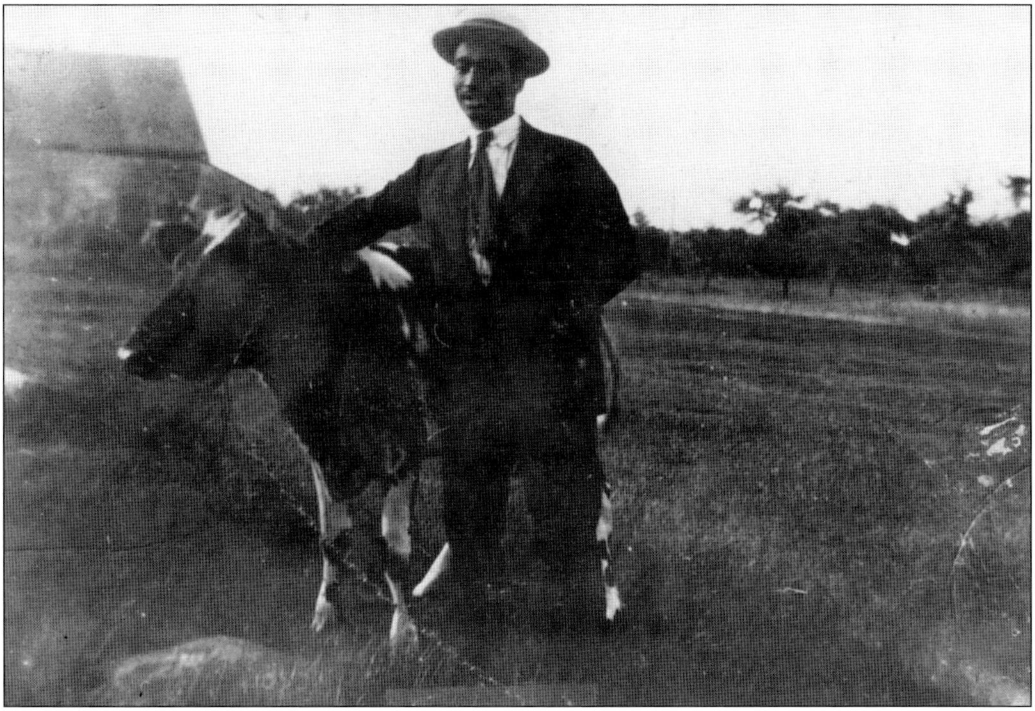

George Gale is walking with his cow in 1920 at his home and farm on Main Street at the corner of James Street. George's father, John, came to Tewksbury after the Civil War, having served under a member of Tewksbury's Spaulding family, of Lee Street, in the US Colored Troops Cavalry in Virginia. George served in World War I with his brother Ernest. George never married.

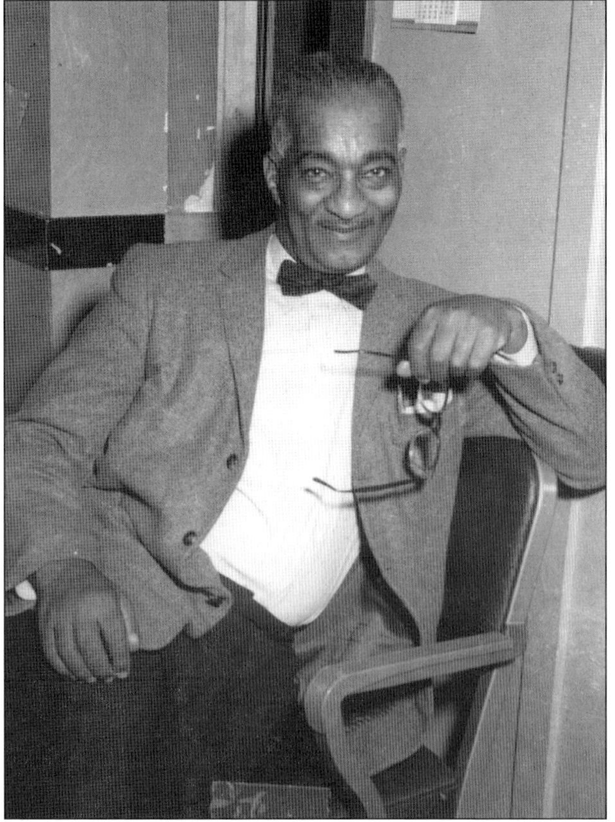

George Gale became a Tewksbury police officer in 1942 and was the town's first Black police officer. He retired in 1958. He had also served the town on the highway department for about 20 years before that. Gale was a 1932 founding member and treasurer of the Tewksbury Athletic Club. He was always supportive of young people and adults in their sporting endeavors, boosting teams from the sidelines. Born in Tewksbury in 1894, he lived in town his entire life and was a friend to many, passing in 1960.

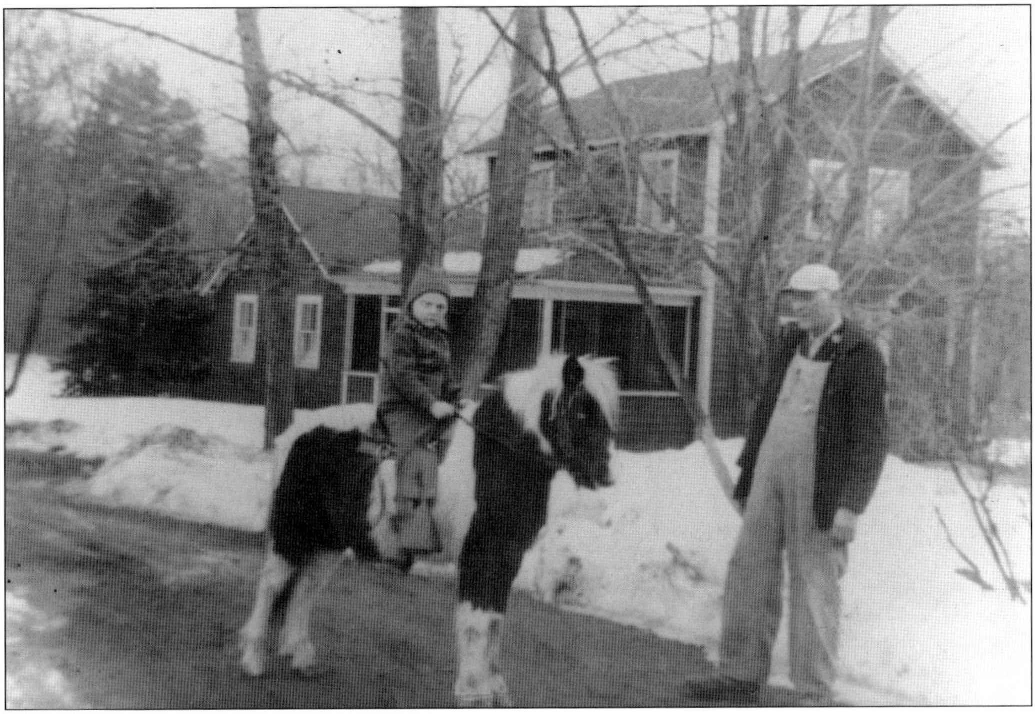

Tom Sawyer, in front of his home on Maple Street, is proudly standing with his daughter Barbara in the early 1900s. Tom was born in 1897 on Trull Road in Tewksbury. He and his wife, Alice, ran the Millstone Dairy Farm on Maple and Lowe Streets for over 60 years. They had up to 200 cows and sold milk to the Tewksbury State Hospital from 1917 to 1945. Tom served the town in numerous ways over the years, such as driving children to school with a horse and wagon and plowing snow. He also worked on the construction of the 1920 Town Hall and the 1922 Congregational church. He was a member of the finance committee for 23 years, a road commissioner for 15 years, a fire warden, and an inspector of animals. Tom passed away in 1997.

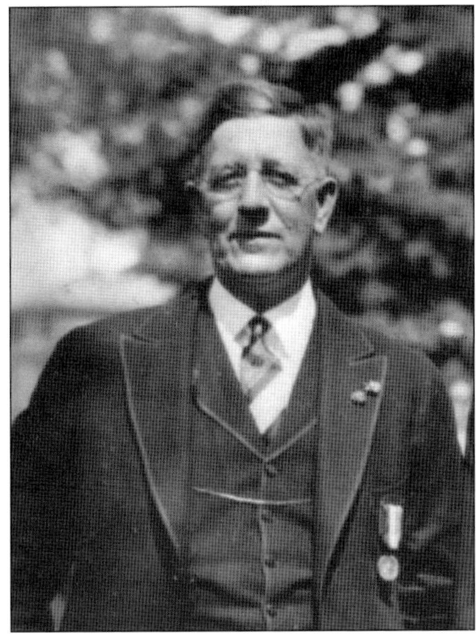

This is Harold J. Patten in 1934 at the 200th Anniversary Celebration on the Town Common. Harold was born to Marcellus and Susan Patten in 1884. He would serve as 1st Lieutenant in the US Army in World War I. Harold also collaborated with his father in the florist greenhouse business on North Street, Patten & Co. Florists, which his father founded in Lowell and relocated to Tewksbury. Harold was innovative in hybridizing and cultivating carnations. His work was instrumental in the town being named the Carnation Capital of the World in 1976 by *Yankee* magazine. Harold served the town in many capacities and committees. He is the author of the town's definitive history book *Ask Now of the Days That Are Past, A History of the Town of Tewksbury, 1734–1964*, published in 1965.

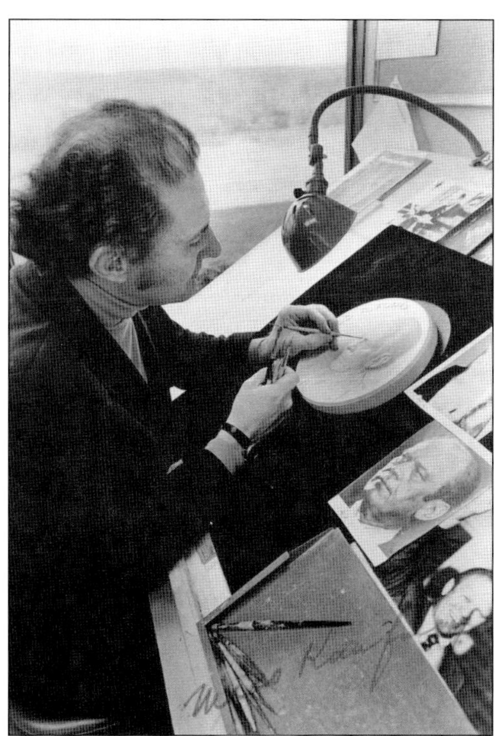

Renowned sculptor Mico Kaufman of North Tewksbury is here putting the final touches on the plaster model for Pres. Gerald Ford's inaugural medal in 1974. He would go on to design inaugural medals for presidents Ronald Regan and George H.W. Bush. Several of his statues are on display in Tewksbury, including "Water," "Muster," "Wamesit Indian," and "Touching Souls." Mico appreciated the public art that populates European open spaces and had a mission to bring sculpture to the public in his adopted communities of Tewksbury and Lowell.

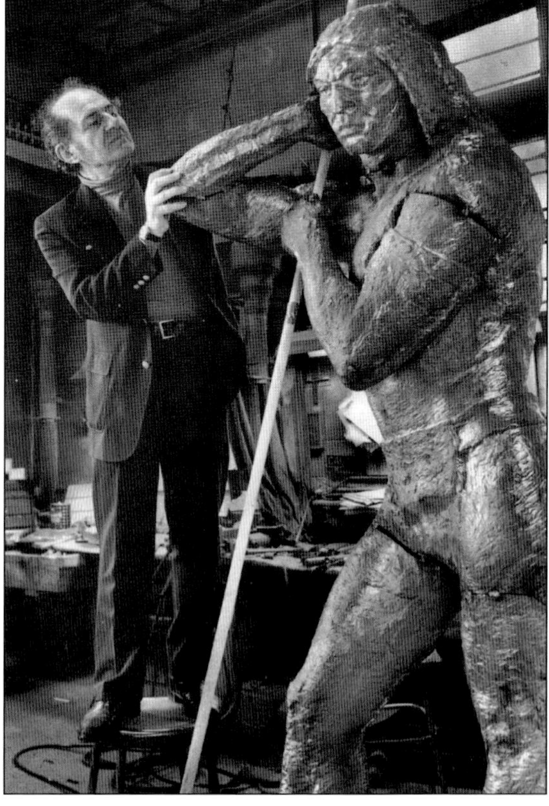

Checking the workmanship on the bronze casting of the Wamesit Indian, is its sculptor, Mico Kaufman. This statue would be unveiled in June 1989 and installed in the Wamesit area on Main Street. Born in Romania in 1924, Kaufman had survived concentration camps there during World War II. Kaufman was educated in the arts in Italy and immigrated to the United States in 1951, moving to Tewksbury in 1964.

Six

Transportation

Prior to the 1800s, modes of transportation in America were limited to horseback or wagons pulled by oxen or horses. Roads were just dirt pathways. At the end of the 1800s and early 1900s, there were more convenient options for travel becoming available. By the mid-1800s, railroads connected cities and states across the country, and the electric street trolley was becoming popular in getting around inside major cities. Tewksbury benefited from these improvements in travel efficiency. With Boston 23 miles south and Nashua, New Hampshire, 22 miles to the north, several rail lines converged in the middle of town. Lowell and Andover, Lowell and Lawrence, Salem and Lowell Railroads all came together at Tewksbury Junction, just off the intersection of Livingston and East Streets. This Tewksbury Junction served the State Hospital, bringing in patients locally from Boston as well as other parts of Massachusetts. In the early 1900s, the trolley came to Tewksbury from the city of Lowell, with the notable grade crossing in Wamesit over the train tracks. The trolley went down Main Street to the Town Center, turned around, and headed back to Lowell. Around the 1930s, Tewksbury High School students used the trolley to go to school in Lowell when the Foster School was used for elementary grades rather than as a high school. With trolleys and trains cutting through all quadrants of town, they had a big impact on the daily lives of the town's citizens and their ability (or not) to get around town for years to come.

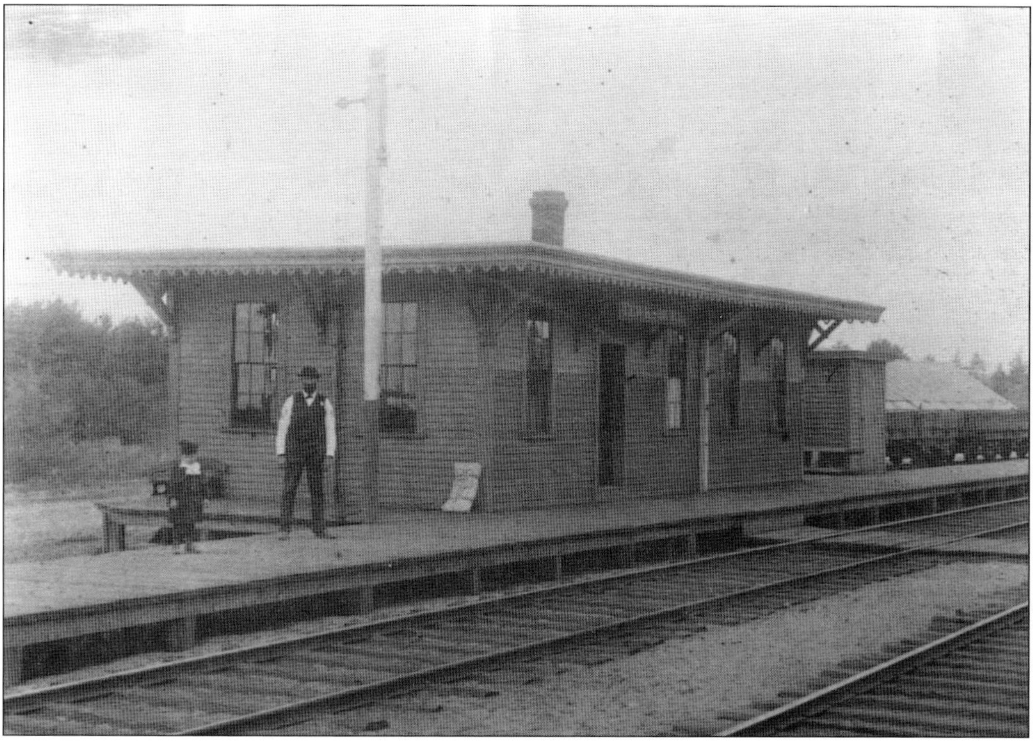

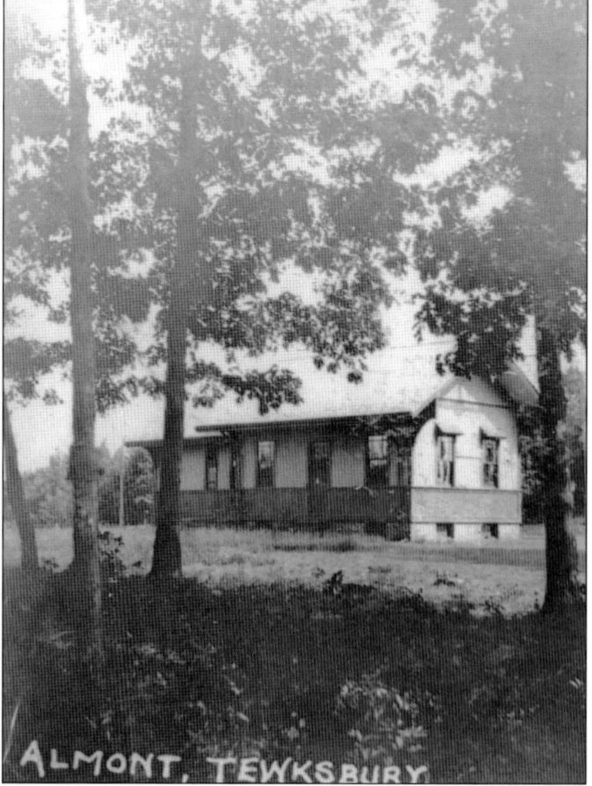

This Baldwin Station photograph is noted as being taken in 1888 with Joel Washington Baldwin as station agent and a young Walter Baldwin. This Boston & Maine station was off Livingston Street near the Pinnacle Street intersection.

Built in 1892, Almont Station was on North Street near Kendall Road near the entrance to the current soccer fields on the Boston & Maine Rail line. This station was on the Lowell branch from Lowell Junction in Andover/Wilmington to Central Street in Lowell. The station remained open until about 1925. After this station was built in 1892, the town's Village Improvement Association installed a sidewalk from the station to Marcellus Patten's home and greenhouses on North Street, using cinders from the railroad and volunteers. After they were finished, the ladies held a dinner for the workers in the Congregational church in the Town Center.

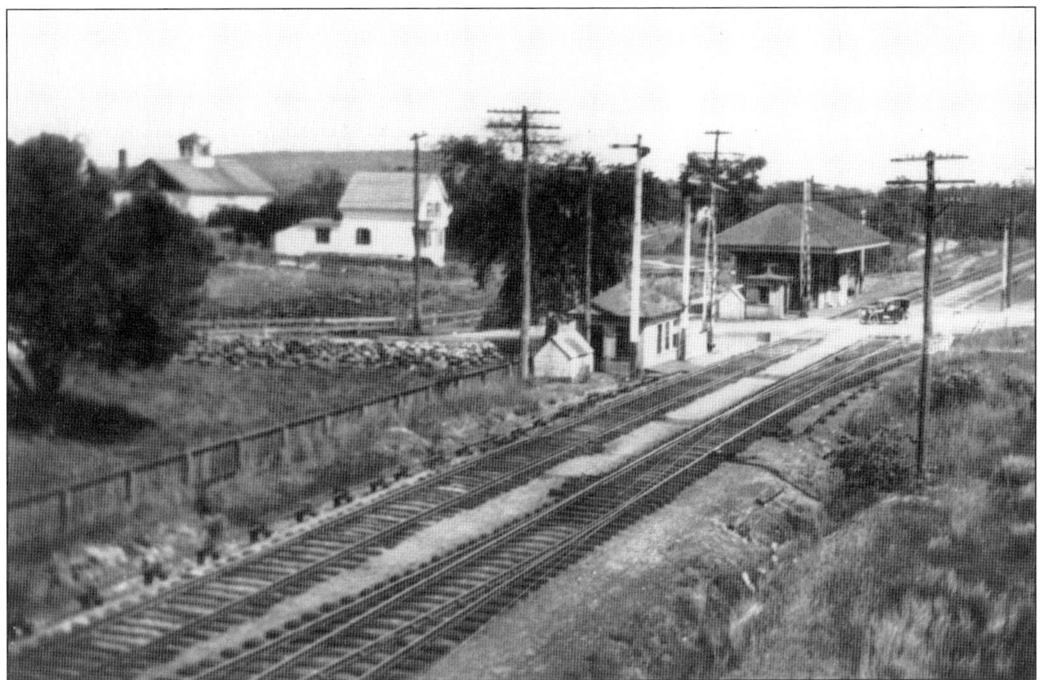

Wamesit Station was located off Old Main Street behind Main Street. The neighborhood was known as Mace's Crossing. Abram Mace built the home on what was Main Street around 1830. The name for Main Street in that area was changed to Old Main Street when the road was altered to make way for the current railroad overpass in about 1940.

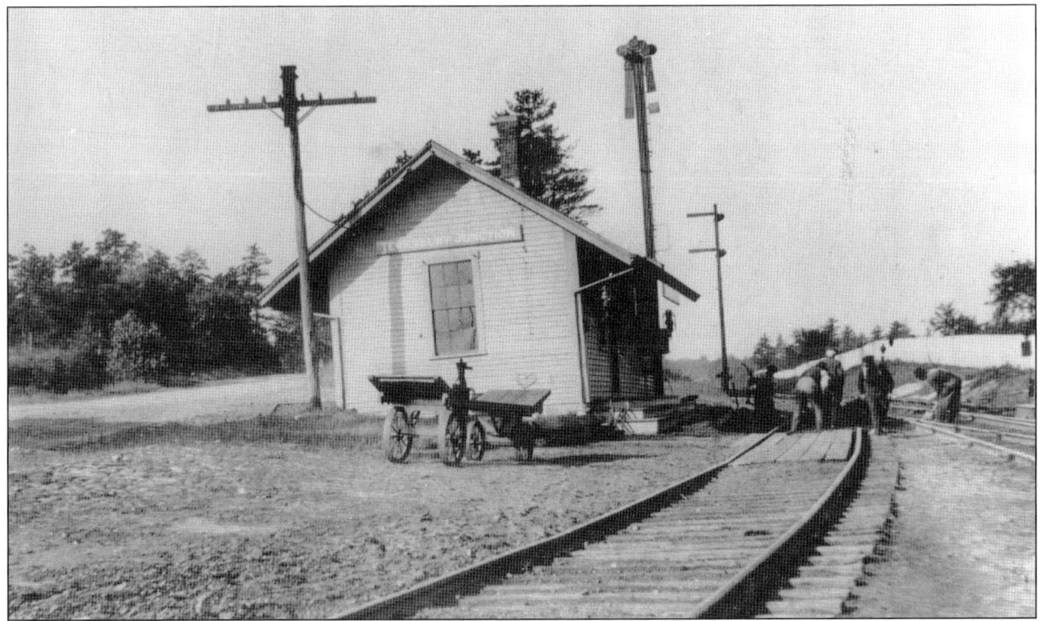

This Tewksbury Junction Station photograph is noted as being taken in 1917. According to a 1902 map, this station was on the west side of Livingston Street near East Street. The actual junction was located on the east side of Livingston Street where three railroads came together, named at that time: Salem & Lowell, Boston & Maine, and Lowell & Lawrence.

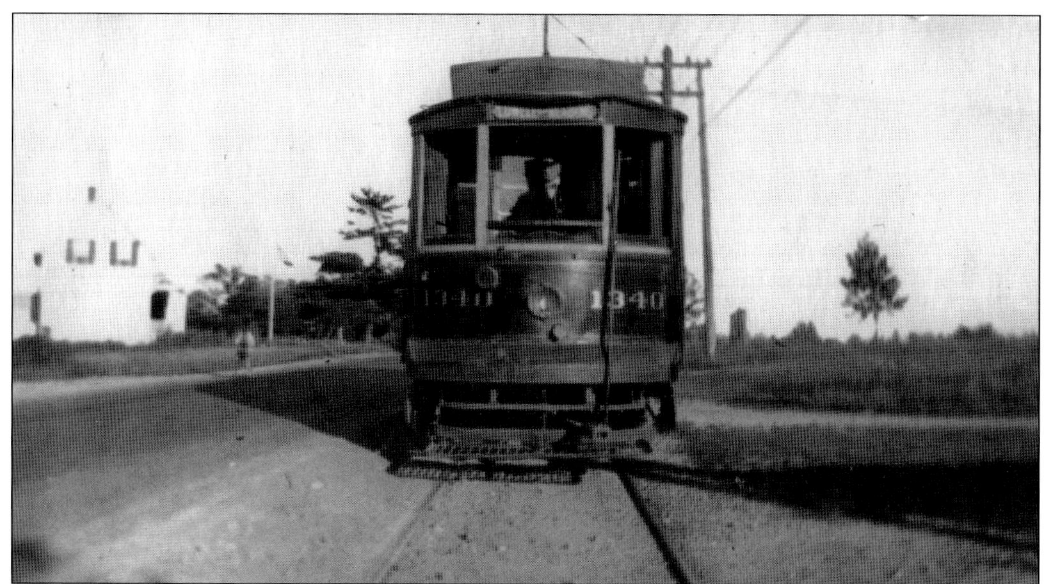

This is a trolley on Main Street heading to Lowell in front of the Hardy-Pike House. Records note that it was in 1895 that Tewksbury granted permission for the Lowell and Suburban Street Railway to build tracks on Main Street to the center of town.

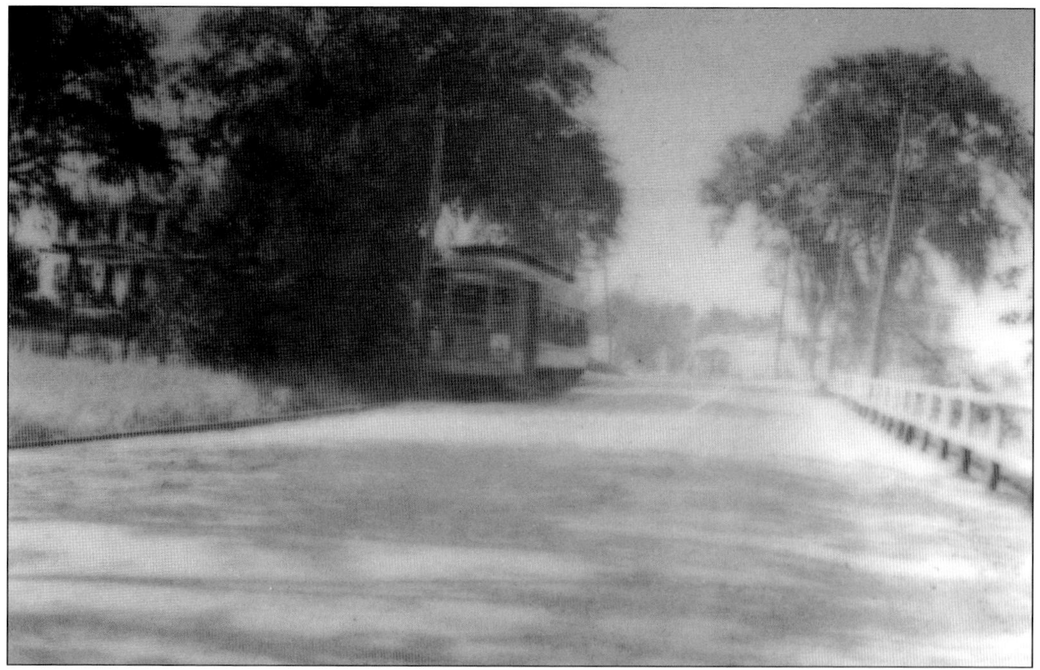

This undated photograph is of another trolley on Main Street, but the exact location is unknown. There was a trolley line to get to Lowell, next door, which started its trolley lines in 1889 as the Lowell and Dracut Railway Company.

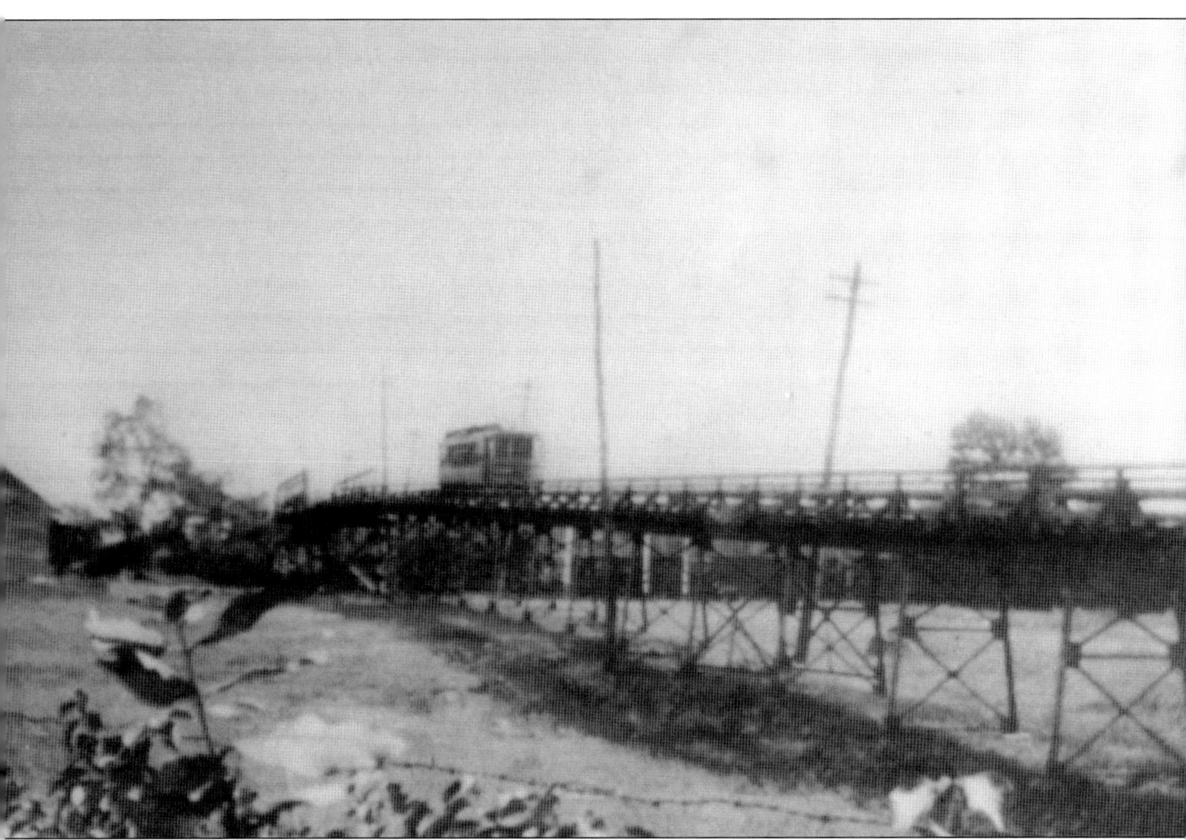

This trolley is on the trestle bridge over Main Street and the railroad line in the Wamesit area. Known as Wamesit Crossing, this bridge was built by the Boston & Northern Electric Railroad Company in 1901. It was noted as the most elaborate grade crossing over a railroad track in the state at the time. Several hundred feet of the bridge on each side went up to two steel bridges over the tracks with an overhead clearance of 19 feet. Years later, in about 1940, the trestle bridge was removed, and a girder-type bridge was built over the railroad, relocating Main Street to how it is arranged today.

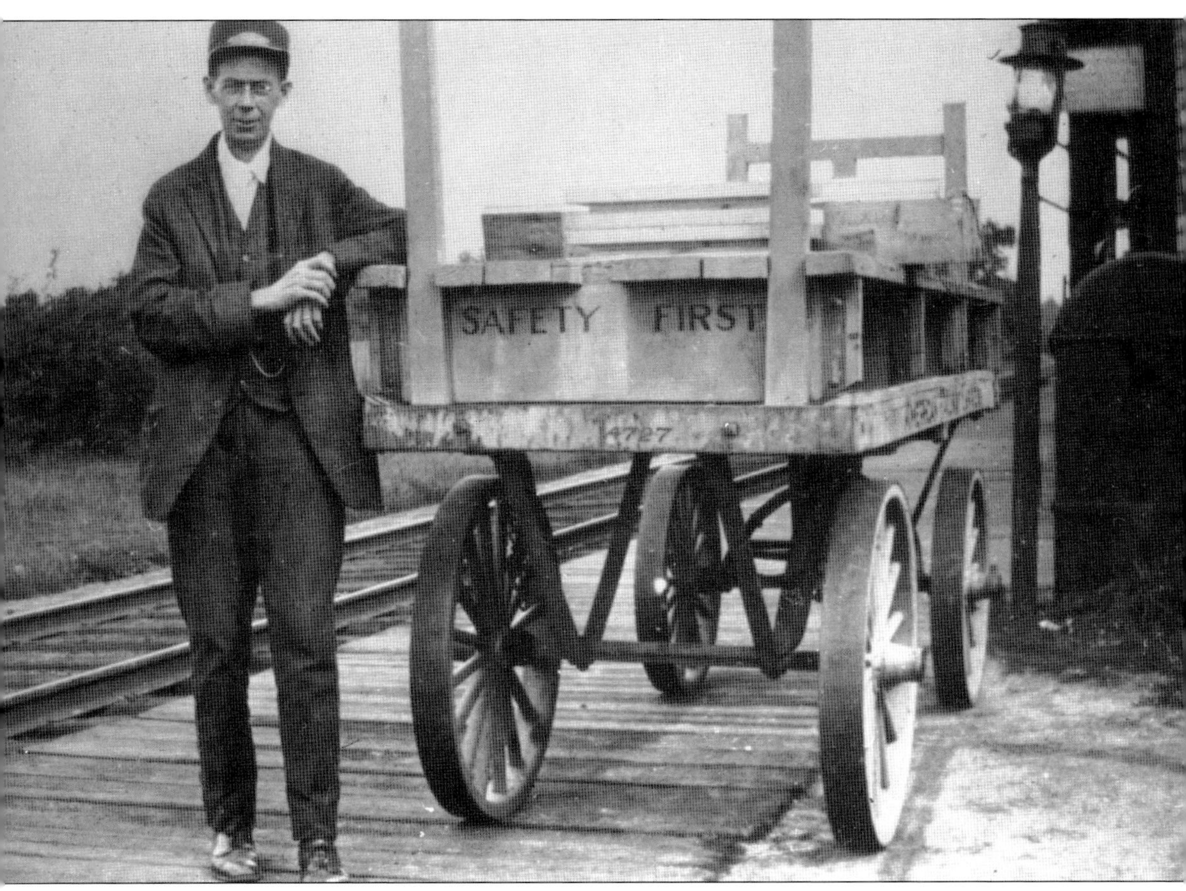

Peter Cameron was the station agent at the North Street location, known as Tewksbury Center Station, just behind the Foster School. This station was on the Lowell & Lawrence rail line, now inactive, which ran parallel to Main Street to Wamesit. The abandoned track can still be seen in the wooded area behind properties on Main Street.

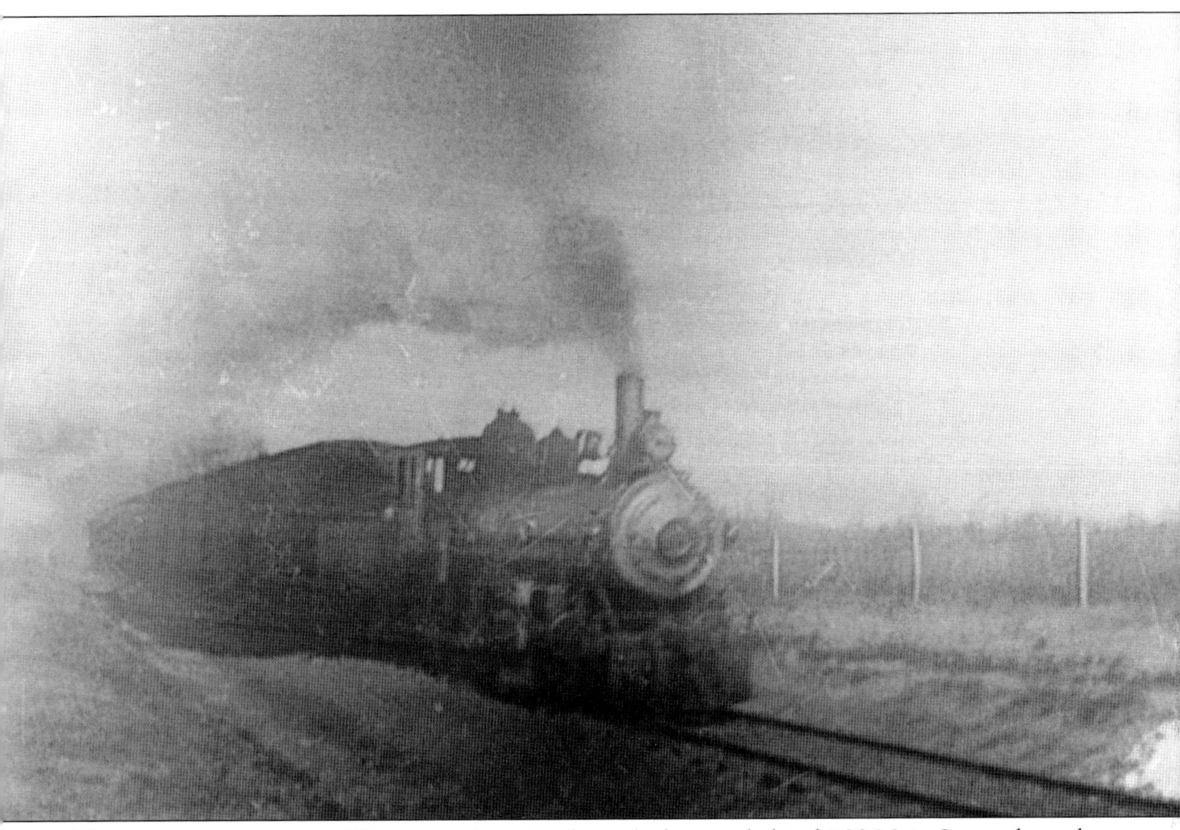

This passenger train in 1907 is seen chugging through the area behind 700 Main Street along the now-abandoned single-track railroad to Lowell. This steam-powered locomotive looks like a Boston & Maine No. 410. The City of Lowell has a restored version on display. It was noted to have held up to 4,500 gallons of water and 7 tons of bituminous coal to fuel the engine.

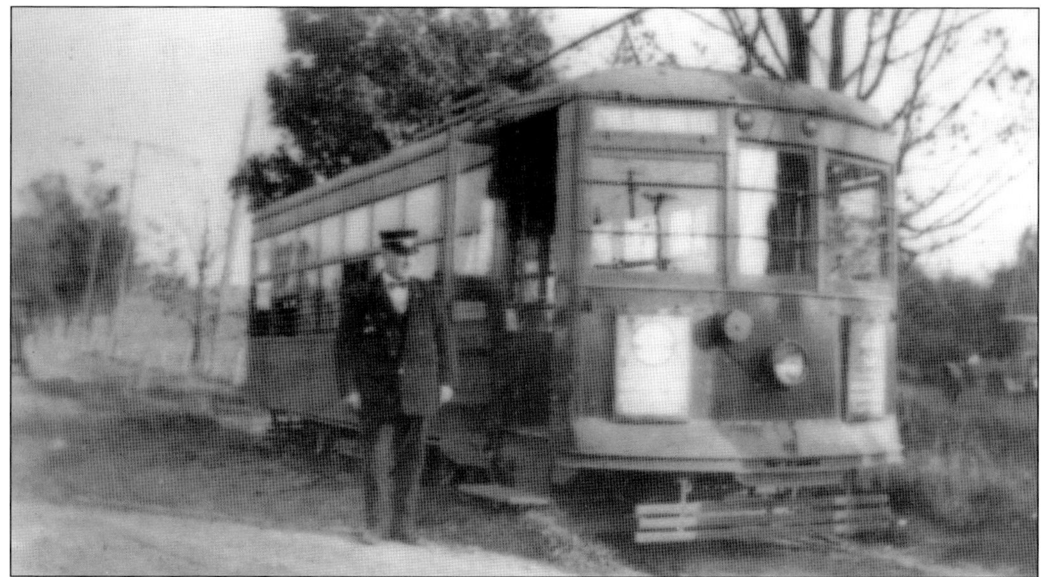

This photograph is undated with a Tewksbury trolley and its engineer. Tewksbury residents would take the trolley to the shopping areas of neighboring Lowell in the early 1900s. Once in Lowell, there was a grid of overhead wires over the streets, and the trolley would make stops at each block so that passengers could go to their destinations while others would climb aboard. In the 1920s, the popularity of the trolley declined with the coming of the automobile. Trolley operations in the Lowell area stopped around 1935.

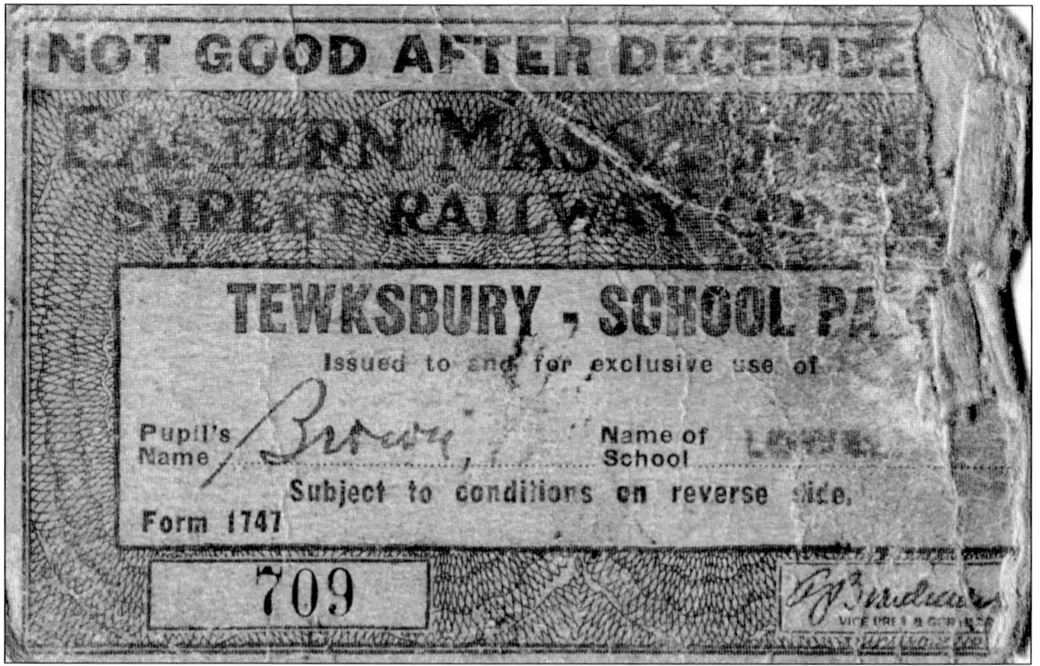

This trolley ticket was used by Francis "Taddy" Brown (page 71) to go to high school in Lowell around 1930. The ticket reads, "Eastern Massachusetts Street Railway Company, Tewksbury School Pass, Lowell." Tewksbury students went to Lowell for high school grades starting in 1900 until 1935, when the Center High School on Pleasant Street was built.

Seven

POLICE AND FIRE

Tewksbury's police and fire departments are a vital part of the town's history. From the early times of 1798, when volunteer firefighters formed in Belvidere using the Wamesit hand pump and bucket brigades to fight fires, to now the town having three fire stations with engines, ladders, and emergency medical equipment. The town's firefighters have always worked to do the best for the town. In 1734, the town's first constable was appointed, as the police had not yet come into practice. Constables were the peacekeepers in the community back then. Later, in 1886, the first police officer, James Manley, was listed in town records. Manley would go on to serve as the first town police chief from 1902 to 1907. In 1942, Tewksbury appointed its first Black police officer, George Gale, whose father served in the Colored Union Army in the Civil War. In 1988, the town's first woman to serve as deputy police chief, Denise Rosen, a Tewksbury High School graduate, was sworn in. Today, police officers operate in all aspects of public safety, including a criminal investigation unit, a drone unit, a K-9 unit, a SWAT/regional response team unit, and school resource officers, all engaged in keeping the peace in our community and maintaining good government. It is notable that many who serve in fire, emergency, and public safety also serve in the military, protecting us here and in wars overseas, the ultimate calling.

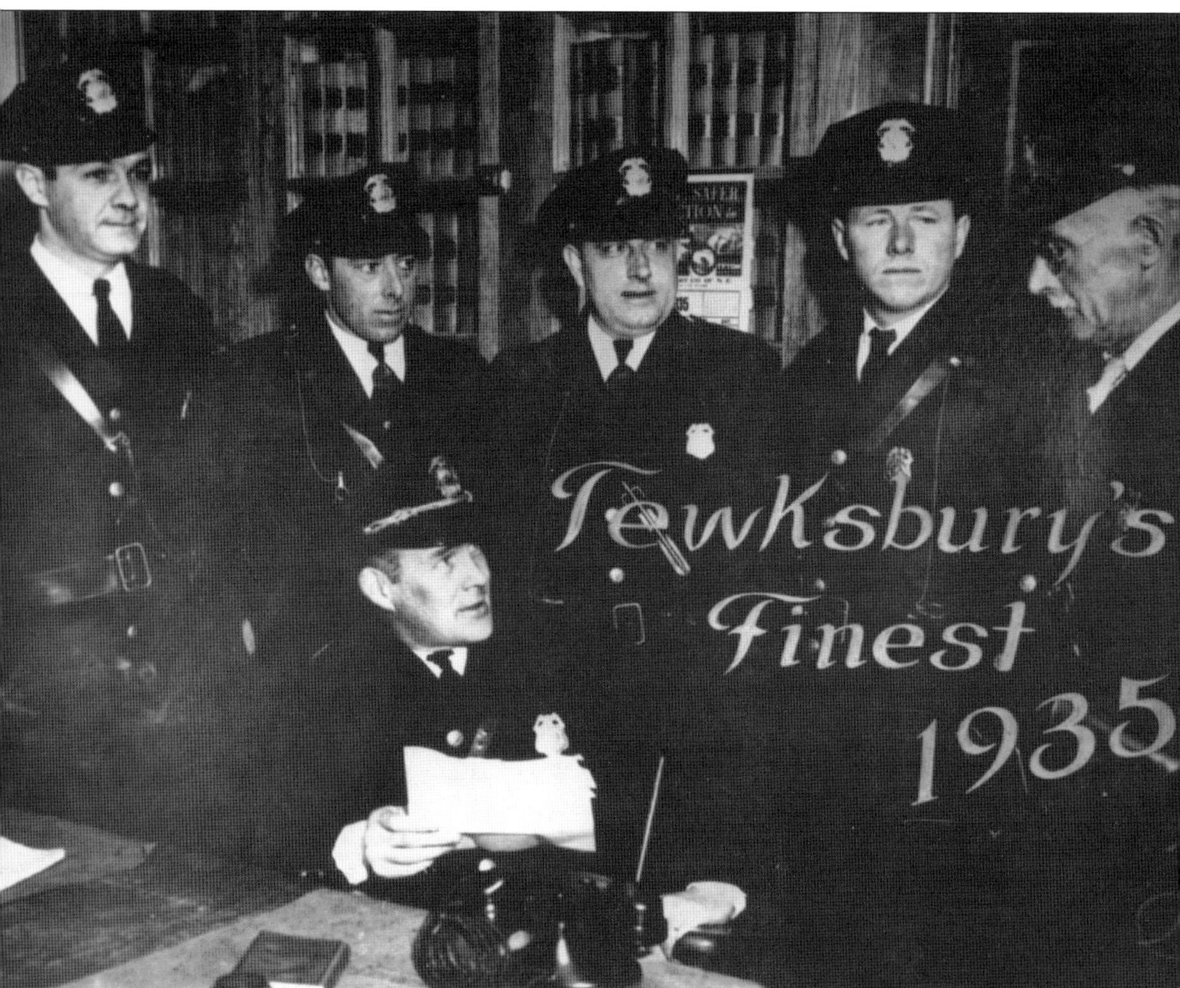

Tewksbury's finest in 1935 included Police Chief Cyril Barker, seated, and police officers, from left to right, Bernard Greene, Abbott Battles, Ross Sargent, Lauchie McPhail, and Warren Bancroft. Cyril Barker joined the Tewksbury Police Department in 1929 and served as the chief from 1934 until 1952.

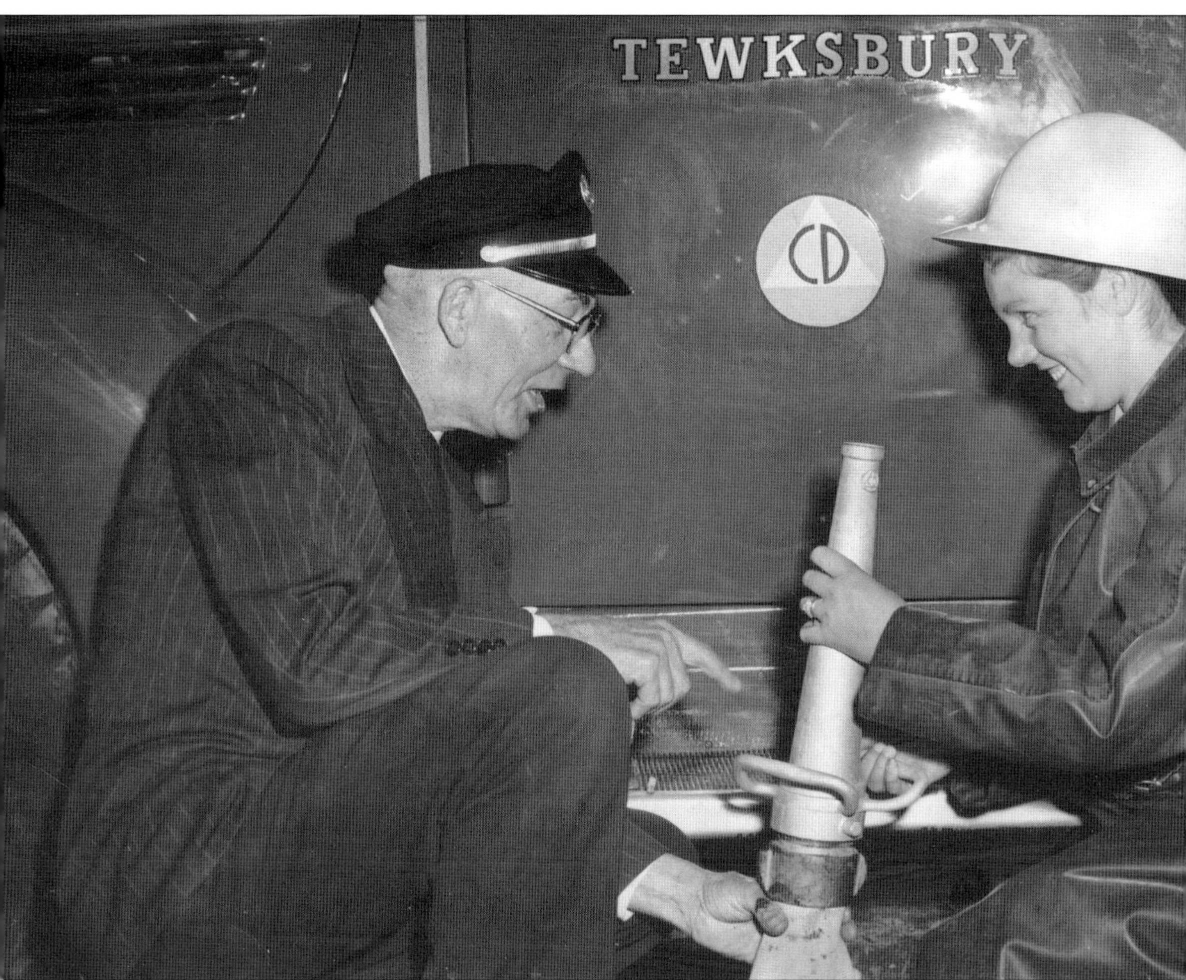

Fire Chief Anthony Obdens, with a Tewksbury Women's Fire Auxiliary of Civil Defense member in the 1950s, is practicing assembling the equipment. The volunteer women's group was trained and qualified in procedures to prepare for military attacks or other disasters during the Cold War. This was at a time when the threat of nuclear attack was at a high, and fire departments were seen as the best mechanism to oversee the training of volunteers who could assist in recovery after extreme events of weather, industrial accidents, or military catastrophes.

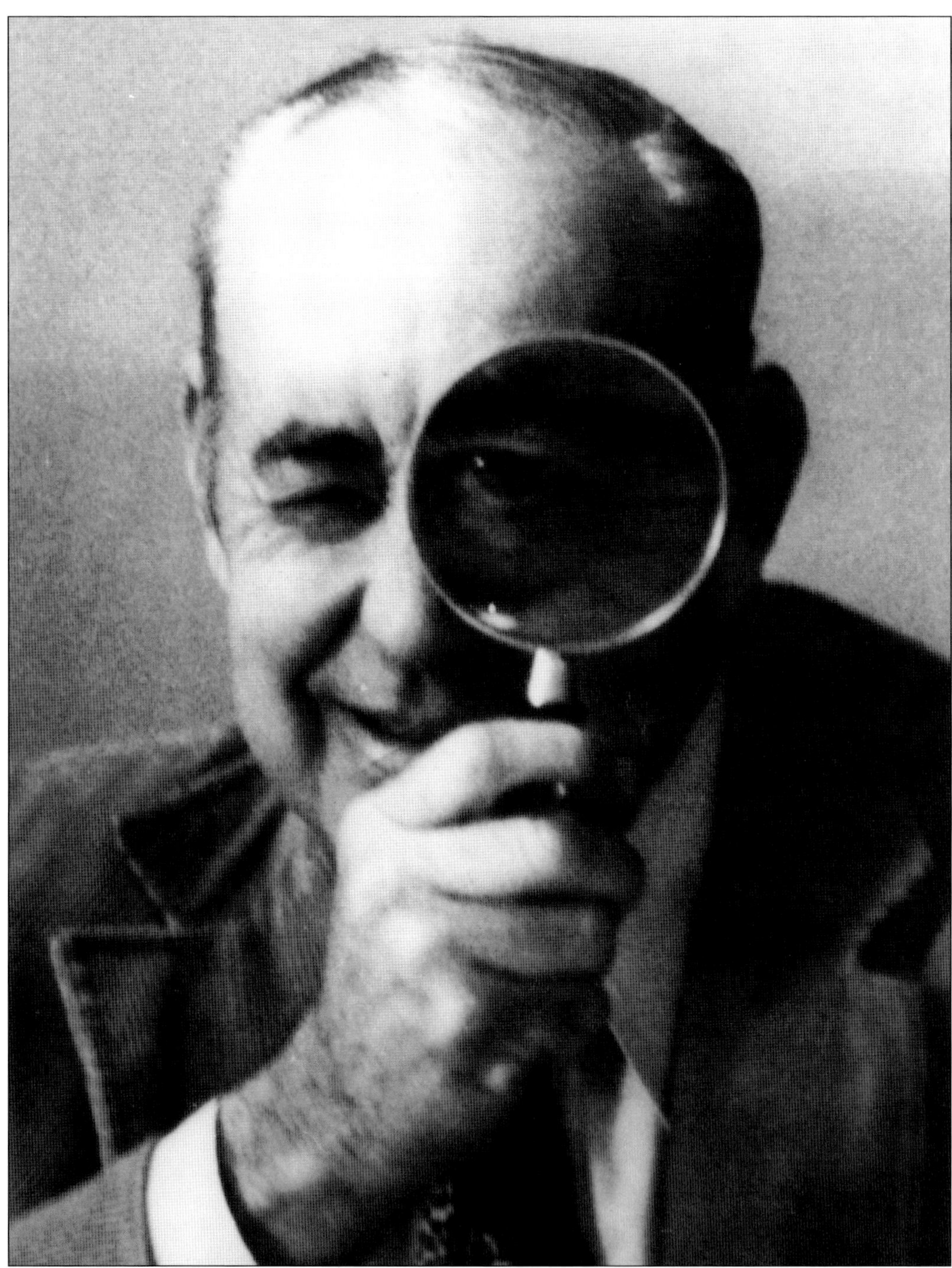

Tewksbury police officer Robert Haines is peering through a magnifying glass, looking like the inspector that he was. Appointed as an officer in 1956, he also served as a call firefighter for 20 years. His grandfather Alden Haines had been a Tewksbury fire chief, and his father, Everett, was also in the fire department. At one point, the three generations served at the same time. Robert has donated many photographs to the Tewksbury Historical Society, including several of the town's police department.

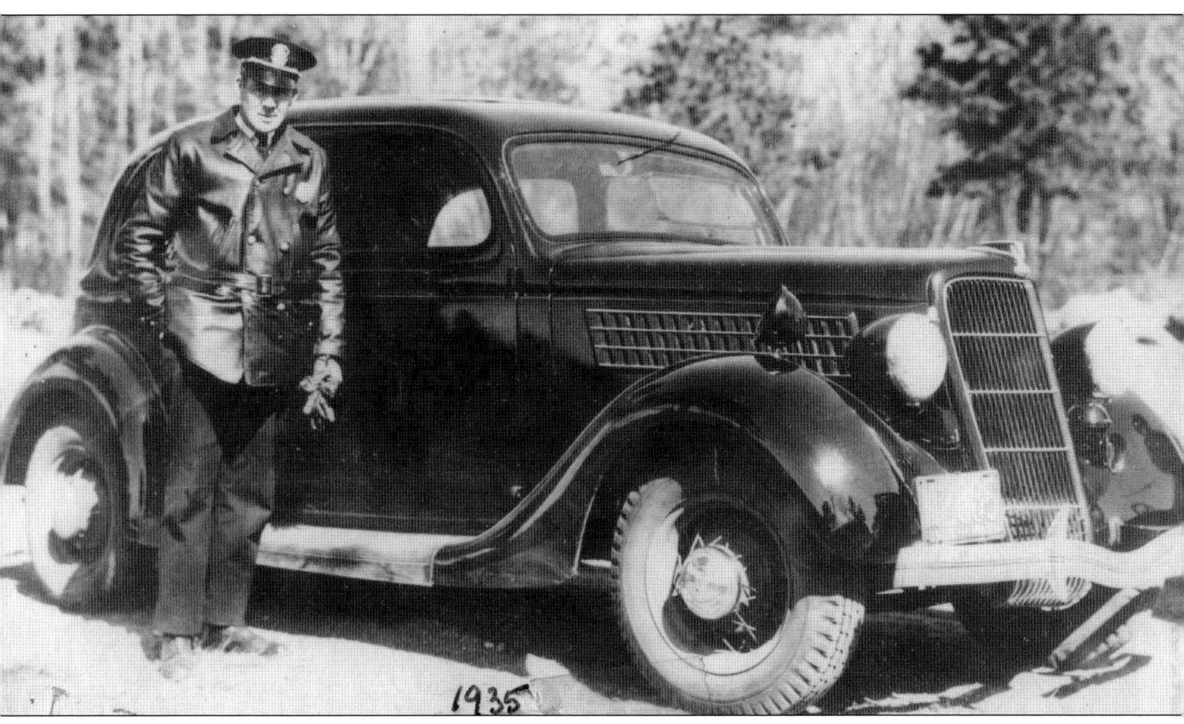

Police Chief Cyril Barker, in 1935, stands with the town's first police cruiser, one of his accomplishments while serving as chief. Cyril was born on what was Martin's Farm on Andover Street at the corner of Sheridan Lane in 1897. He pioneered radio communications in the Merrimack Valley in 1938 and purchased the first police revolvers—.38 Smith & Wesson Specials—in the town as well. In 1945, during World War II, his two sons were in the armed forces, one serving in the Army in Germany and the other in the Navy in the South Pacific.

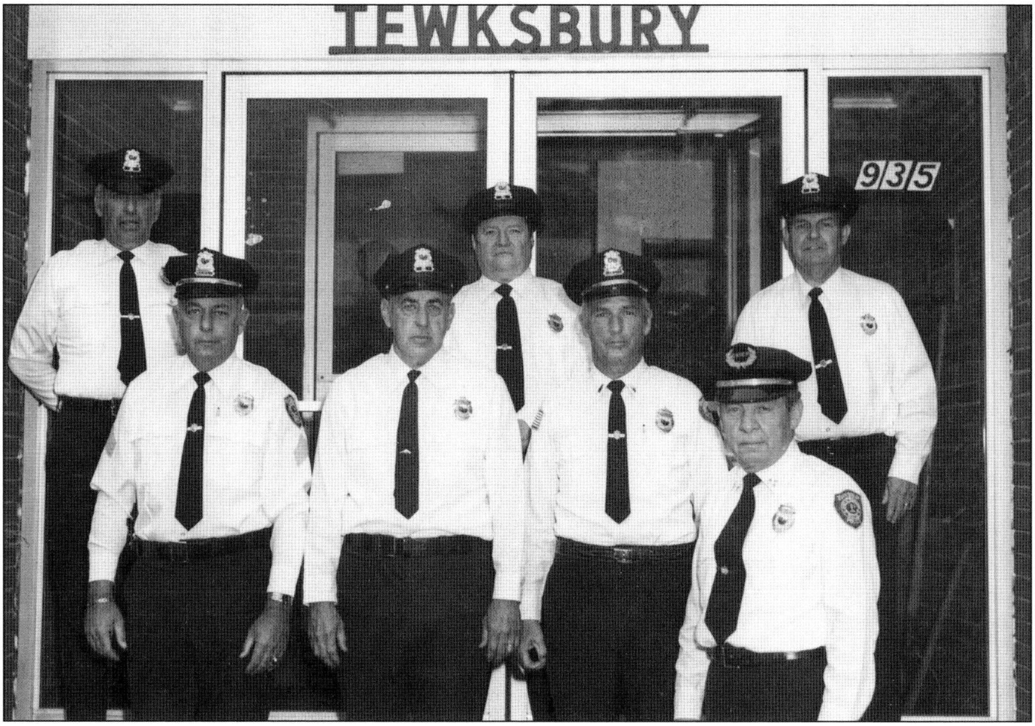

Police Chief John F. Sullivan was appointed acting chief in 1952. At that time, the police force in the town consisted of the chief and two police officers. Chief Sullivan served in the Navy from 1943 to 1947. He worked for the town as a police officer starting in 1948 and went to police school in Boston. Police officers pictured are, from left to right, (first row) Paul Johnson, Robert Haines, Richard Mackey, and Chief John Sullivan; (second row) Martin "Joe" Cormier, James Jones, and Frank Sullivan. Chief Sullivan served until 1987 as the chief of police of Tewksbury.

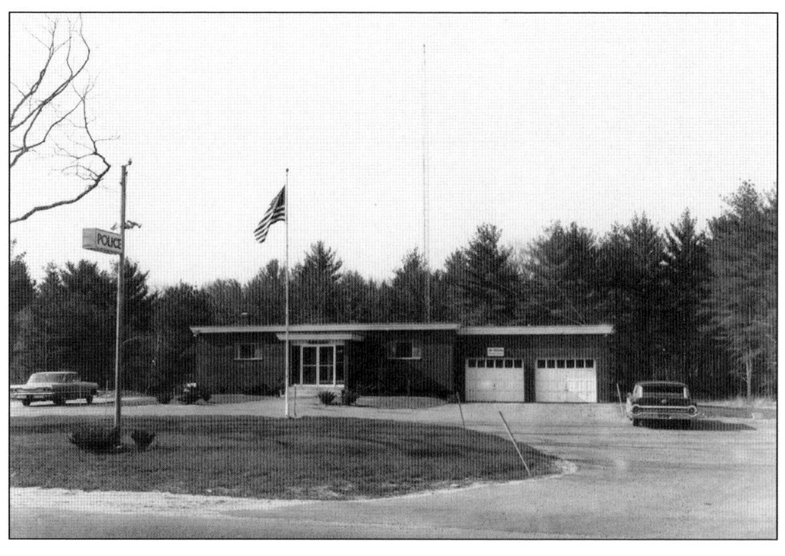

Tewksbury's former police station, new in 1962 and located on Main Street, served the town until 1996, when the new police station at 918 Main Street, across the street, was constructed. Before the 1962 station was built, the police headquarters had consisted of two rooms in the Town Hall.

Tewksbury Police are shown measuring tire skid marks on Trull Road after an automobile accident. This undated photograph looks to be from the 1960s. At that time, police used the distance of tire skid marks and the "drag factor" of the surface to calculate the speed of the vehicle. Today's anti-lock braking systems make this review more complex, and experts are needed to make the analysis.

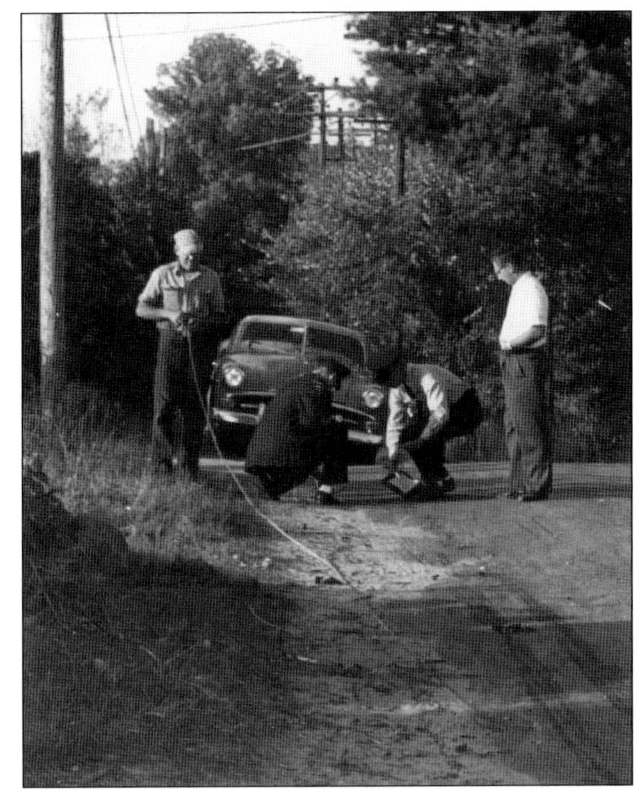

These are the Tewksbury Police officers in 1934. Retired Chief Anthony Kelley had been the chief from 1921 to 1934. Chief Cyril Barker would serve as chief from 1934 to 1952. In the front row are Chester Burgess, Ross Sargent, Abbott Battles, and Lauchie McPhail. Along the back row are Asahel Jewell, Warner Bancroft, Chief Cyril Barker, Retired Chief Anthony Kelley, and Bernard Greene.

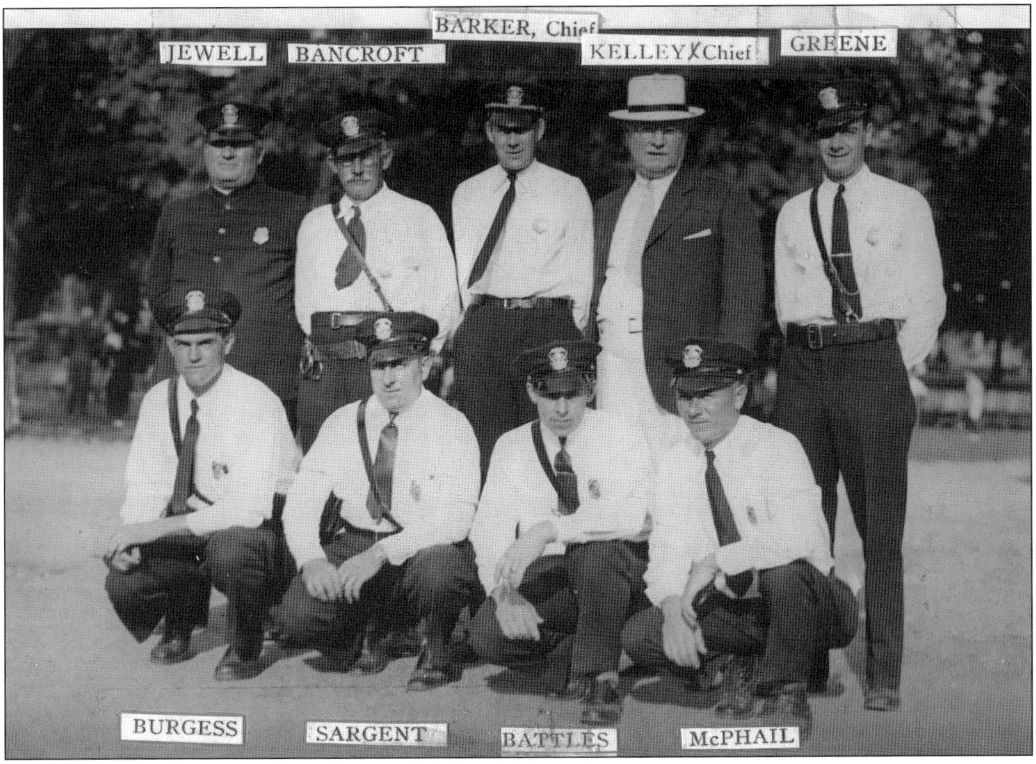

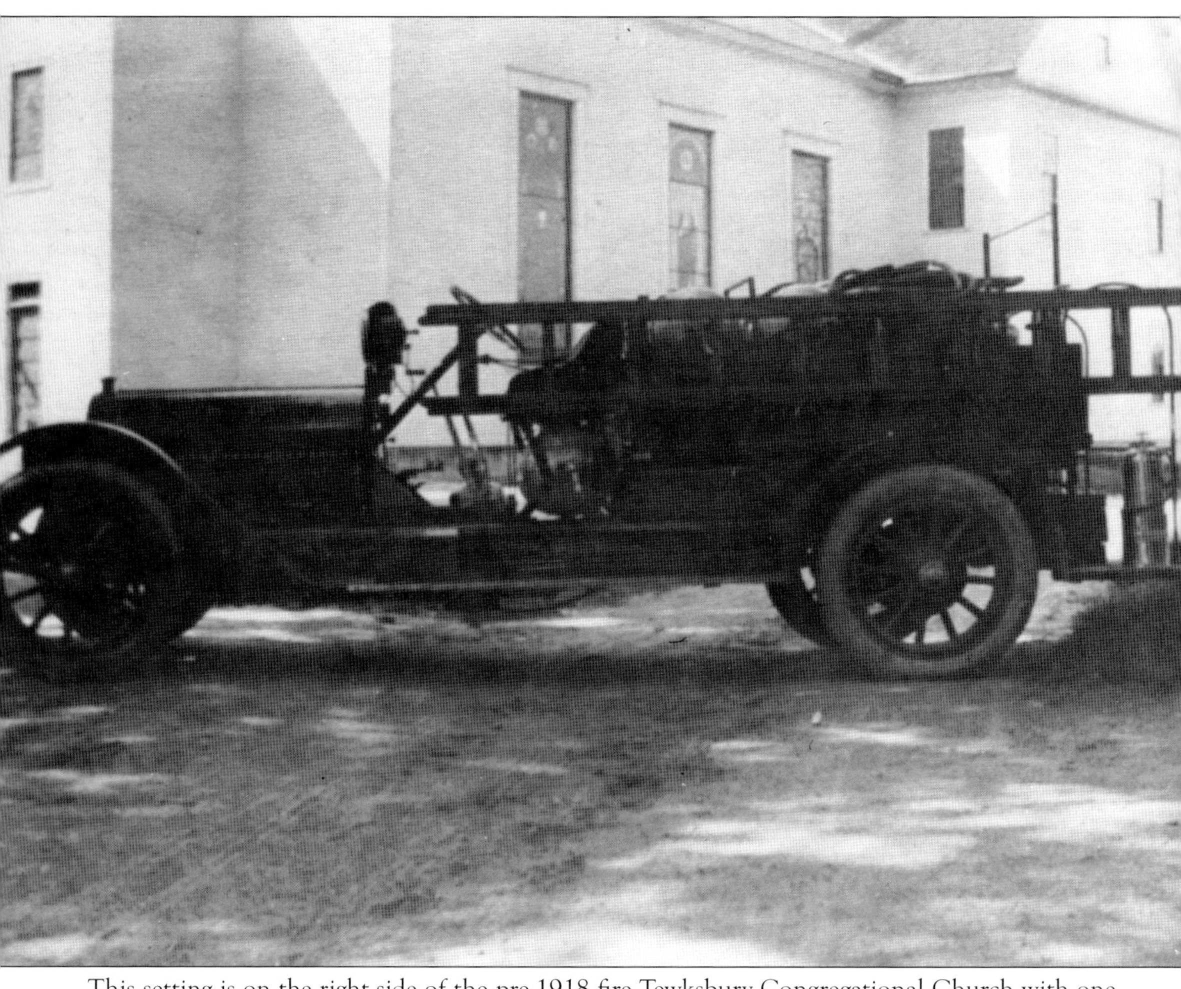

This setting is on the right side of the pre-1918 fire Tewksbury Congregational Church with one of the town's first fire engines. This model looks like an American LaFrance Type 12, which first came out in 1912. The New York company's roots started in 1832 and continued to provide fire and emergency apparatus until 2014, when this leader in the industry closed its doors.

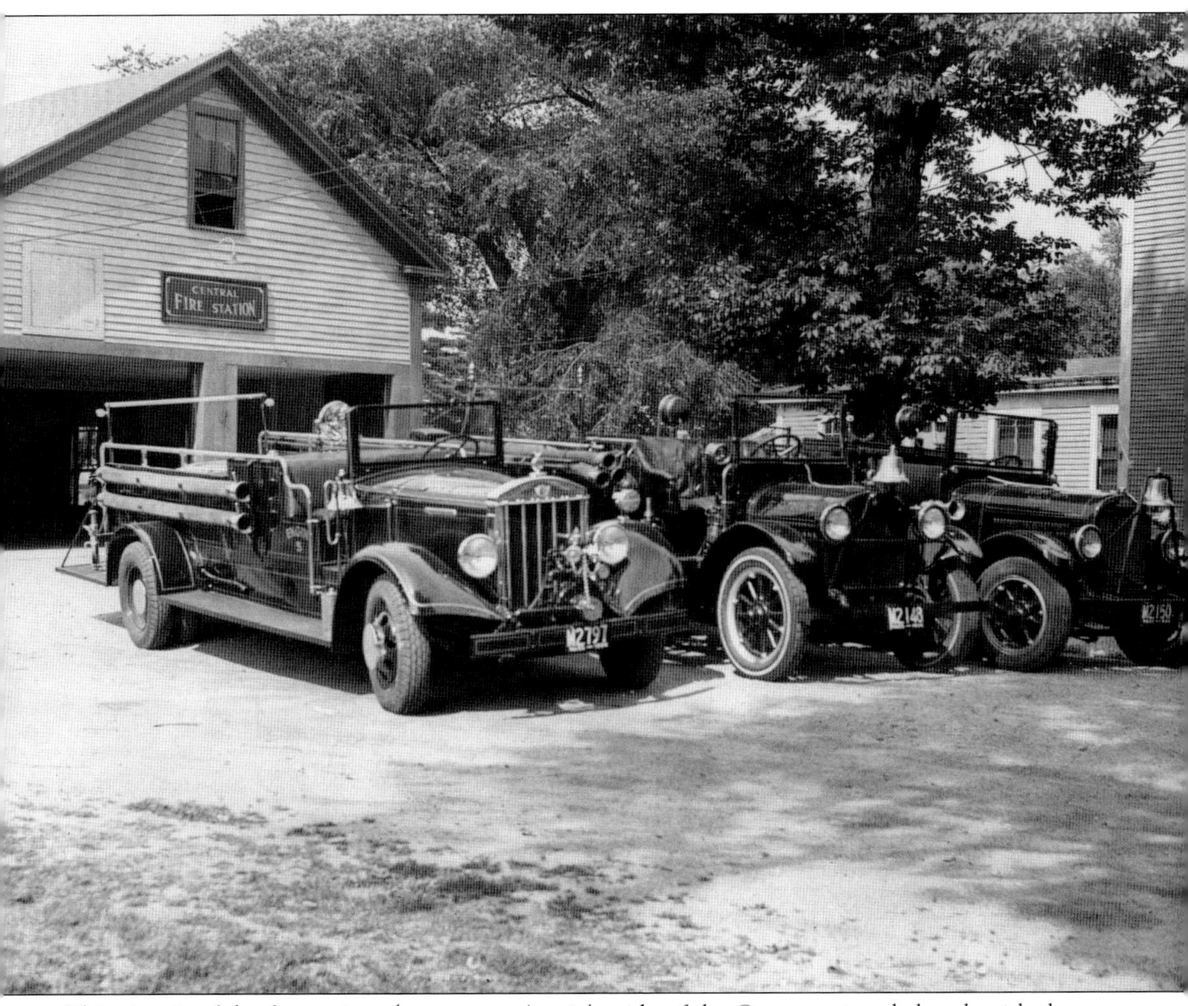

This view is of the fire station that was on the right side of the Congregational church with three REO fire trucks from the 1920s to 1930s, engine Nos. 5, 4, and 2. The REO Motor Car Company was located in Michigan, in business from 1905 to 1975, where building fire trucks began in 1909.

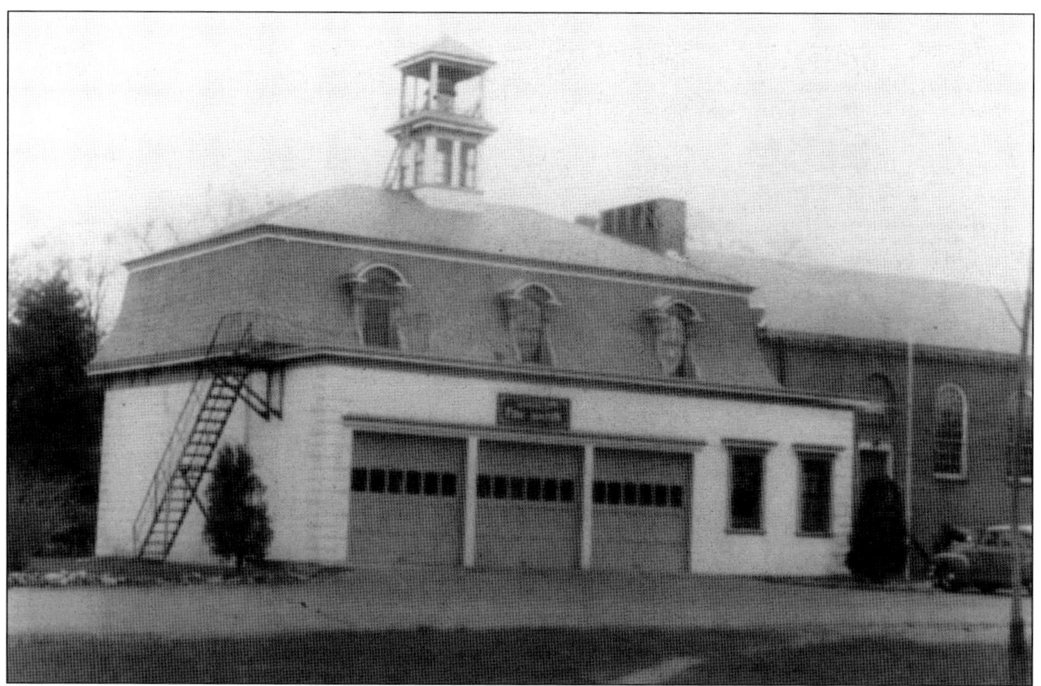

The barn from the Foster homestead remained in place to be used as a fire station when the home was taken down to make way for the new Town Hall in 1920. Here is a view of that fire station with the back of the new Town Hall seen on the right.

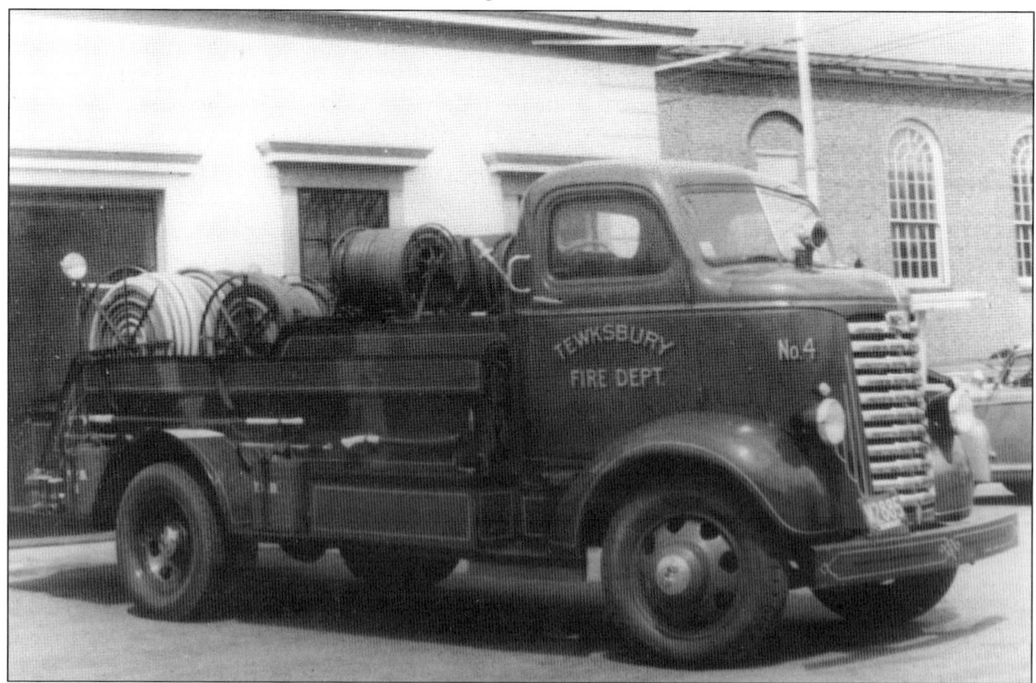

This undated early fire engine is shown in front of the Foster Barn fire station behind Town Hall. The engine looks to be a c. 1939 Ford COE (cab over engine) fire truck. These trucks were known for having better visibility and versatility due to having a shorter length than conventional vehicles.

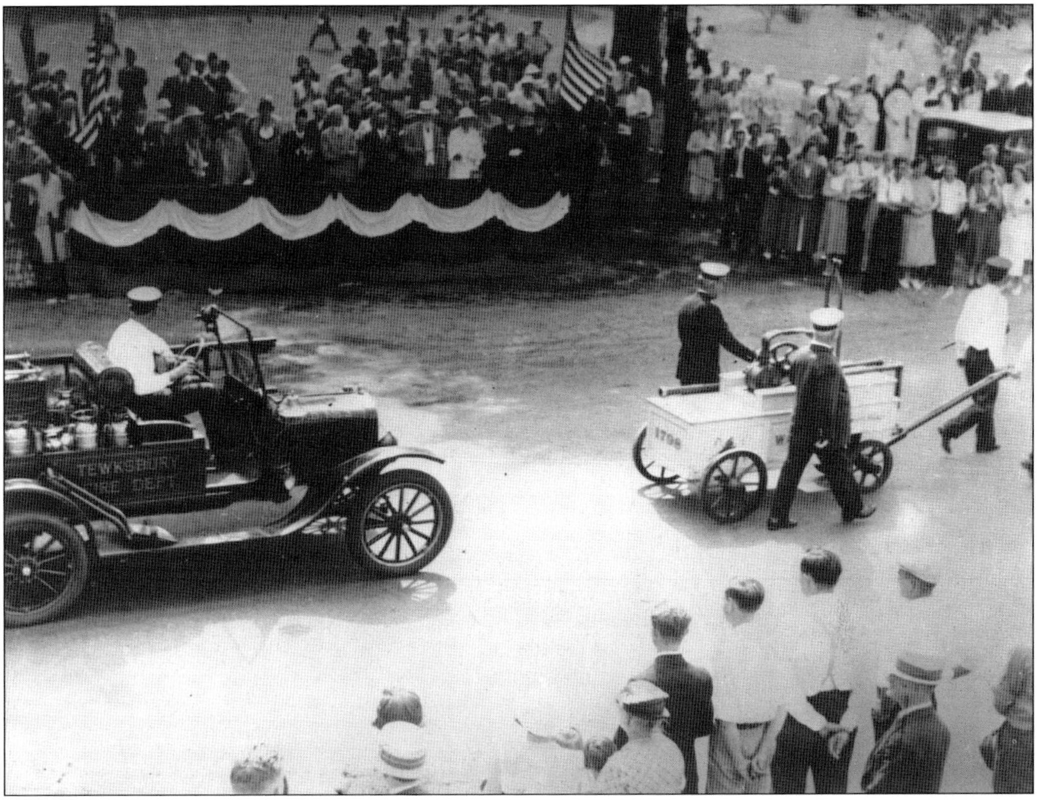

Firefighters are pictured in 1934 marching in the 200th Anniversary Parade with the Wamesit hand pump. Volunteers had purchased this pump to be used in the Belvedere section of Tewksbury in 1798. When that section of town was annexed to Lowell in 1834, the hand pump stayed with Lowell. Tewksbury asked for the return of the hand pump for the 200th Anniversary Celebration, and Lowell agreed. The hand pump is on display at the new fire station in Town Center.

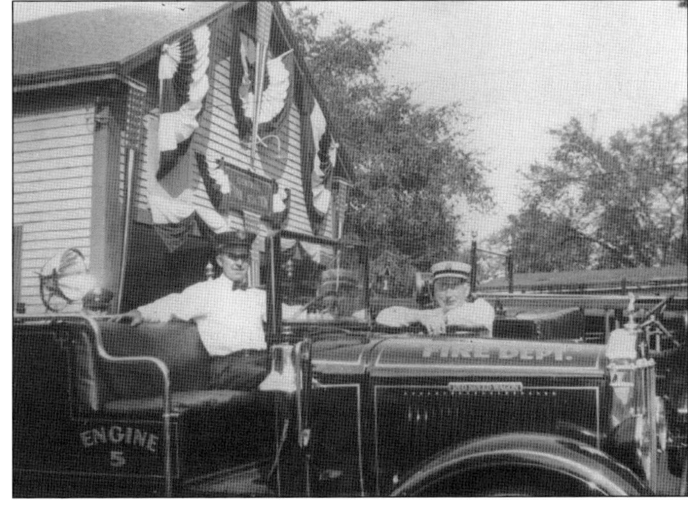

Ready for the 200th Anniversary Celebration parade in 1934 are two unnamed Tewksbury firefighters and REO fire engine No. 5. The REO fire truck was known as a combination fire engine because there were two methods of pressurizing the water. One was by mixing water with acid and soda in a tank, and the other was by a rotary gear pump, which could produce between 300 and 400 gallons of water per minute to assist with firefighting needs.

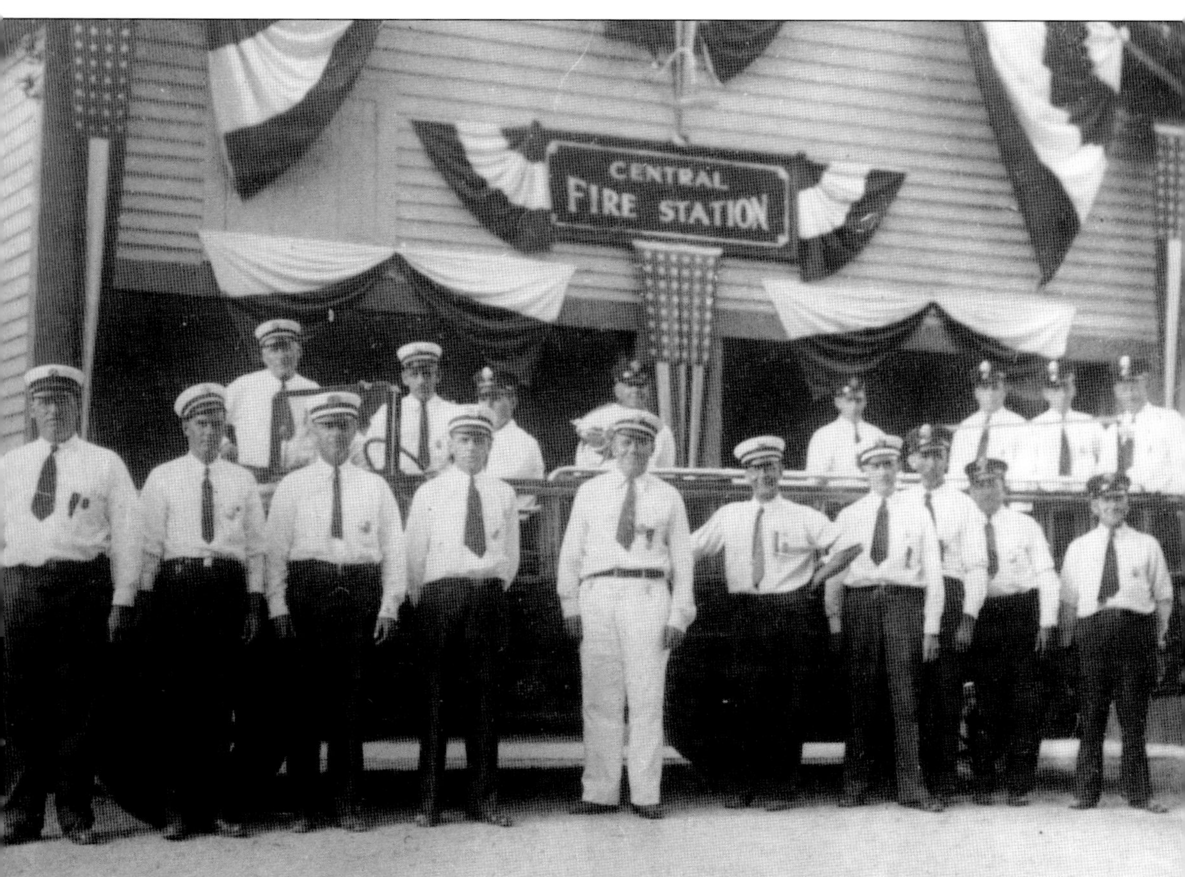

The Tewksbury Fire Department poses in front of the fire station when it was beside the Tewksbury Congregational Church pre-1920. From left to right are (first row) Irving Bailey, Chester Burgess, Omar Blanchard, Russell Millett, Edward Walsh, George James, William McGoogan, Wallace Farwell, Ross Sargent, and Andrew Kohanski; (second row) Chief Alden Haines, Everett Haines, Harold Mills, Daniel Stirling, Clifford Edgecomb, Leonard Gath, Harry M. Patterson, and Francis Corr.

Eight

Churches and Schools

Tewksbury's historic churches and schools illustrate the founding and growth of the town. Varying architectural styles define the trends of the day and address the needs of those who would use the buildings. Both building types, government and religious, served as community places to gather, celebrate events, and provide support to each other. One example that cannot be understated is the linkage of the 1854 State Almshouse opening and the arrival of the Catholic Missionary Oblates of Mary Immaculate from Canada to Lowell when they began to serve the poor at the Almshouse in 1868. The Oblates later purchased the nine-acre Kittredge Farm on Chandler Street in 1883. The property had two houses, a pond, and a barn for the Oblates to use as places for Catholic services. The purchase of the large Kittredge Estate on Chandler Street was also the first step that led to the establishment of the parish of St. William of York Catholic Church in 1935 on Main Street, its school, and rectory. The Oblates' buildings would suffer destruction by fire and changes in use, but the lovely campus and buildings remain today as a retirement residence for them. Their story is just one that shows how the interrelation of different endeavors by the government and church can benefit the community at large for many years.

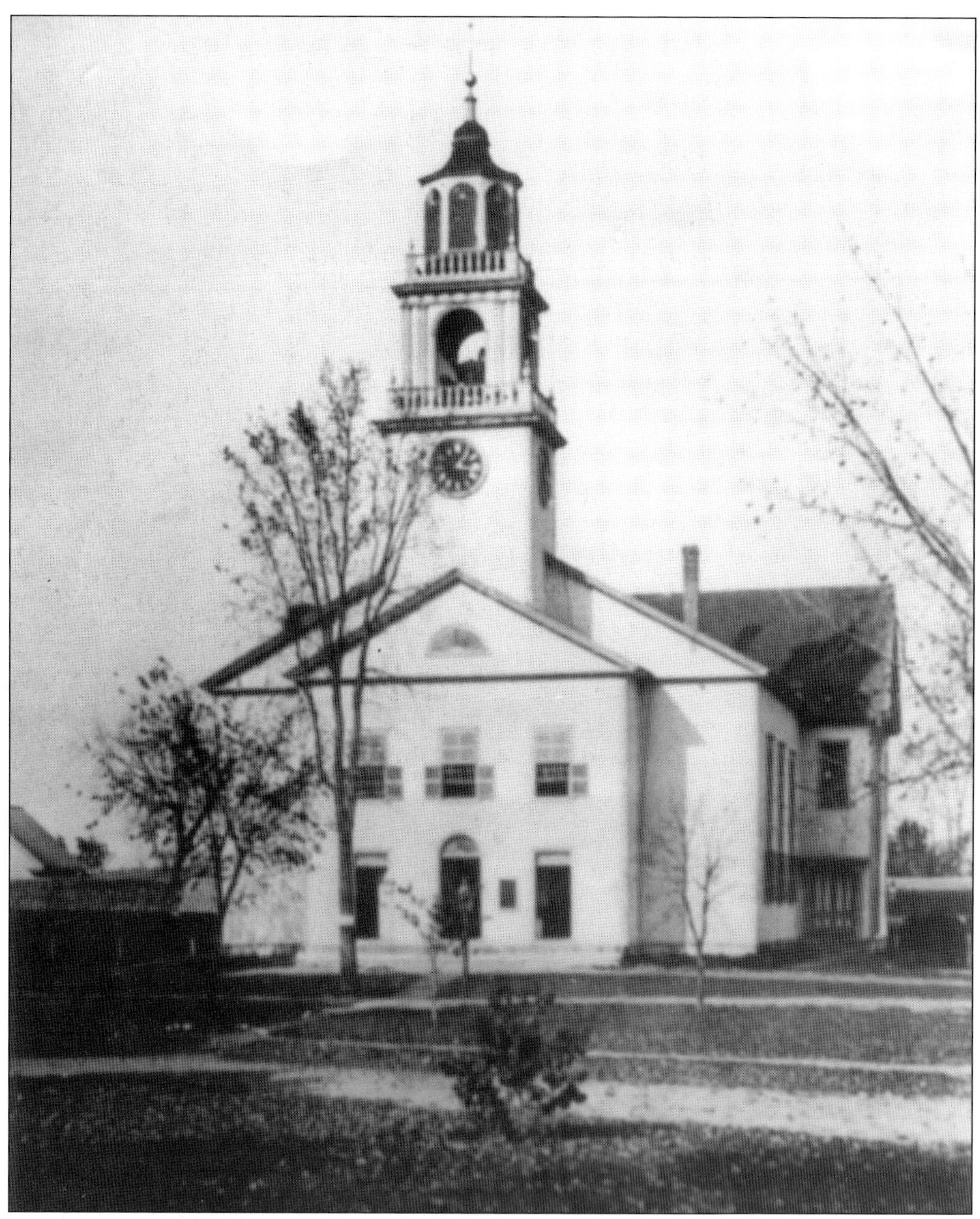

This is the Tewksbury Congregational Church, built in 1824, as it stood before the fire of 1918. It was the second church built on the site of the first church, established in 1735 after Tewksbury's incorporation. Notice the Vestry Hall on the right.

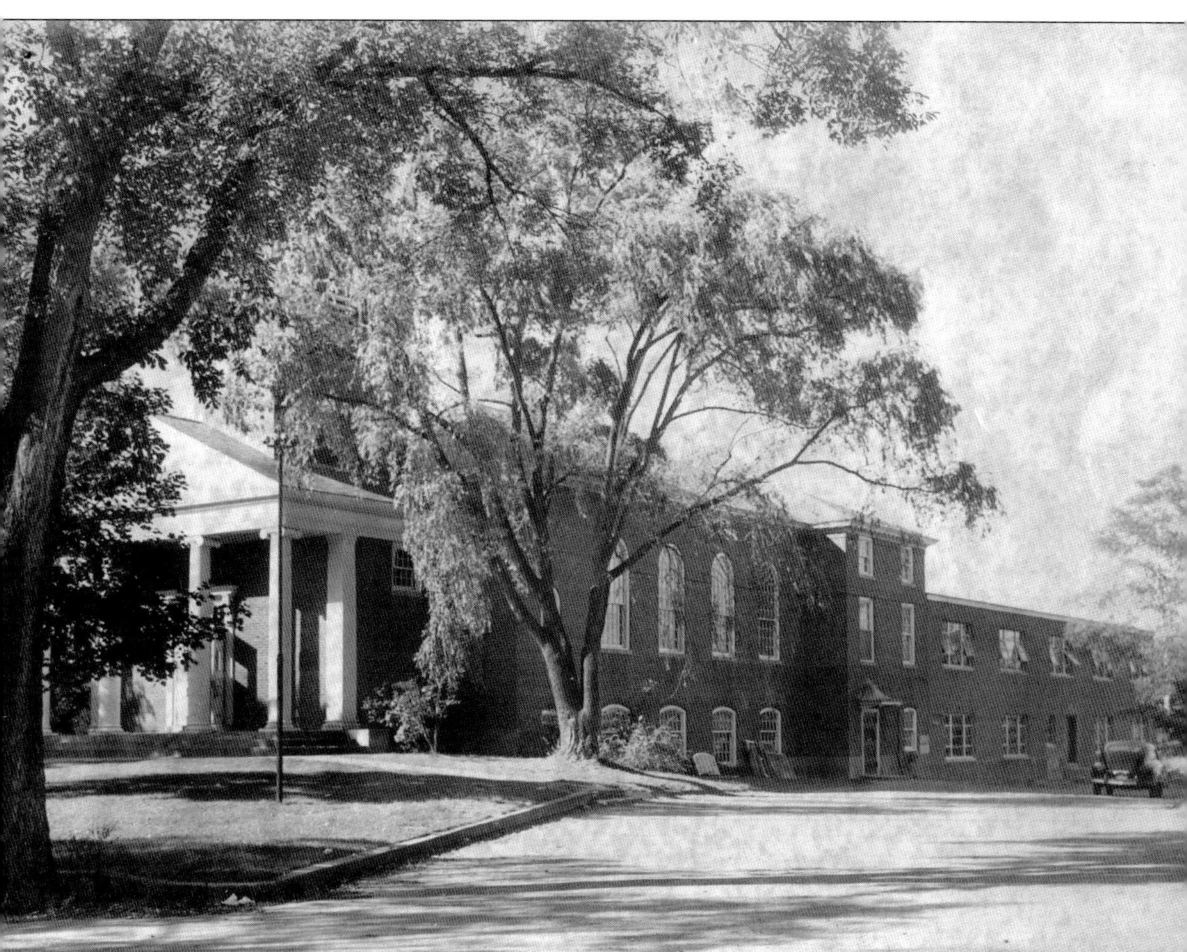

The Tewksbury Congregational Church was built in 1922 to replace the former building. The rear portion was added in 1961, including a fellowship hall that can seat 300 people, Sunday school rooms, and a large lobby.

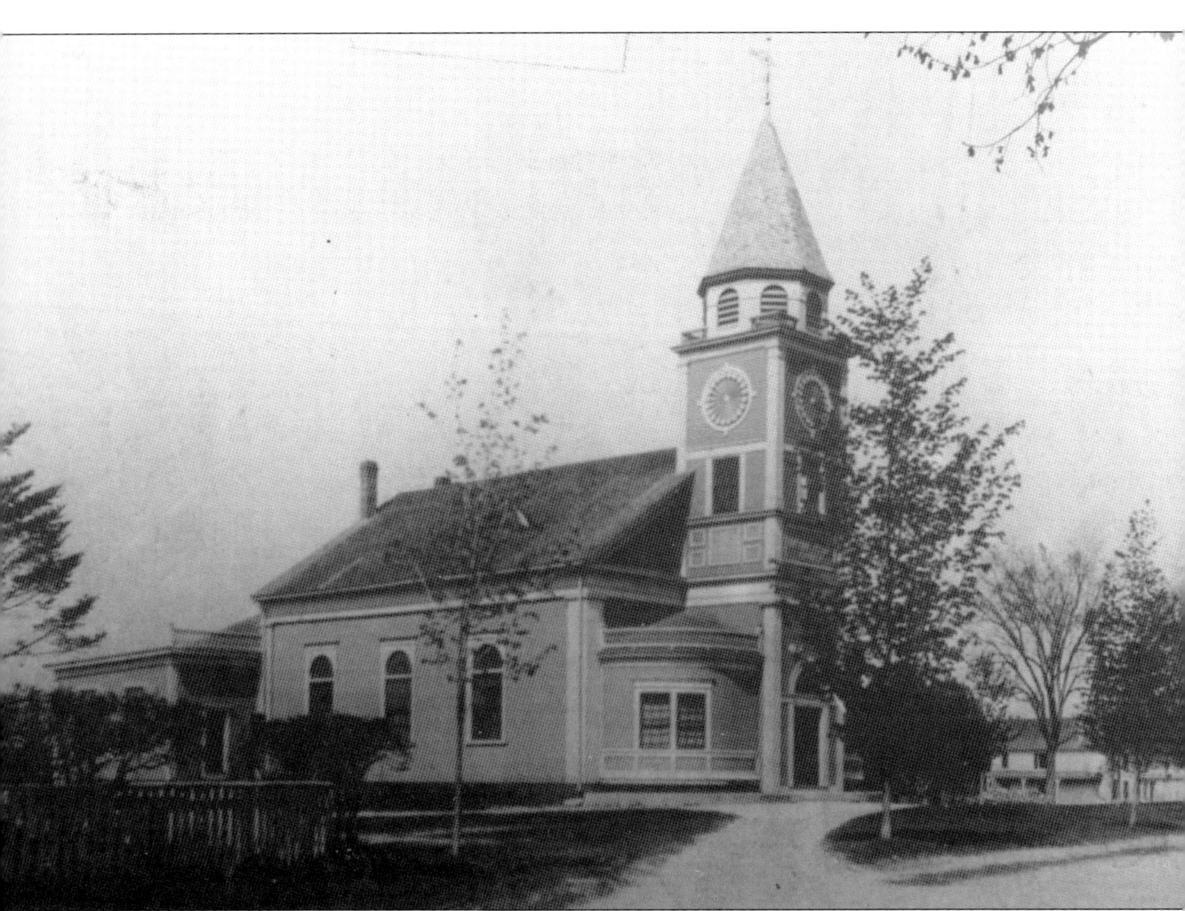

The First Baptist Church on Andover Street was formed in 1843. The current building was moved there from nearby in 1867, then it was expanded, and the new entrance was added in 1887. In the late 1950s, the Parish Hall was added with classrooms, a large function hall, and a kitchen.

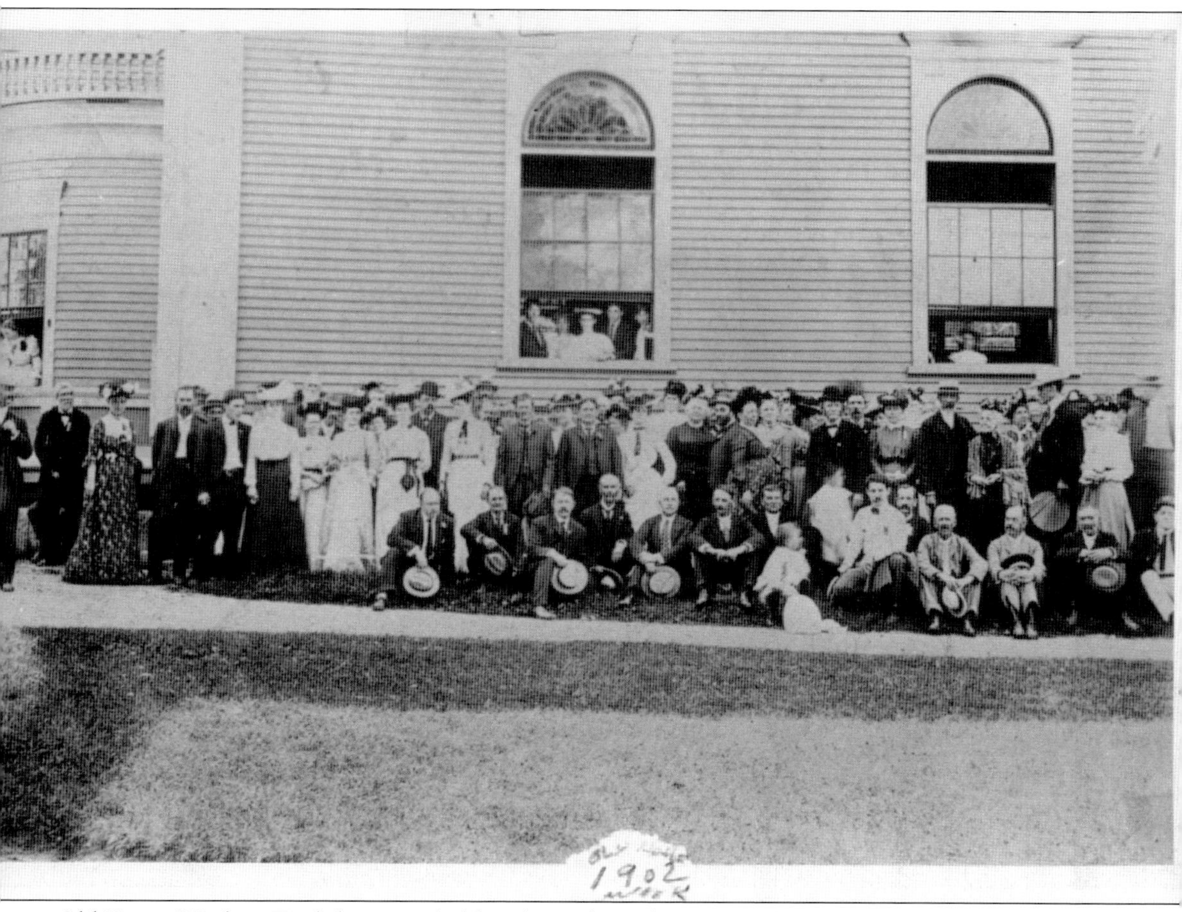

Old Home Week in Tewksbury was held at the end of July 1902. Celebration gatherings were held in Town Center and in North Tewksbury. Here at the event at the First Baptist Church, people gathered for a photograph after a clambake.

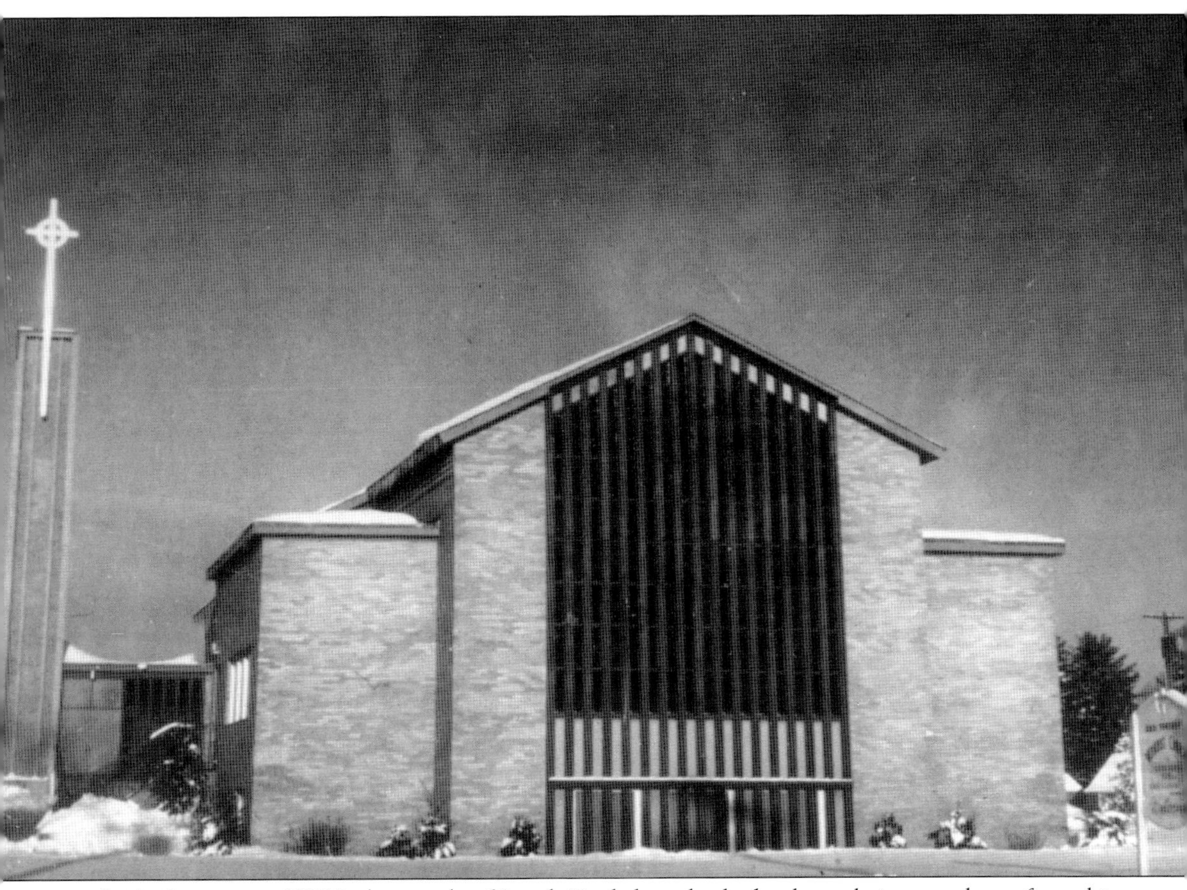

In the later part of 1910, the people of South Tewksbury looked to have their own place of worship. In 1911, a plot of land on Main Street was purchased, and open-air meetings were held. It was a Methodist minister who had led them, which steered their decision that the church would be a Methodist Episcopal Church. A wood-framed white church was built and dedicated in 1916. In 1956, the corner of Main and South Streets was purchased for the new larger church pictured here.

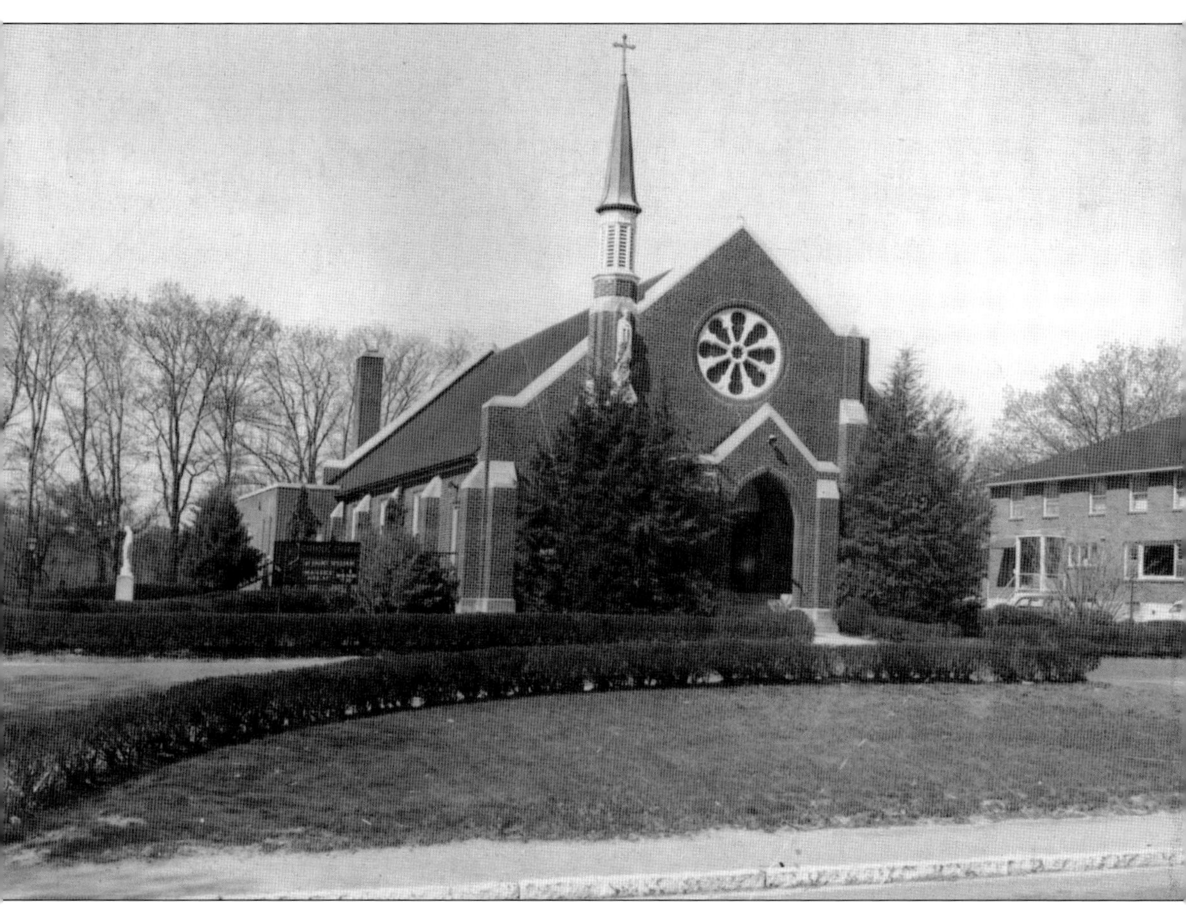

Dedicated in 1939, St. William of York Catholic Church is part of a complex that includes a rectory, a former convent, and a school. The parish was named for the patron saint of Cardinal William O'Connell, the Archbishop of Boston at the time. The Missionary Oblates of Mary Immaculate had established their location on Chandler Street in 1883 after serving the State Almshouse starting in 1868. In 1934, the Boston archbishop deemed that the Oblate order would lead this new Catholic Church.

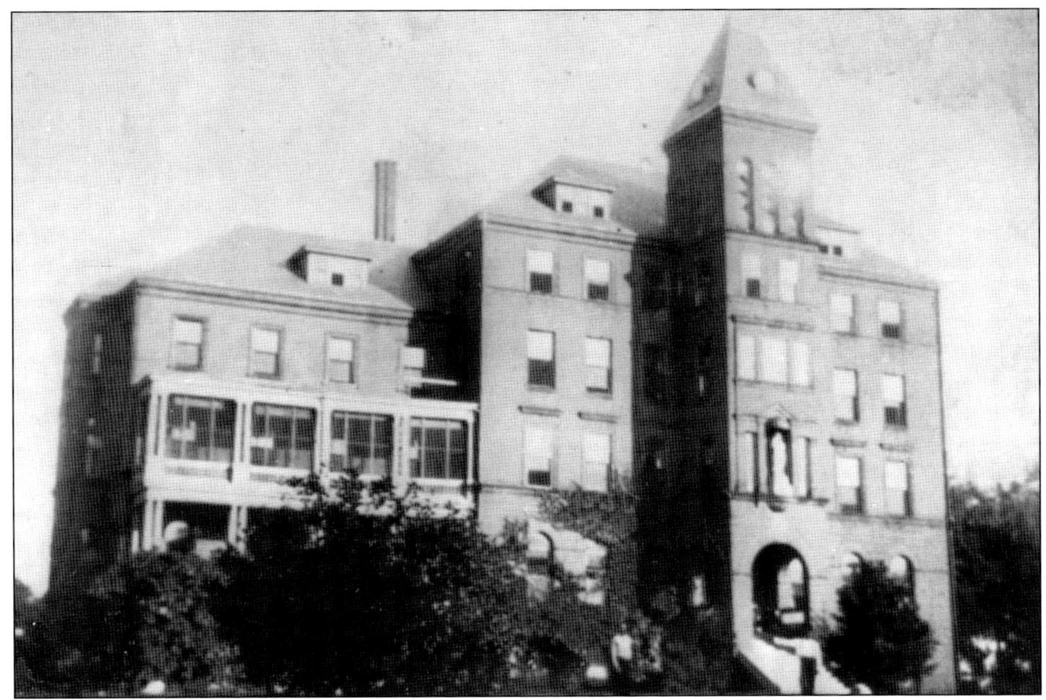

In 1883, the Missionary Oblates of Mary Immaculate purchased land and buildings on Chandler Street, known as the Kittredge Estate. In 1895, the house being used for worship burned down, and a second house on the property was then used temporarily. In 1896, this five-story Queen Anne–style building opened on Chandler Street.

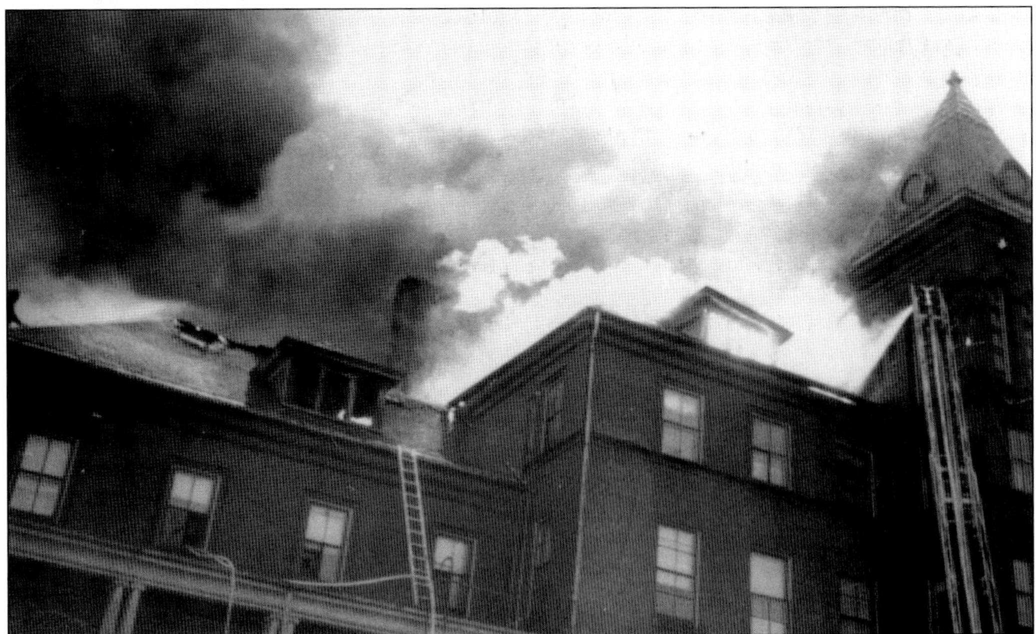

This photograph shows the Chandler Street 1896 Oblate Novitiate building's unfortunate destruction by fire in January 1959. This building housed the priests for St. William's Church, and plans for construction of a rectory next to St. William's began immediately.

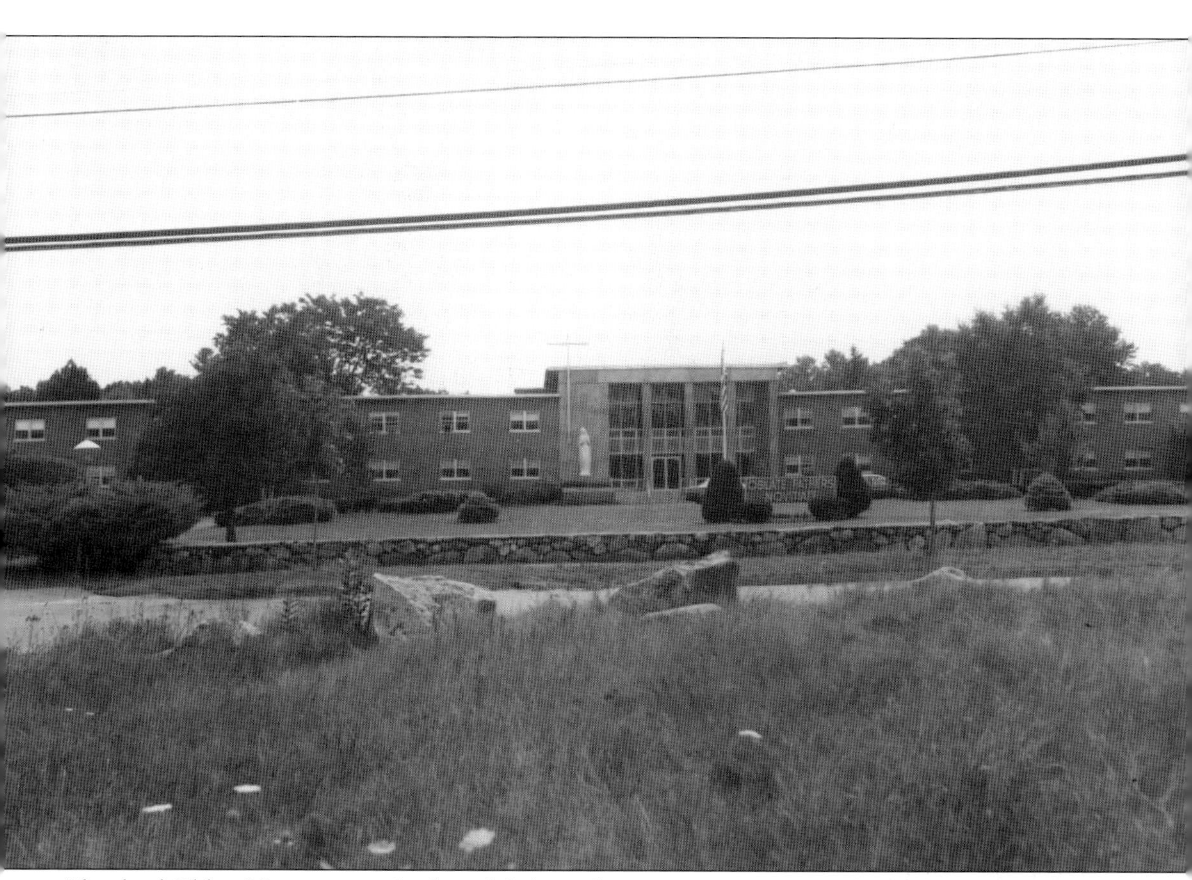

The third Oblate Novitiate was built and dedicated on January 17, 1962. This building now serves as a retirement residence for the Oblate of Mary Immaculate order of priests. The grounds of the campus provide beauty, walkways, stations of the cross, and a cemetery where Oblates who have served the town and those at the almshouse are buried.

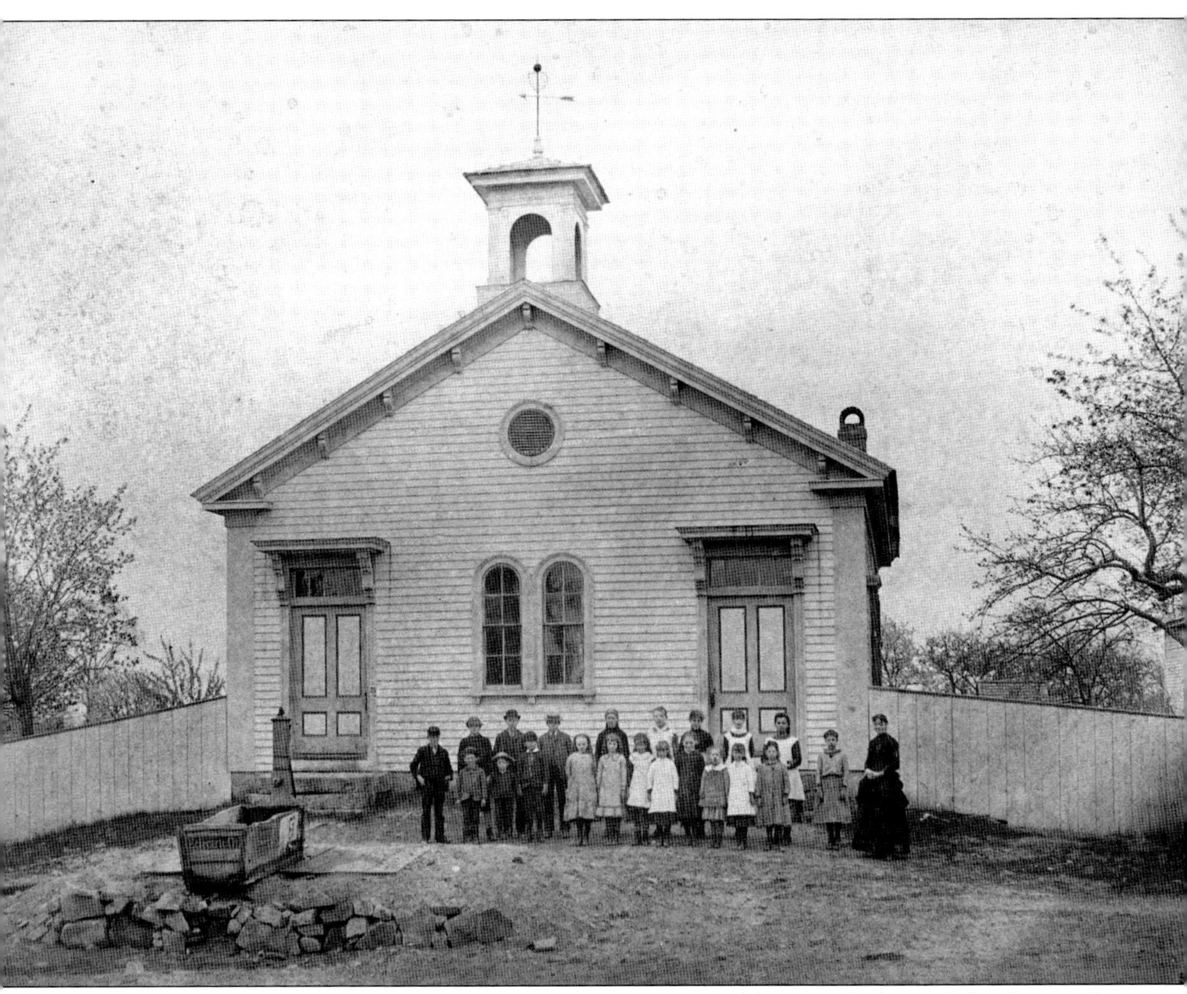

The District No. 3 North School on Andover Street, pictured here in the late 1800s, depicts the early days of a one-room schoolhouse in North Tewksbury. There was no running water, heat, or indoor plumbing, but the building had a wood stove and two outhouses—one for the girls and the other for the boys. Two doors in the front were to separate the girls and boys as entries for each. Once inside, boys and girls would stay on either side of the one-room schoolhouse. Ella E. Flemings attended the school in 1878 and started teaching there in 1885. The school would be named after her in 1935 at a town meeting. This image is from *The Ella E. Flemings School: Tewksbury's Little Red Schoolhouse* by William Pavao, published in 2023. (Courtesy of Beverly A. Bennett.)

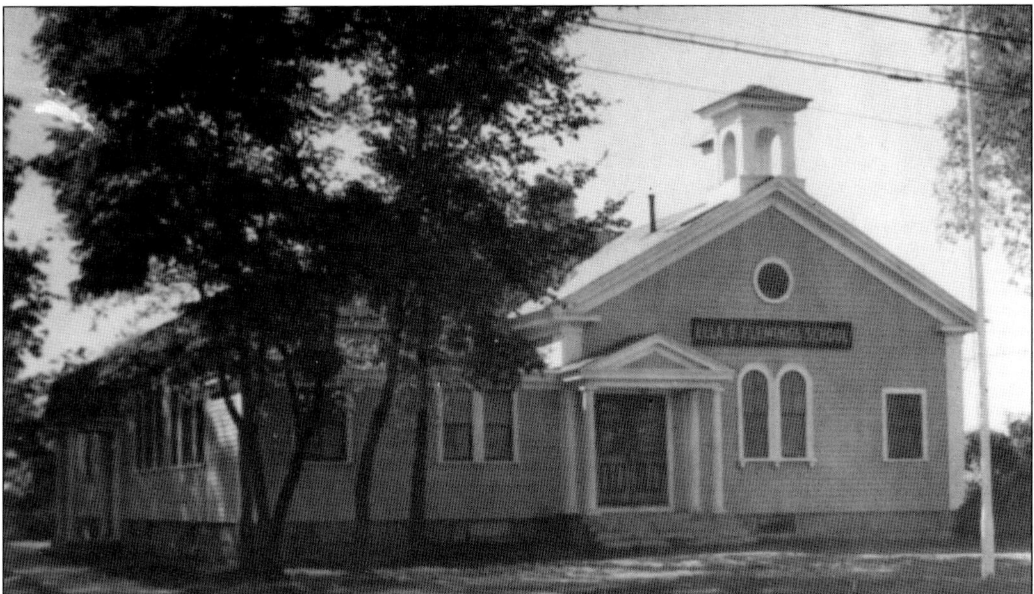

In 1911, an addition on the left side of the District No. 3 School was built. These two extra rooms were used for student teachers from the Lowell Normal School, now UMASS Lowell. This cooperative effort was one of the first of its kind in Massachusetts. Plumbing, electricity, and restrooms were added at this time.

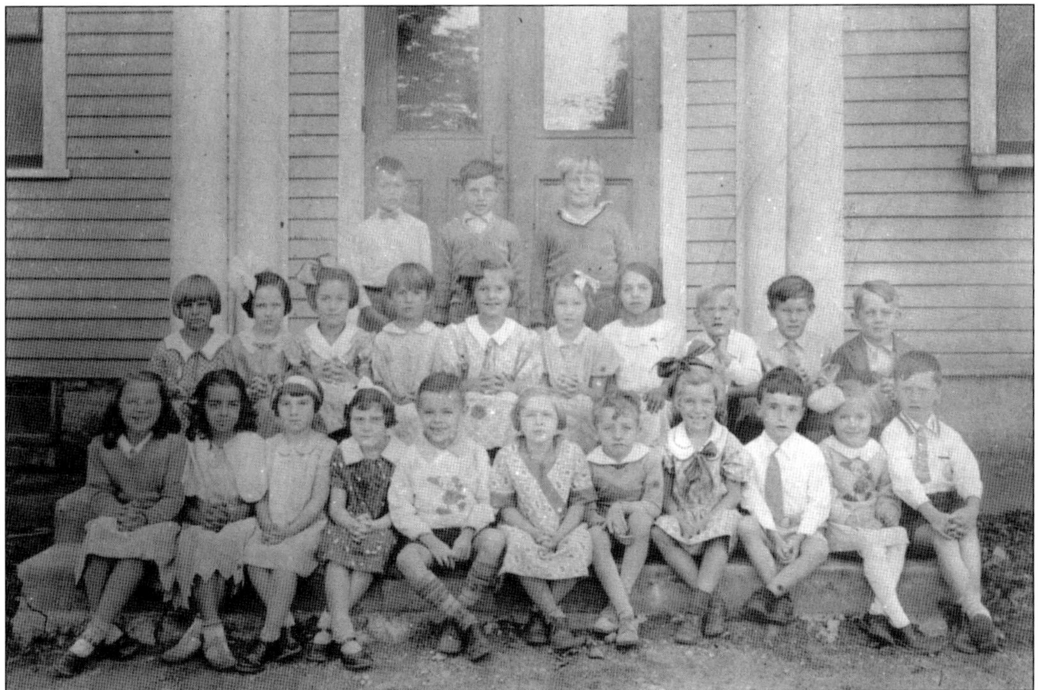

The District No. 3 North School pictured with students in 1933, including a young Beverly Bennett, second row, third from the left. She lived next door to the school on Andover Street her entire life. Her passion for the preservation of the school and town history inspired her to establish the Tewksbury Historical Society in 1993.

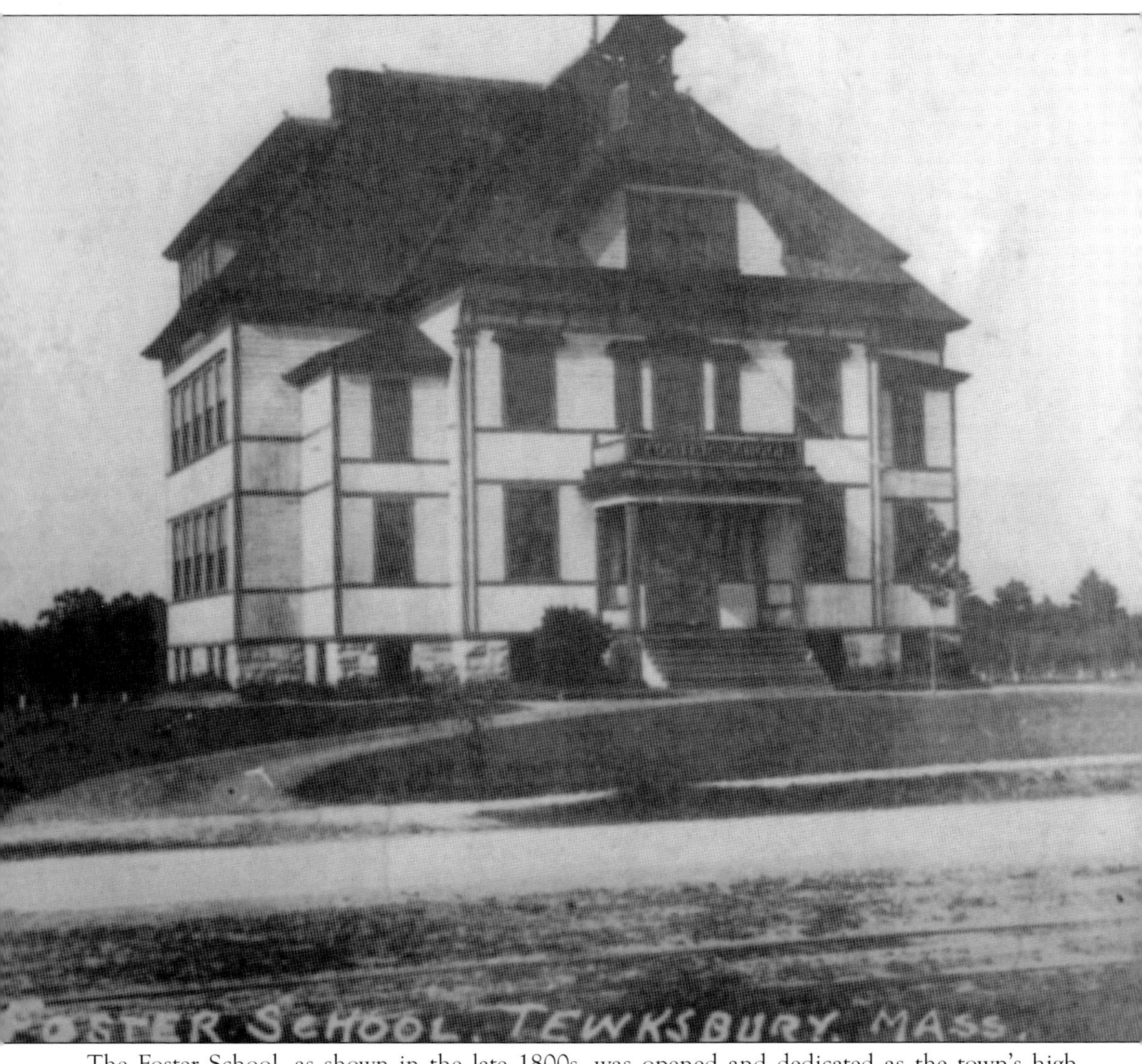

The Foster School, as shown in the late 1800s, was opened and dedicated as the town's high school in February 1894. The dedication was held in Pickering Hall, on the third floor. There was a chorus by students and a key presentation to the chair of selectmen, Frank Farmer. A prayer dedication was made by Rev. E.W. Pride, author of the 1888 book *Tewksbury, A Brief History* and pastor of the First Baptist Church from 1878 to 1891.

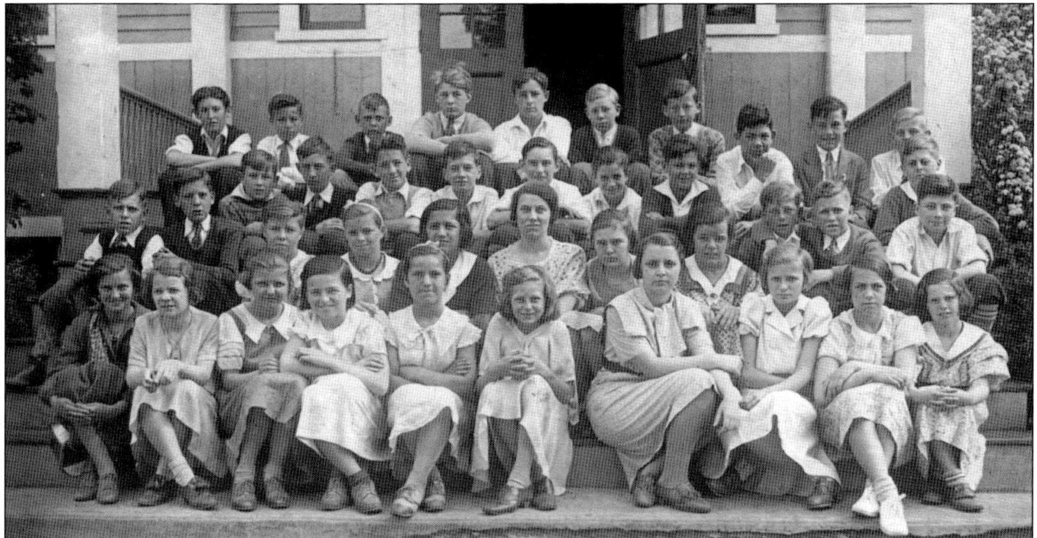

This is the seventh-grade class of 1936 at the Foster School. The photographer has captured the youth and spirit of the times with this image. In 1933, Franklin Delano Roosevelt was inaugurated as president of the United States and began to deal with the issues of the 1929 Great Depression. Among his accomplishments were the New Deal social and economic programs, the Social Securities Act, and the Historic Sites Act, establishing National Historic Landmarks. Roosevelt overwhelmingly won reelection as president in 1936.

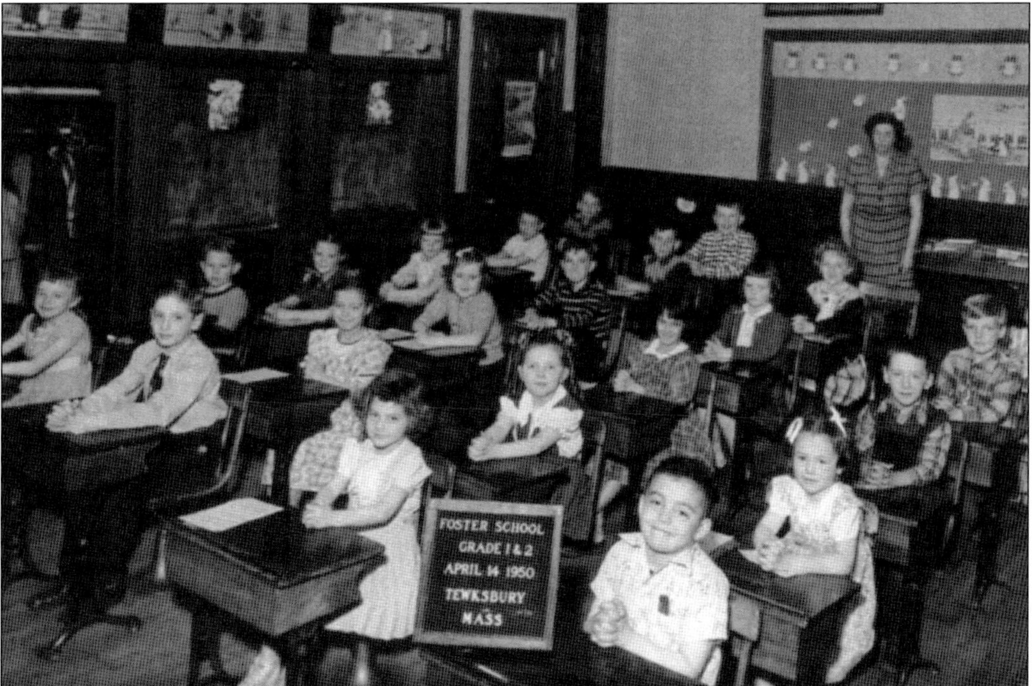

The class of 1950 students are smiling at the Foster School with their teacher, Ruth Tingley Anderson. Anderson taught in Tewksbury schools for over 30 years. She taught in the old Shawsheen School in the 1920s, the Foster School, and, after retirement, the North Street School. At one time, there was a plaque at the North Street School, now closed, in her honor.

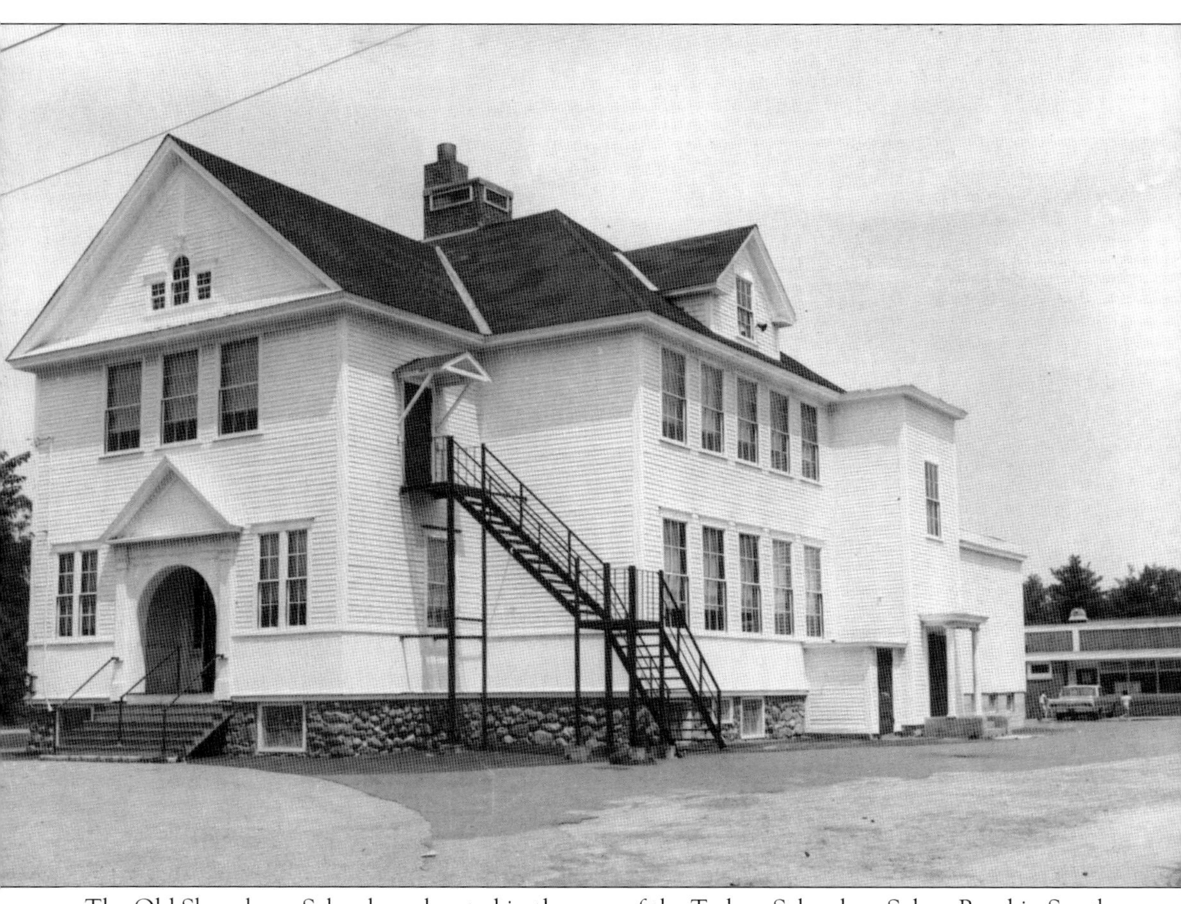

The Old Shawsheen School was located in the area of the Trahan School on Salem Road in South Tewksbury. Shown here in about 1950, there is little history on record about this school, which was demolished to make way for the newer elementary school in the area named the Shawsheen School and later named the Louise Davy Trahan School.

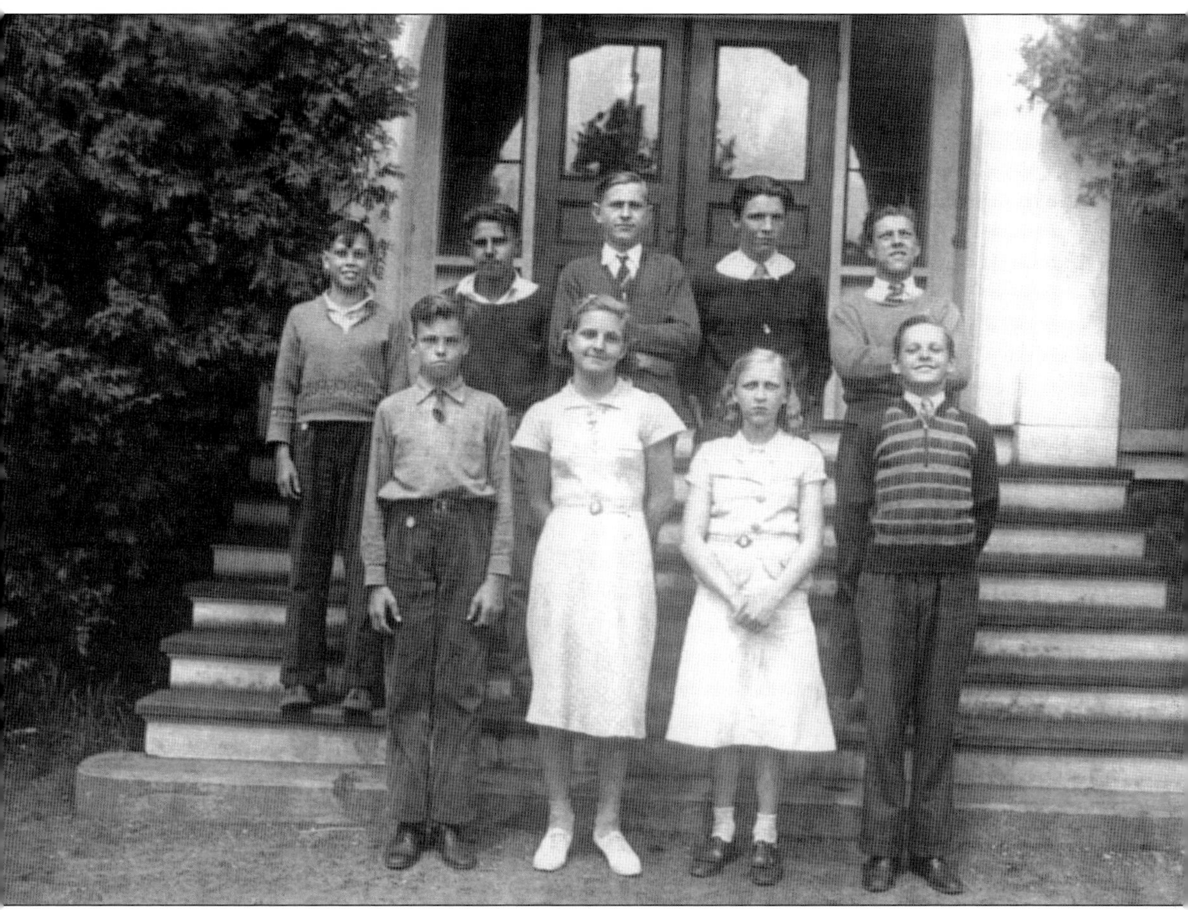

The Old Shawsheen School class of 1938, with Elsie Haas shown in the first row, second from the left. Elsie grew up to be Elsie Haas Howell, life companion to sculptor Mico Kaufman (see pages 68 and 74) and an active member of the United Methodist Church (see page 100).

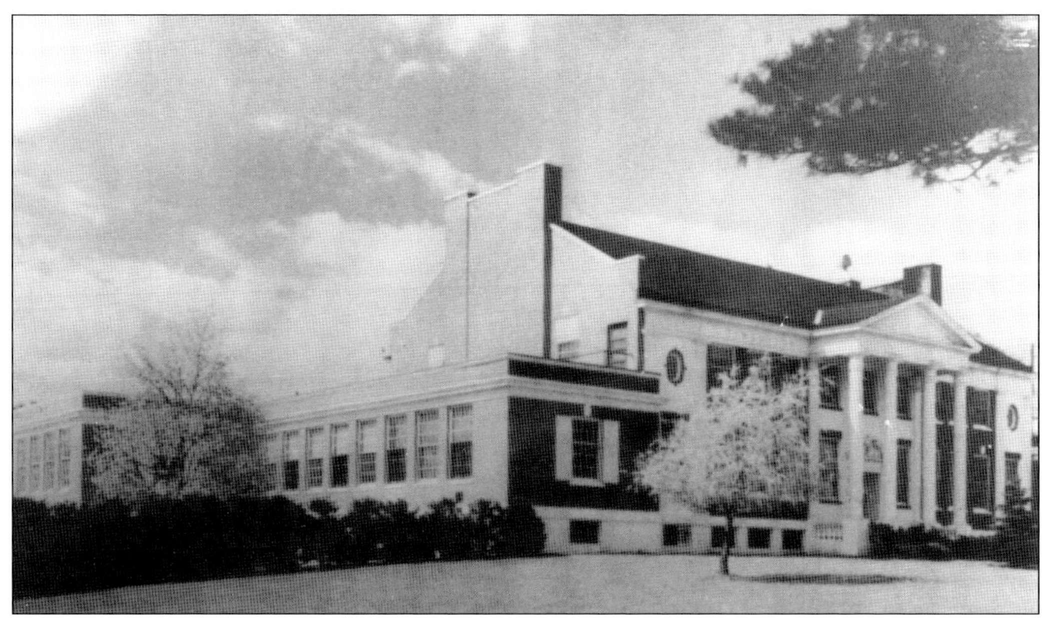

The 1935 Center School on Pleasant Street was built as a high school for Tewksbury and was home to many firsts for the town, including the first football team and football stadium. It remained a school until 1959, when another high school, now demolished, was built at 320 Pleasant Street.

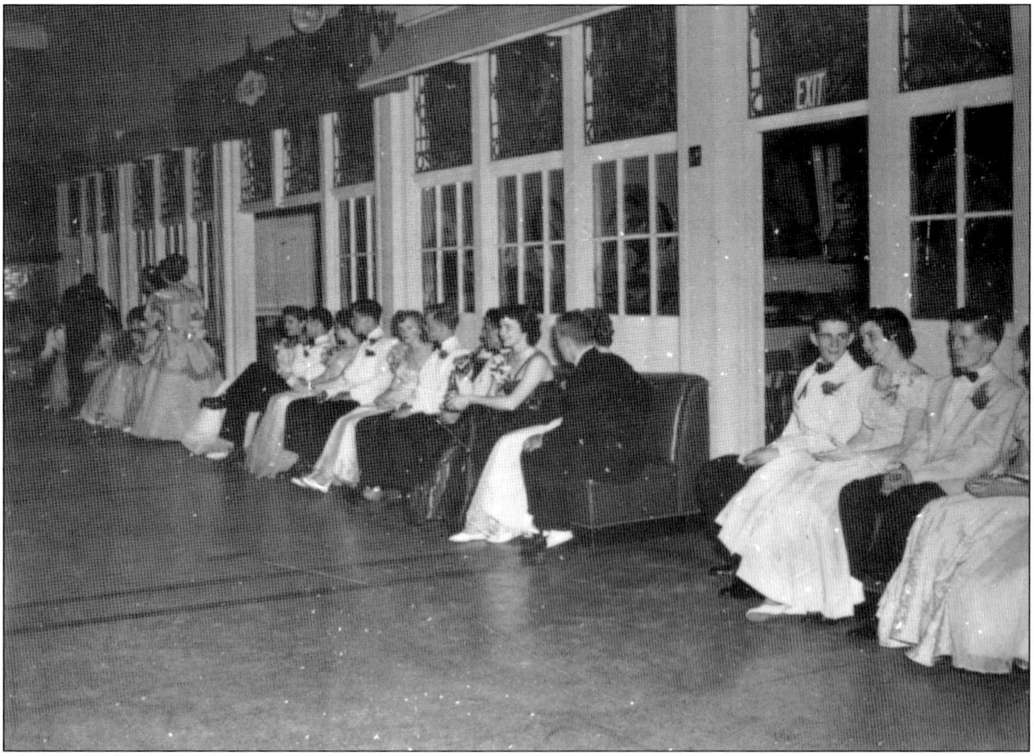

This undated photograph is of a high school promenade, or prom, setting in the third-floor gymnasium of the Center High School on Pleasant Street in about 1950. This was just one of many social occasions to take place at the school.

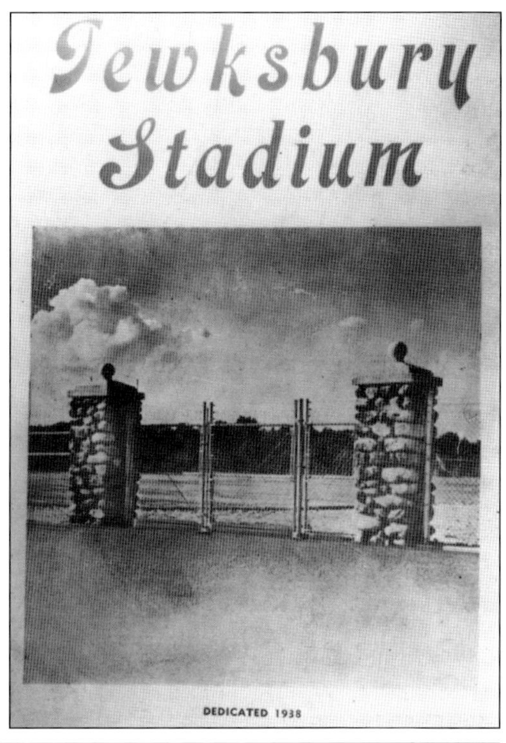

This is the cover of the dedication booklet for the stadium at the Center School in 1938, which was a Works Progress Administration (WPA) project. Complete with seating for over 900 people, a fieldstone ticket booth, and a fieldhouse, this facility was said to be one of the best in the area at the time.

Everyone is smiling on the Tewksbury Center High School's first football team in the years 1935–1936. The team members are, from left to right, (first row) Walker McCausland, William Powell, Louis Nolan, William Seekins, Capt. Frank Livingston, Mason Alexander, John Nolan, Billy Houlihan, and Philo Dewings; (second row) Joe Traveis, Vernon Darby, Joe Neveska, Stuart Mitchell, Leonard Glen, Bob Briggs, James Roper, James Manley, and Joe Kane; (third row) Robert McCann, Bernard Marion, John O'Neil, Frank Borgardo, Al Lucas, Robert Mills, and coach Donald Dunnan. Notice the "T" logo on their team shirts.

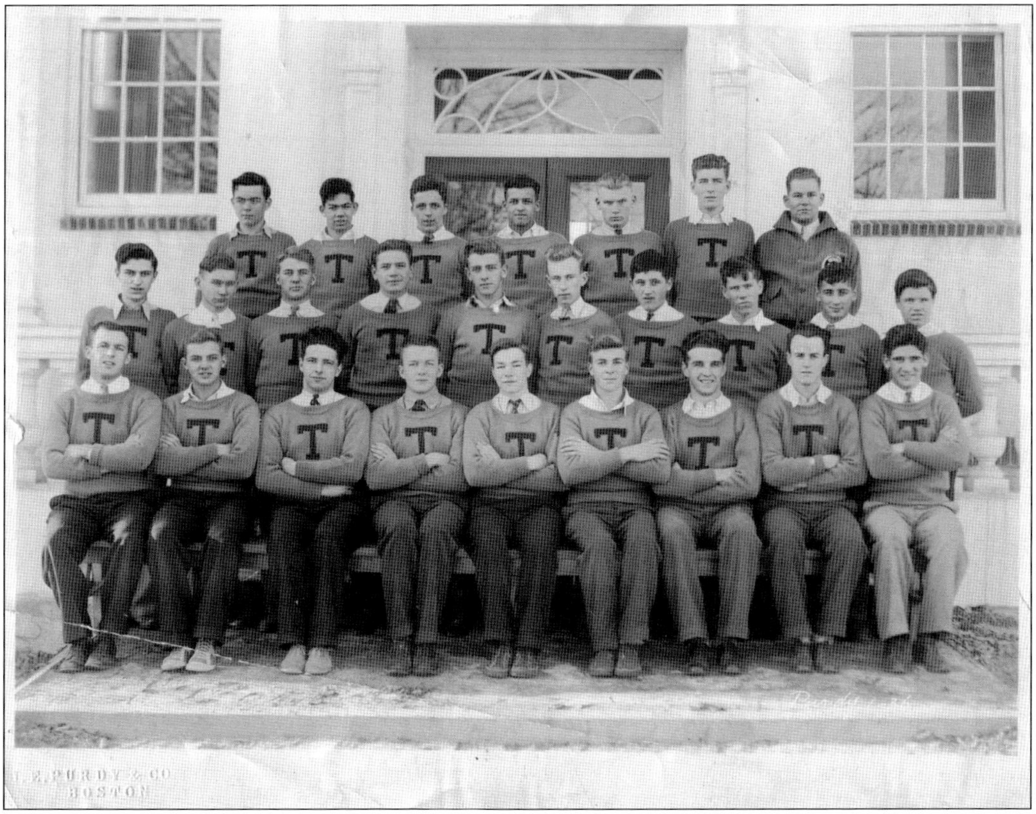

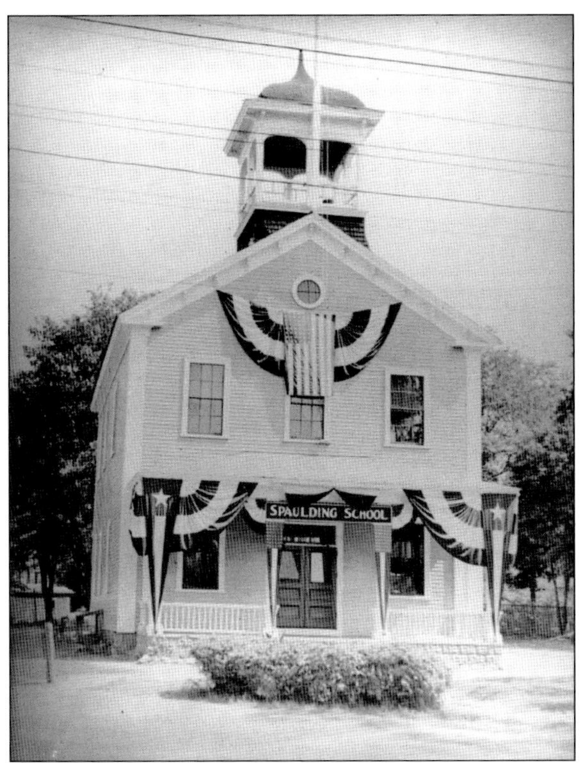

The Old Center Schoolhouse was once a town high school, built around 1865. The town's library was, at one time, housed in this building until it went into the new Town Hall in 1920. The school was named the Spaulding School after Benjamin Spaulding (see page 62) for his efforts with the Village Improvement Association in the Town Center. As shown here, the building is decorated for the 1902 Old Home Week. This school stood at the corner of North and Main Streets.

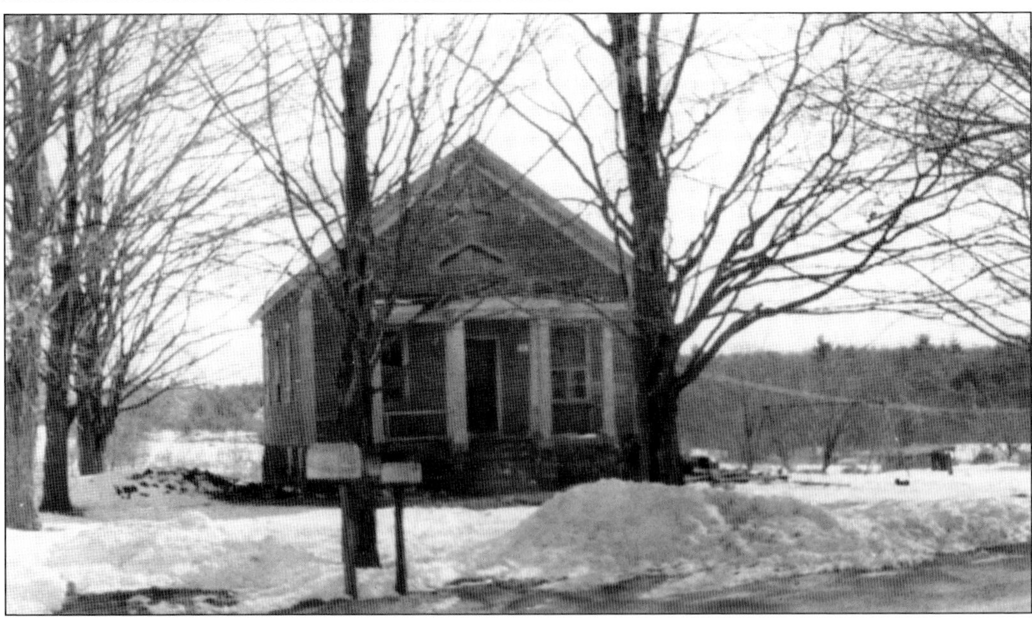

The West District No. 5 School, at the corner of French Street and Whipple Road and built around 1865, is shown in this c. 1950 photograph. In 1887, for Arbor Day, trees were planted around the school, and a large rock was inscribed, "TREES SET 1887." The rock and the inscription are still there, shaded by trees, and can be seen on the side of the road on French Street. The school's foundation was beside the rock. The school closed in 1935. Memories of the school are found in Marie Georgia Ruckledge's booklet *Just One Room But Many Memories*, published in 2004.

Nine

Tewksbury Hospital

An image book about life in Tewksbury would not be complete unless it had photographs of the State Almshouse that was established by an Act of the Massachusetts General Court in 1852. The state saw the need to open three almshouses to address those in poverty due to several factors, including increases in immigration and low wages at the start of the Industrial Revolution. The site was chosen due to its location in the northern part of the state, its high ground on Stormwater Hill, fertile soil, and nearby Stormwater Brook. All elements that would support a self-sustaining facility that included farming. In 1866, the hospital component was added, and the mentally challenged poor, as well as tuberculosis patients, were able to be treated at the site. Much has been written about events at the Almshouse, from politically motivated accusations of mismanagement in 1883 to the rise of a partially blind girl in the 1880s who became a pioneer in improving life for the deaf and blind. Through overcrowding and pandemics, the leadership stayed focused on improving the lives of those who sought care within their reach. To assist with staffing needs at the overcapacity facility, an onsite training school for nurses started in 1894, and in 1921, the School of Practical Nursing was opened and continued through to 1997. Many residents of town have worked at the hospital over the years in roles including the medical field, administration, farming, and facility management. The Tewksbury Historical Society is fortunate to have a photograph scrapbook from one nurse with images she saved from her experiences, dating from about 1903 to 1918. The images in this chapter are from her scrapbook, with the exception being the last image of a Tewksbury Hospital baseball team from the 1920s.

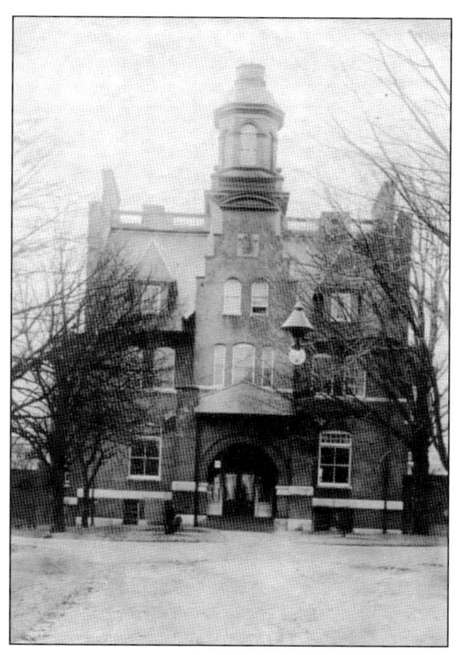

This is a c. 1904 look at the Tewksbury Almshouse Administration Building. This building is the hallmark of the site, upgraded in 1892 and designed by John A. Fox to include a brick façade and steep-pitched slate roofs along with three additions. This replaced the outdated original wood-framed building.

In this c. 1904 photograph are three doctors; from left to right are Dr. Howland, Dr. Romney, and Dr. Nichols. Dr. John H. Nichols was the superintendent of the hospital for 38 years, starting in 1897. The two-story Nichols Building, bearing his name, was constructed in 1939, with a brick exterior and slate roof, to address overcrowding in other male hospital buildings. It is located near the 1962 Saunders Building.

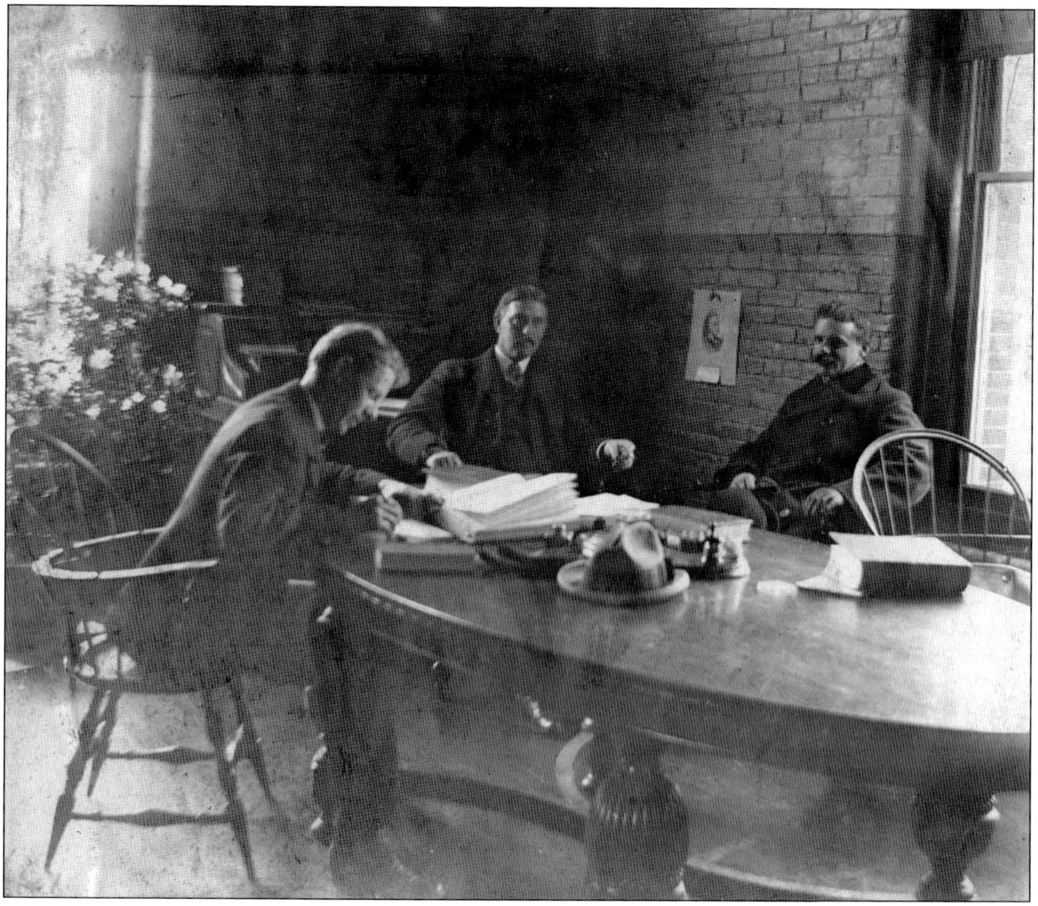

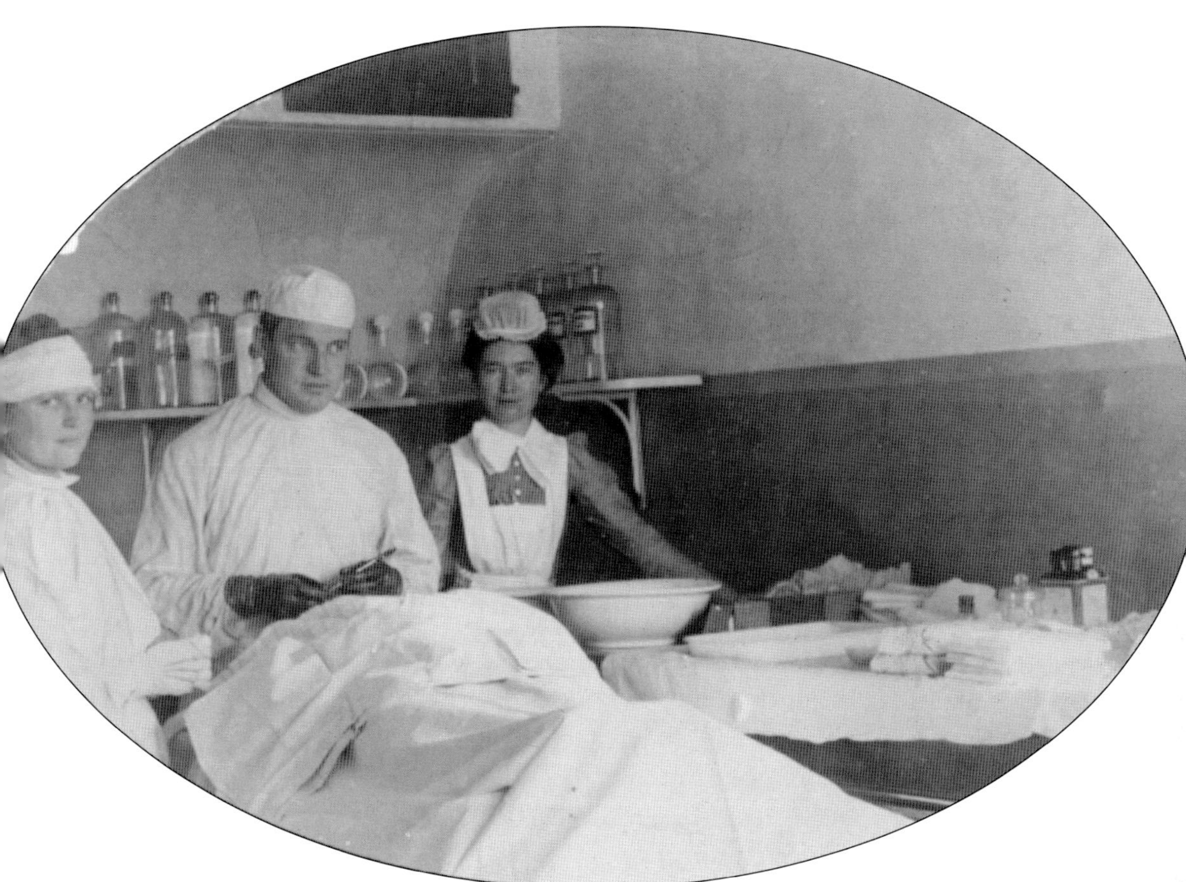

This is a glimpse at a doctor and two nurses with a patient in a gurney. The doctor is noted as named Dr. Holmes and they appear to be in an operating room. Most surgical procedures at the hospital were performed to address the needs of onsite patients' needs and diseases; however, on occasion, some outpatient accidents were addressed.

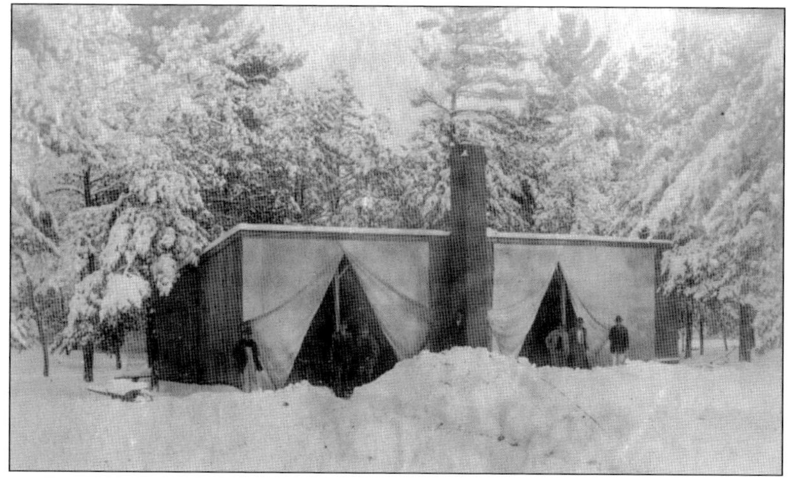

This image shows the use of outdoor therapy for tuberculosis patients. These three-sided buildings had canvas fronts that could be opened to let fresh air in for patients to breathe, thus improving their lung function and hastening recuperation from the disease.

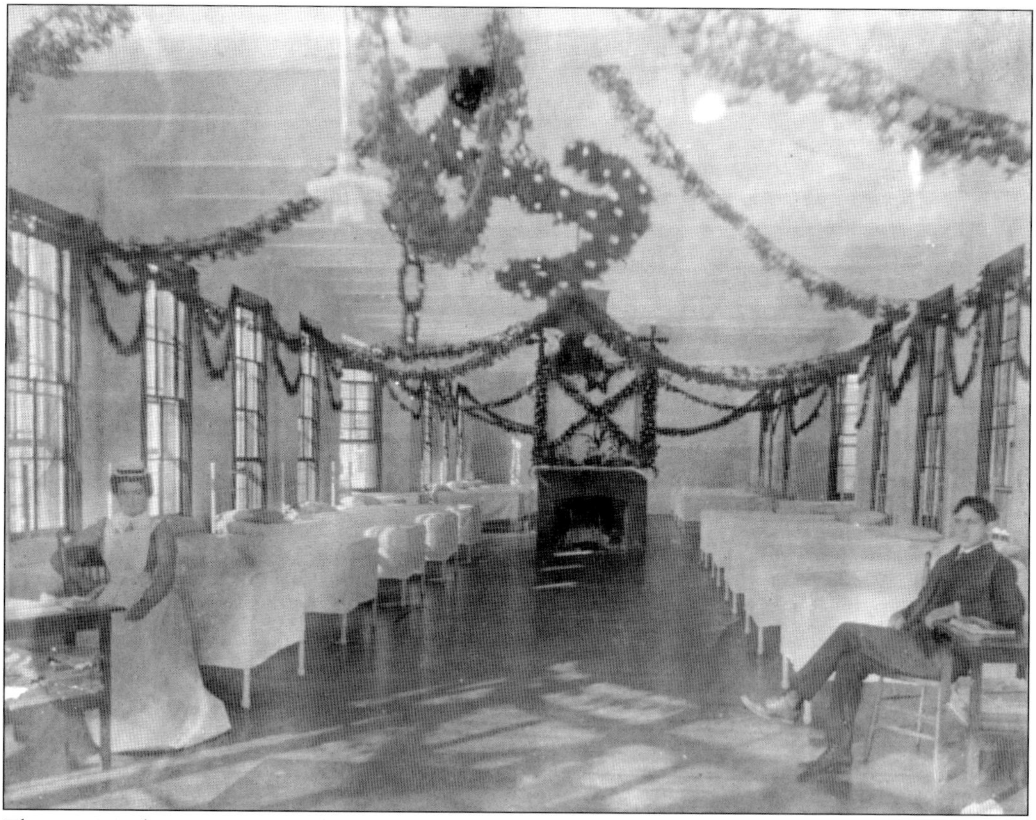

This is a Men's Consumption (Tuberculosis) Hospital ward decorated for Christmas. The hospital administration needed to address the growth in tuberculosis patients being sent to the hospital. In 1899, the building was constructed and later was named the Bancroft Male Tuberculosis Hospital after hospital board of trustees member Cecil Bancroft. Bancroft had been the principal of Phillips Academy in Andover, Massachusetts from 1873 to 1901. A Dartmouth College graduate, he later became a trustee of the college as well as the Andover Theological Seminary and the State Farm in Bridgewater, Massachusetts.

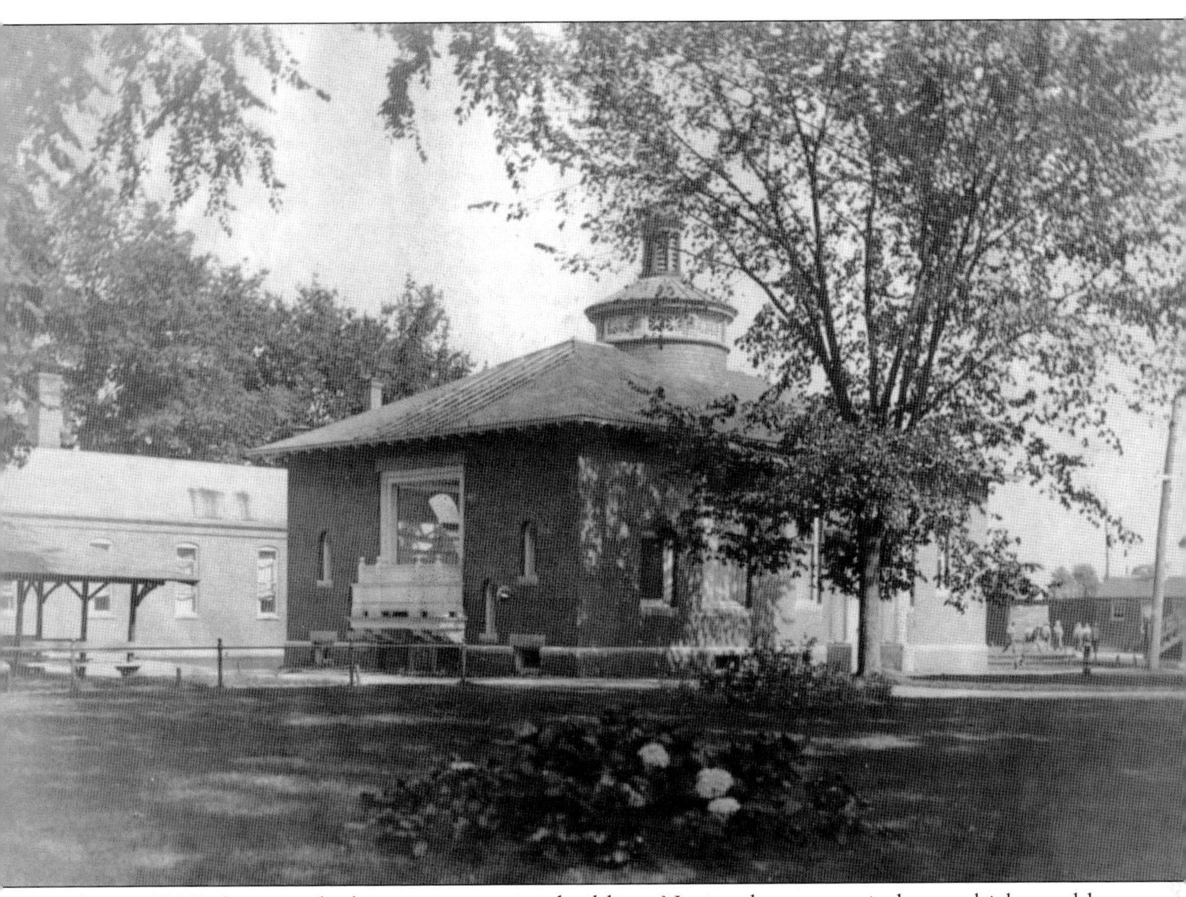

This c. 1905 photograph shows an operating building. Notice the many windows, which would allow natural light to be used during operations. With the addition of this building, doctors were able to perform more surgeries than in the past, with over 1,000 per year by 1906. Training for doctors and nurses could take place in the operating theater from the viewing area above the operating room.

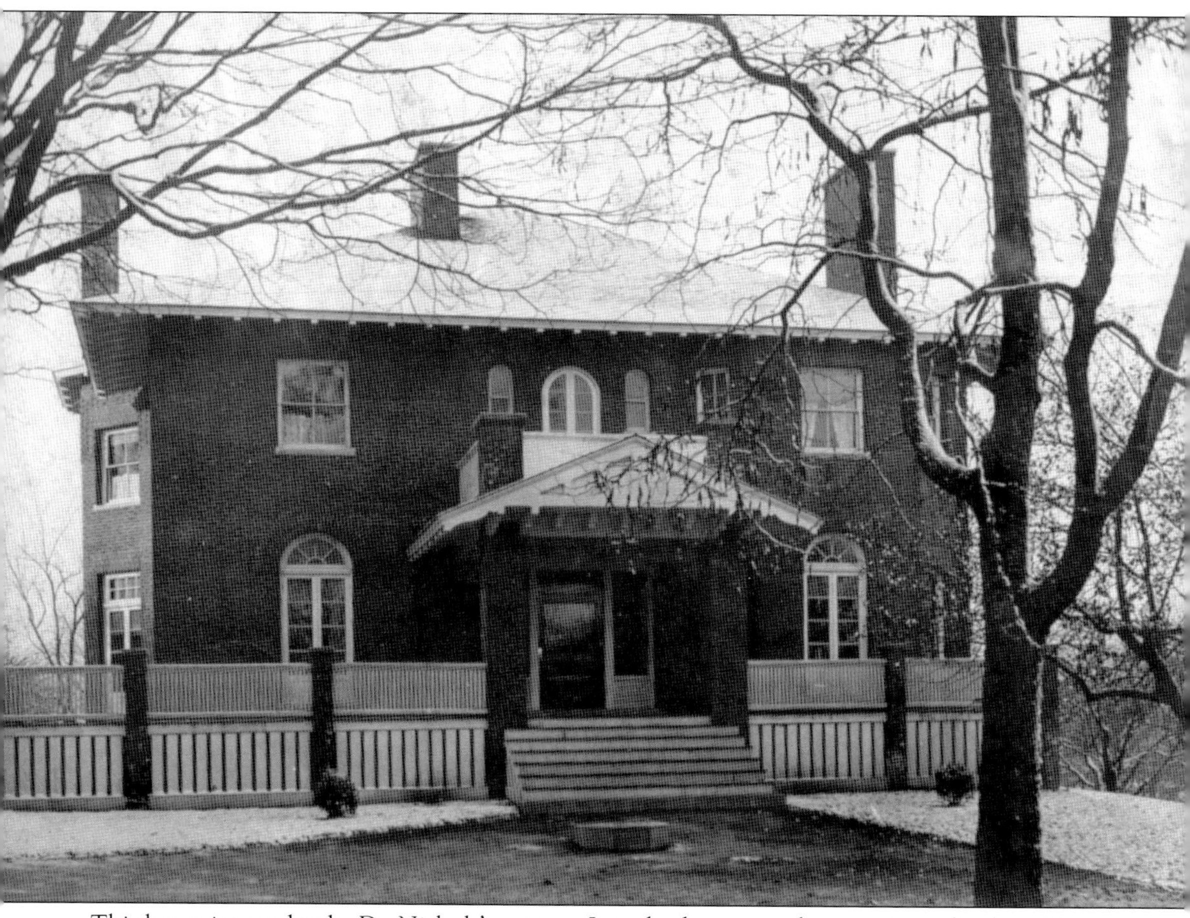

This home is noted to be Dr. Nichols's cottage. It is also known as the superintendent's residence, built in 1894 and designed by John A. Fox. Dr. Nichols is credited for many new buildings, improvements to existing structures, and medical advancements during his 38-year tenure, beginning in 1897. Buildings were improved with more windows for sunlight, better heating systems, ventilation, and fireproofing. It was Nichols who, in 1900, had the name of the almshouse changed to Tewksbury State Hospital to reflect its use and character.

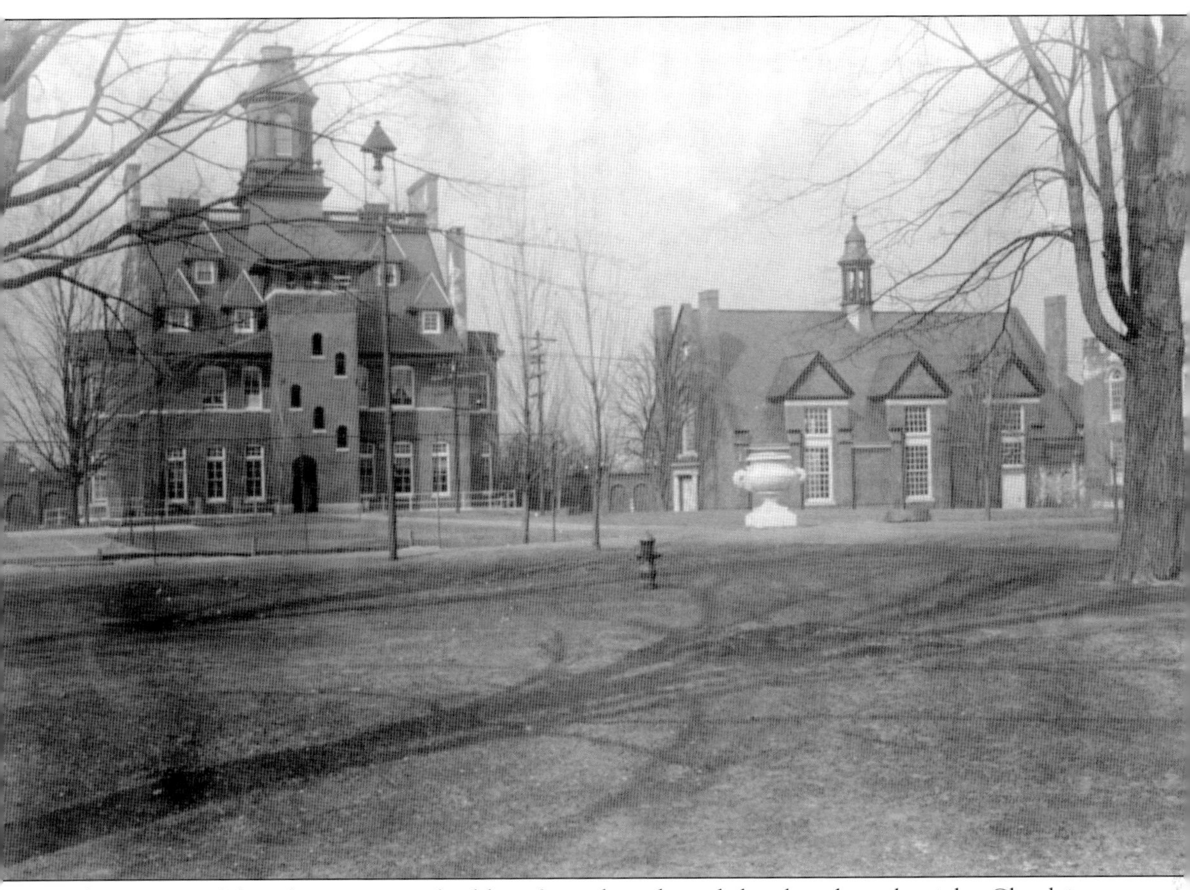

This view is of the administration building from the side and the chapel on the right. Chaplains of the Oblates of Mary Immaculate, a Catholic congregation, first arrived in Tewksbury in 1868 to serve the spiritual needs of the poor at the State Almshouse. The relationship between the Oblates and the hospital had a lasting impact on the town.

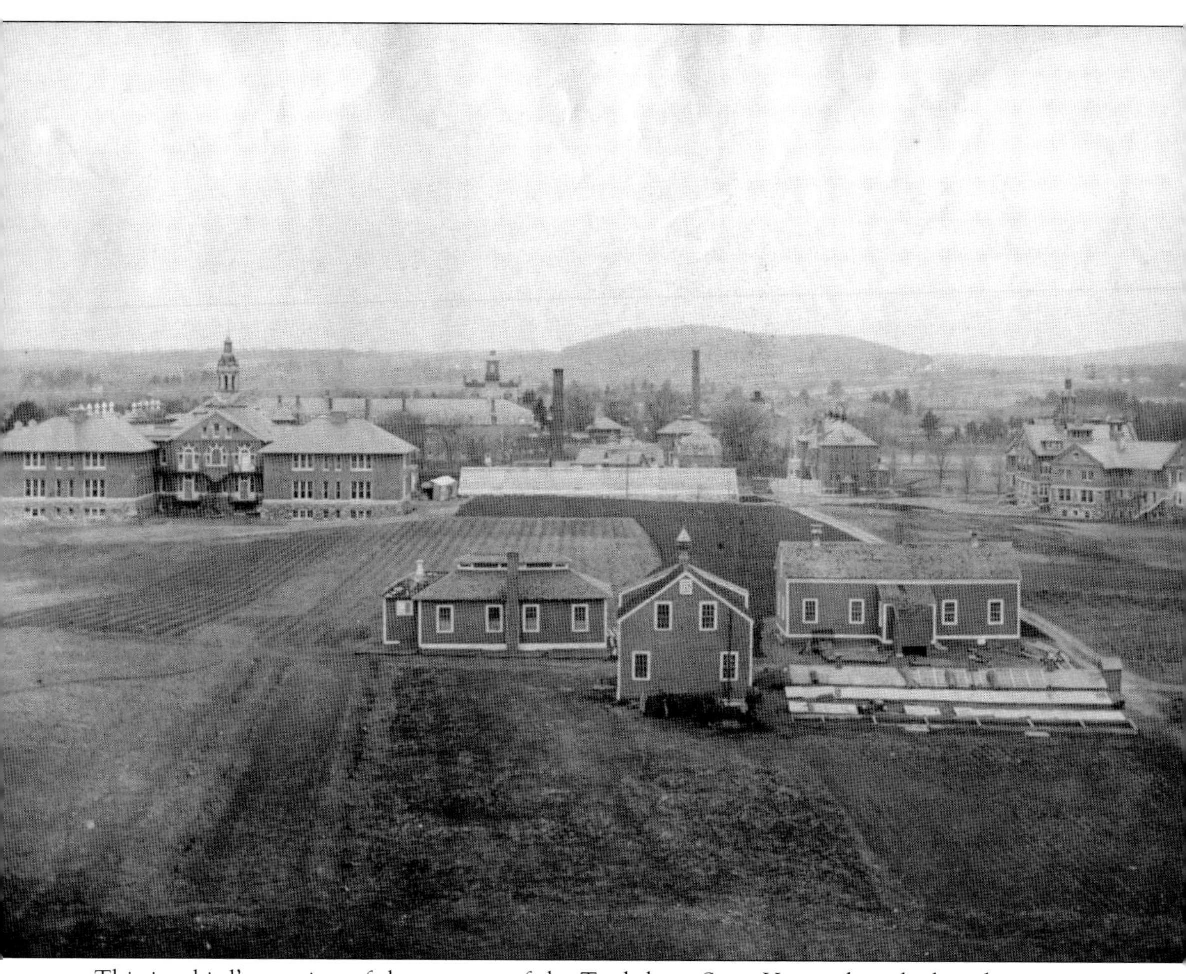

This is a bird's-eye view of the campus of the Tewksbury State Hospital, with the administration building and Prospect Hill in the background. The greenhouses and planting areas are in the foreground. These were used to provide food at the site as well as work therapy for patients. This image is dated 1918.

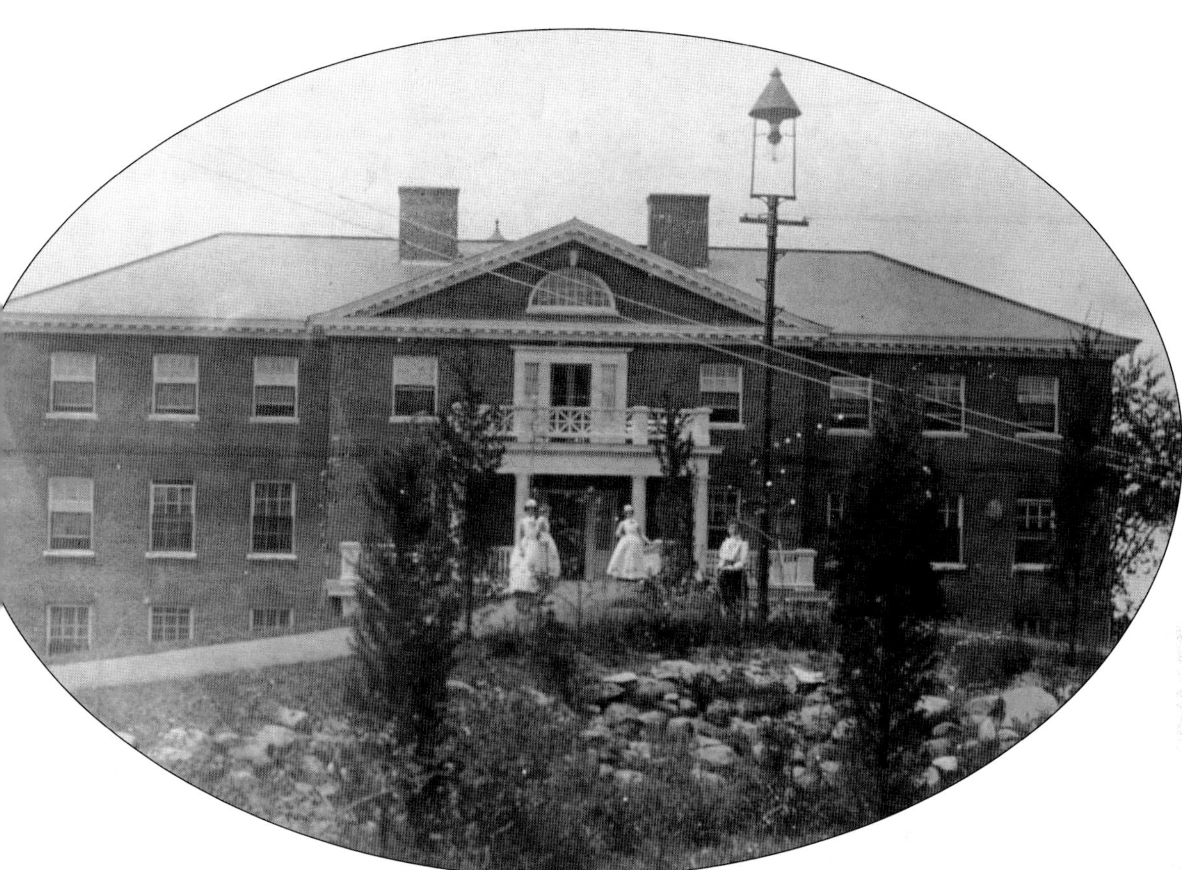

This is noted in the scrapbook as the Nurses Hall view of the front facade. Notice the nurses in their starched uniforms outside the front door. Nurses in the training school typically spent three years attending lectures and being exposed to a wide variety of patients with diseases, surgeries, and mental illnesses. They were paid and provided housing in the Nurses Hall during this training time.

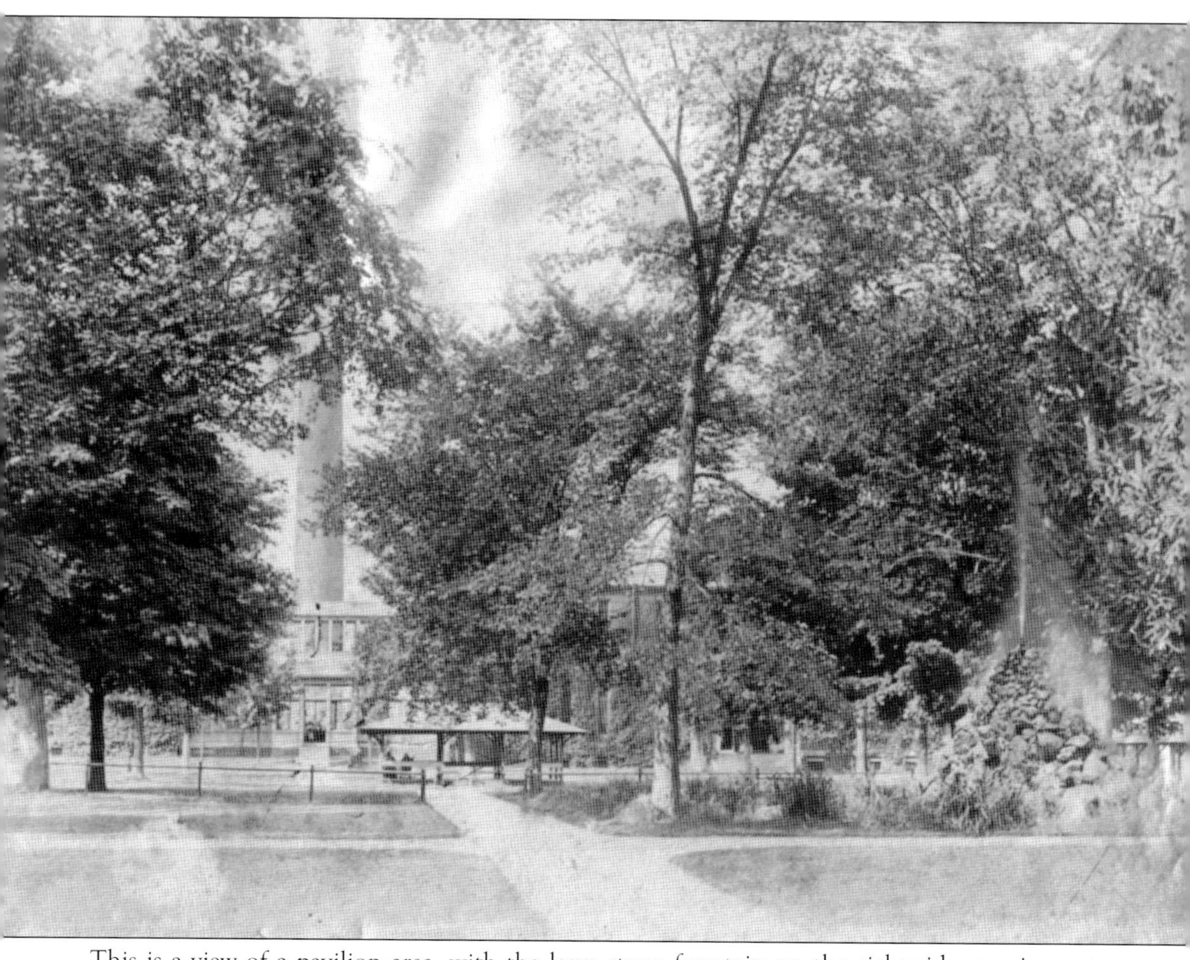

This is a view of a pavilion area, with the large stone fountain on the right side spraying water about 10 feet into the air. There is a smokestack on the left in the distance, which was for the coal-burning water pump station and steam heat system for the hospital campus.

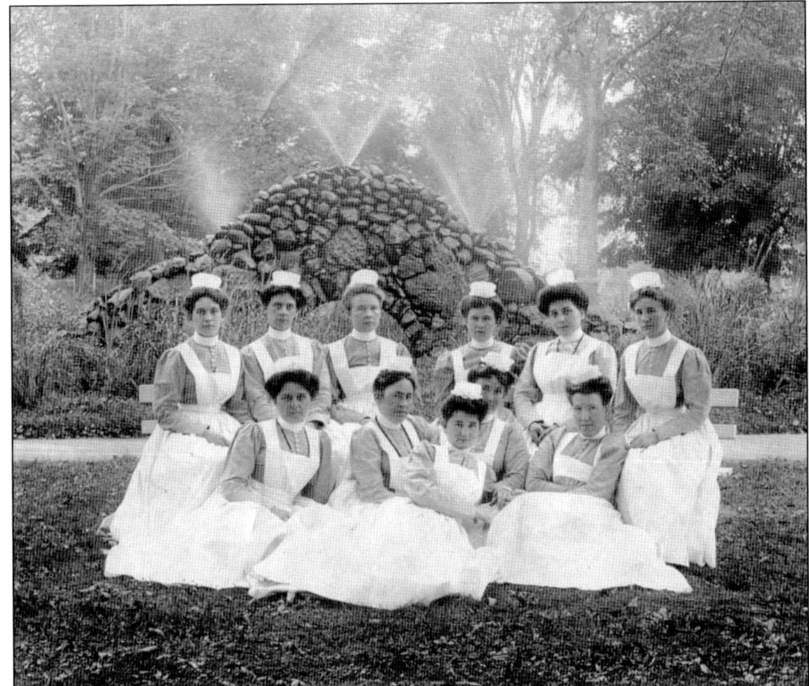

This is a group of nurses with the large stone fountain in the garden. The fountain was a very popular feature in the pavilion. Patients were encouraged to take walks in the well-manicured gardens for fresh air and enjoyment.

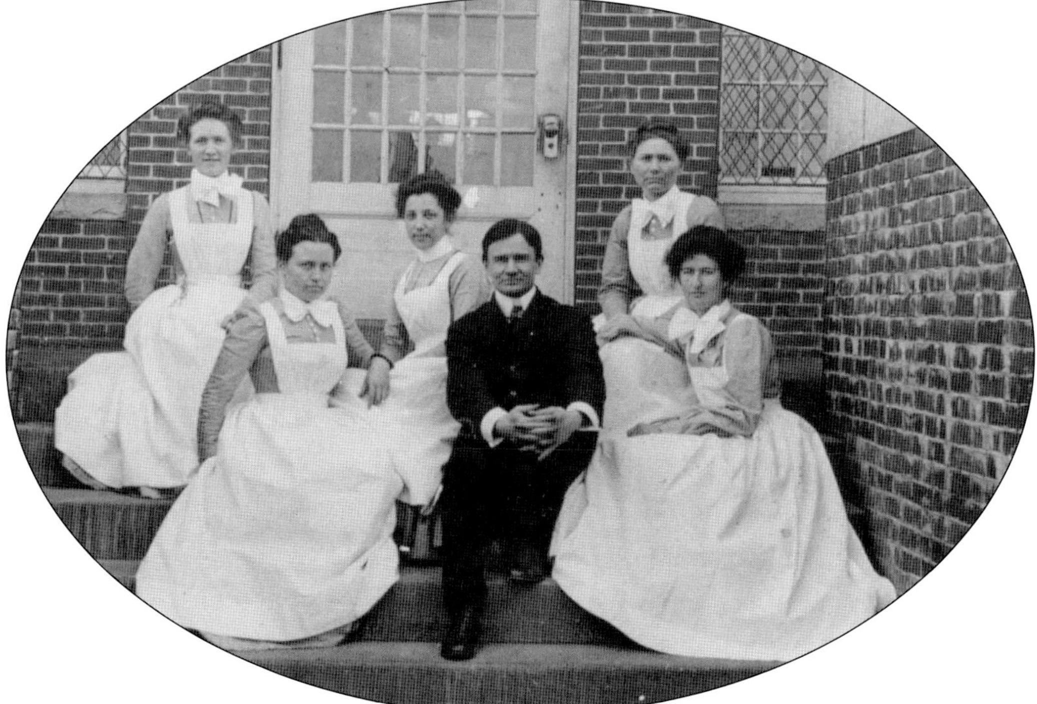

This group is noted as the "class of 1903." Dr. George Pierce is seated in the middle, with several nurses. Having been trained at a facility with such a wide range of patient illnesses positioned the graduates to serve the institution well. Tuberculosis was the disease that dominated attention at the hospital in the early 1900s, and these well-educated graduates were greatly needed.

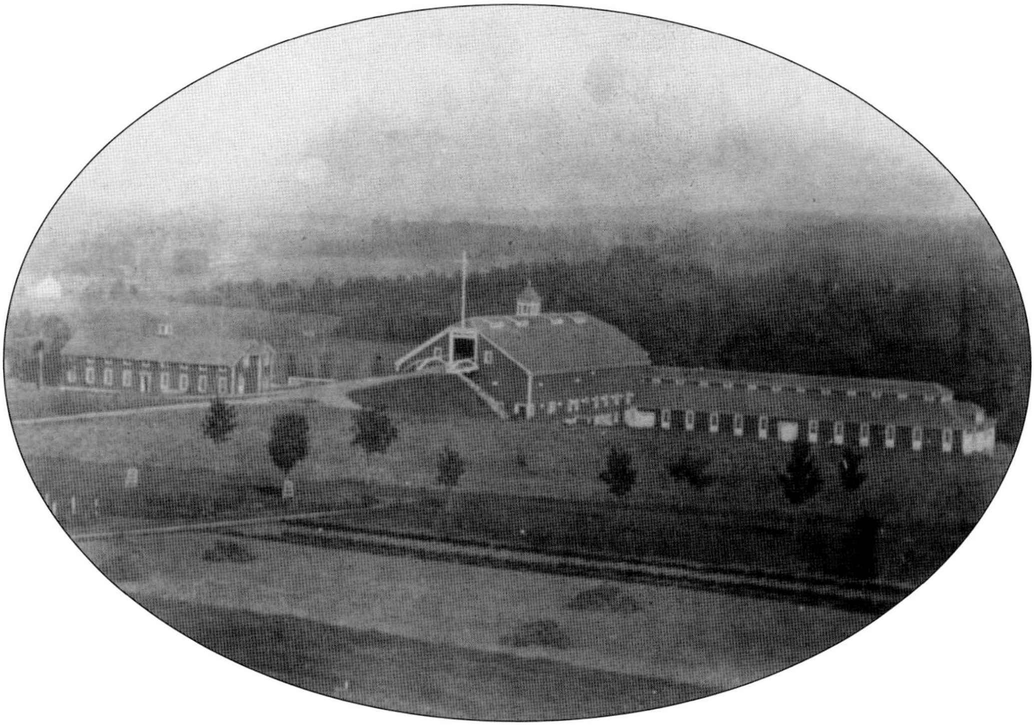

These are views of barns on the campus. They would have been used for dairy cows or pigs, as both were used as part of the self-sustaining farm of the hospital campus. As the number of patients at the hospital grew, so did the need for more dairy and poultry products. Hen houses and a new cow barn, with high ceilings for plenty of fresh air, were built around 1900 to address the increased need.

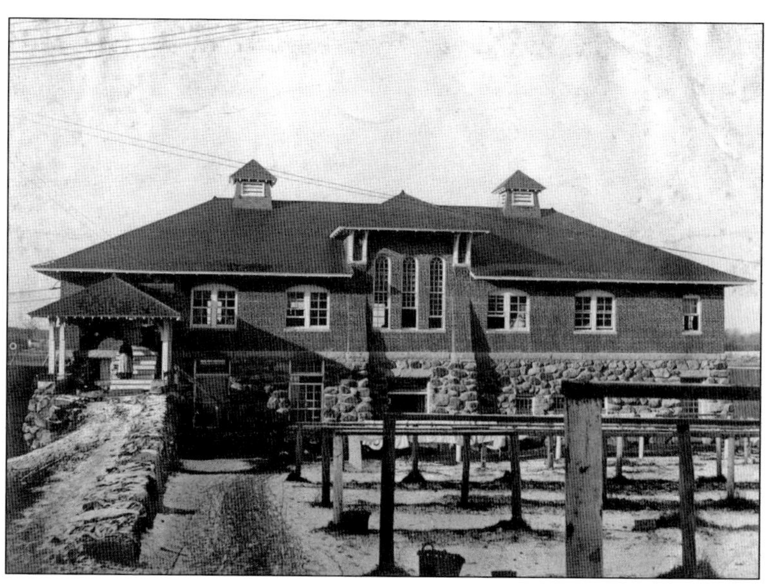

This is a view of the laundry building showing the numerous large drying racks that were used to air out the washed bedding and other items. Women patients were said to have worked in the laundry as part of mental rehabilitation. Inside the building, there were ironing and folding stations where they would complete the laundry process.

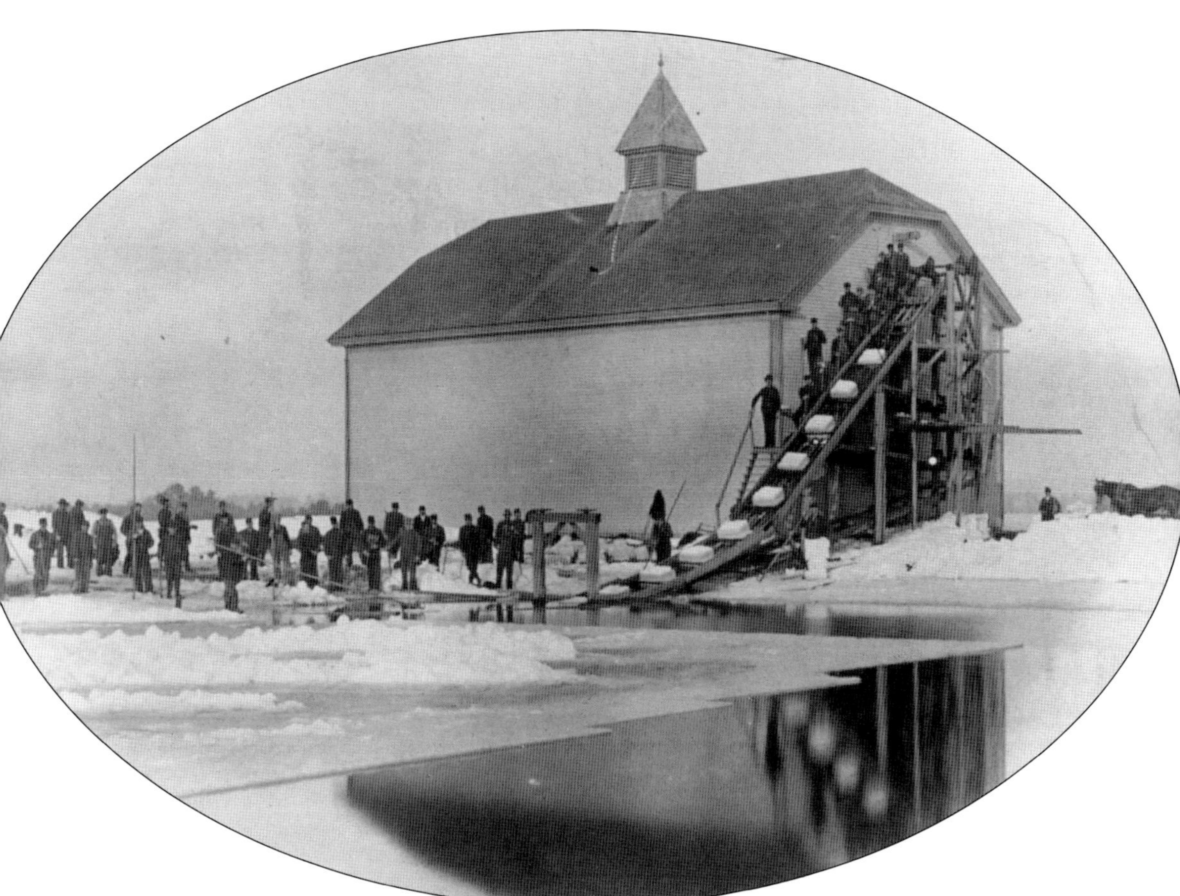

This is a look at the icehouse, with patients passing the ice blocks from person to person to move the ice to the food storage areas. This was one form of work therapy that was seen to improve patients' mental attitudes. In addition, their work served the needs of the hospital and also provided them with a skill for employment so they could be self-reliant when they left the hospital.

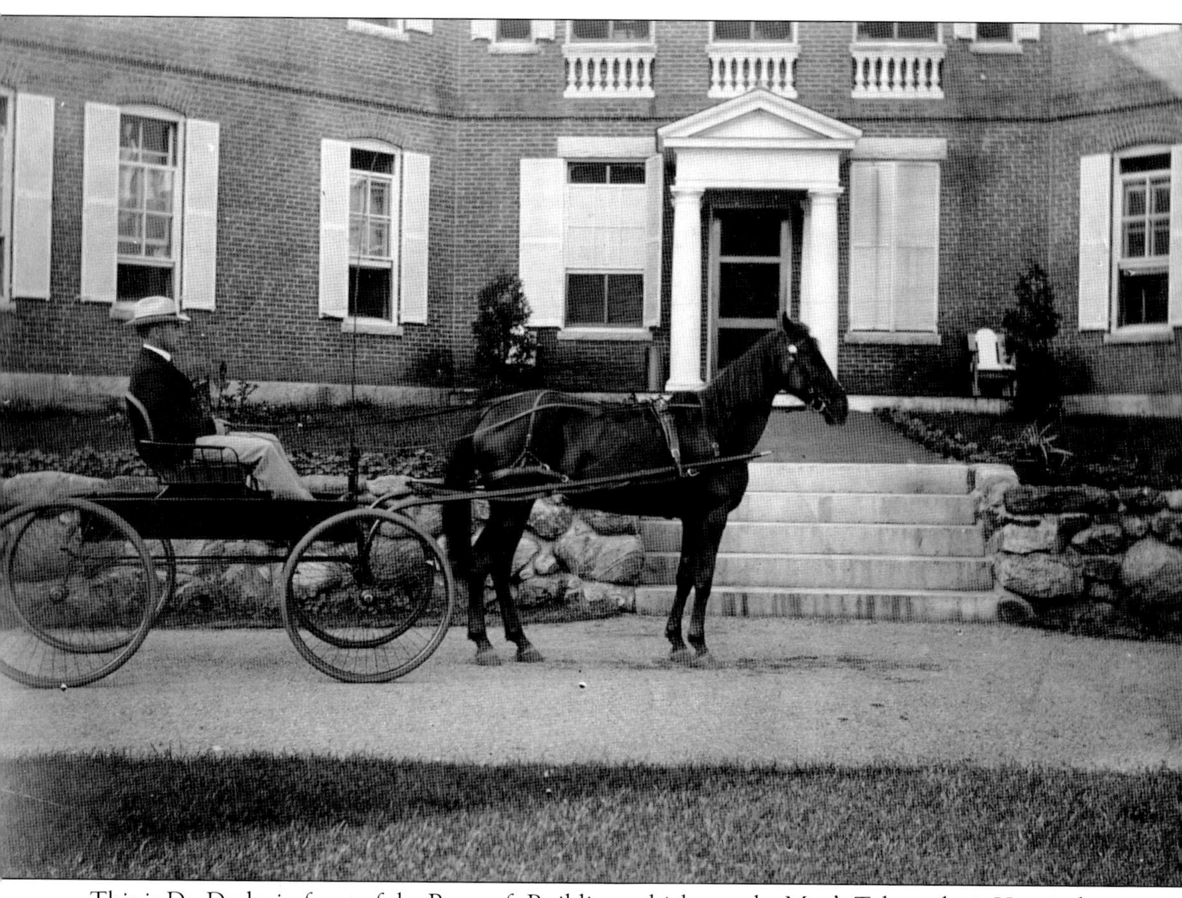

This is Dr. Drake in front of the Bancroft Building, which was the Men's Tuberculosis Hospital, in about 1903–1904. This building had space for 100 patients and was designed so that there were plenty of windows for fresh air and sunlight—both needed to help recuperation from the disease.

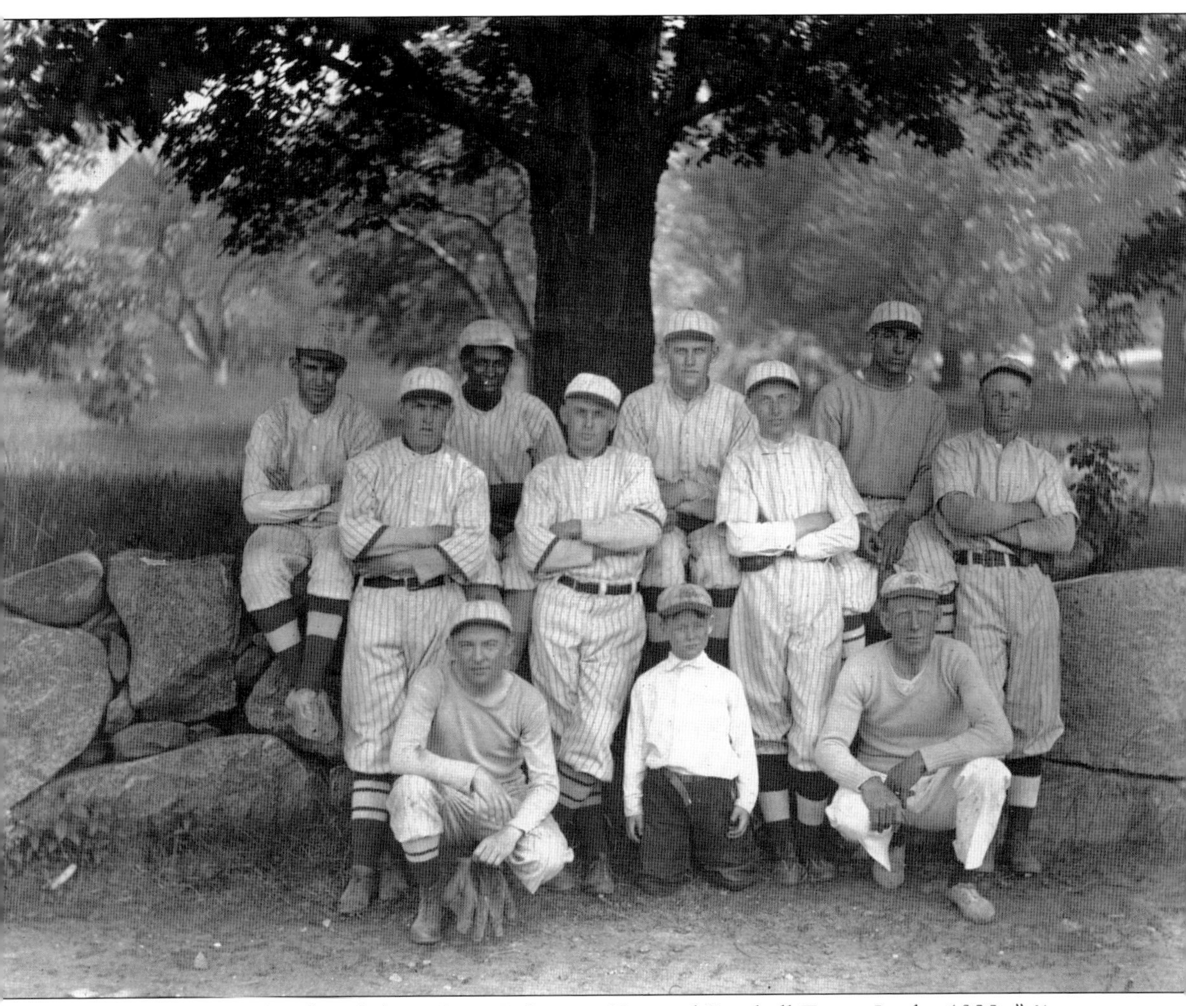

This image is noted as "Tewksbury State Infirmary Hospital Baseball Team. In the 1920s." From left to right are (first row) Walter Quinn, George Pierce (batboy), and Taxi Watson; (second row) John Hickey, Russell Millett, Chuggie Nash, and Bub Harden; (third row) ? Snyder, a patient from the farm, unidentified, and Lester Holt. Little did these players know, while sitting on the stone wall that still exists today along East Street, that 50 or more years later, hospital land would one day be used for about a dozen baseball and softball fields for youth and adult players of Tewksbury and enjoyed by their families, both day and night.